PRAISE FOR *FROM MARG*

M000290245

Essential reading for any organization seeking growth in today's difficult economic environment. Full of practical tools and examples.
Costas Markides, Professor of Strategy and Holder of the Robert Bauman Chair in Strategic Leadership, London Business School

Every business is desperate for growth but few know where to find it. In this exhaustively researched book, Helen Edwards encourages us all to look to the margins, to the marginal behaviours that will become mainstream in time. But this is no theoretical perspective, it's a practical playbook, offering a clear approach to finding the future of our businesses. As Edwards says, 'The margins matter and they can be read'.
Richard Huntington, Chief Strategy Officer, Saatchi & Saatchi

Any book that teaches you how to market insects for food, understand the rise of witchcraft, and the techniques for recovering an additional 21 years of life is well worth reading. This is an eye-opening analysis of an increasingly powerful aspect of successful brand and marketing strategy – one that will become ever more key to the evolution and growth of the great businesses of the future. For marketers, the tools, techniques and frameworks present an excellent guide to navigating the otherwise high-risk challenges of identifying future markets, trends and categories for investment.
Cheryl Calverley, Chief Executive Officer eve sleep, consultant, advisor, coach

I almost want to keep this book under wraps: it feels like the best-kept secret for growth is now well and truly out! Explained, codified and laid out – taking the best thinking to the mainstream... please DO NOT read... a few of us want this all to ourselves!
Jon Wilkins, Global Chief Strategy Officer, Accenture Song

Marketers talk a lot about wanting to break out from being a fringe discipline and be right at the heart of the business. Well here is a way to get there: ironically, by understanding the margins of human behaviour. Helen Edwards gives us the behaviours to explore, a way to understand them better, and practical ideas to apply.
Sara Bennison, Chief Marketing and Product Officer, Chief Executive Officer of The Mortgage Works

Where there is asymmetry there is opportunity! One of the greatest pieces of marketing advice I have ever seen by one of the most thoughtful writers on branding going. Helen Edwards rightly identifies the limits to growth faced by brands and identifies a solution. Extracting value from fringe culture is not new, but Edwards goes further in identifying the ways in which brands can mainstream the causes of marginal groups of consumers in a way that creates value for all. Recommended for brand marketers looking for new ways to address the imperatives of growth.

Professor Michael Beverland, Head of Strategy and Marketing, University of Sussex Business School, author of *Building Brand Authenticity: 7 Habits of Iconic Brands.*

Marketers talk a lot about growth and about change. But they are remarkably silent on where these two crucial concepts actually originate. From Marginal to Mainstream provides wonderful insights on these issues and suggests that by looking to the wings of the market, in the correct ways, marketers can predict and prepare for both. Strongly recommended.

Mark Ritson

This is a game-changing read for anyone wanting to win in business today. As marketers, we need to be on the front foot, finding new opportunities to connect with our customers in highly competitive markets, and this book gives you all you need to further turbo your performance.

Peter Markey, Chief Marketing Officer, Boots UK

One perhaps overlooked problem with 'evidence-based, accountable marketing' is that money tends to be spent too late on things which are already successful – casting a spotlight on things which are already centre-stage. How much more powerful would marketers be – and how much richer would society be – if we instead learned to identify and illuminate the best among those many great ideas which have been unfairly left too long lurking in the wings or in the shadows backstage? Well, thankfully, in this book you will learn how to do exactly that.

Rory Sutherland, Vice Chairman, Ogilvy

How can we find dynamic growth if we're all scrabbling in the same pit for the same customers and using the same methods and insights? In From Marginal to Mainstream, Helen Edwards shows us a path out of that pit with surprising and compelling arguments for looking broad and deep for new customer growth where we might least expect it. It's time for some bold moves with insightful foundations and the margins may be where we find that.

Sonia Sudhakar, Managing Director, Marketing and Digital, Royal Mail

Growth can come to organizations that correctly identify behaviours and ways of life at the fringes of society that succeed in breaking through into the mainstream. This well-researched and clearly-written book is full of practical tools and excellent examples that will help you identify and exploit these marginal-to-mainstream opportunities. This is essential reading for any organization seeking growth in today's difficult economic environment!

Costas Markides, Professor of Strategy and Holder of the Robert Bauman Chair in Strategic Leadership, London Business School

A fresh and insightful perspective on how to understand the marginal behaviours of today, to identify the mainstream behaviours of tomorrow.

Nils Goller, Senior Vice President, Orkla Marketing & Innovation, Orkla

A rigorous and compelling argument for why marketing needs to radicalize its thinking, and turn common practice upside down, if it is to find the growth it promises.

Kate Waters, Director of Client Strategy and Planning, ITV

From Marginal to Mainstream is a fascinating book which leans into one of the biggest challenges facing marketers today – how to continue driving growth when it seems to be eluding many of even the most successful companies. Helen flips the narrative on diversity and the margins from 'nice to have' side-projects and shows how the brands of the future are grown by better understanding and building on exactly these unique experiences.

Jerry Daykin, Vice President Head of Media at Beam Suntory, WFA Diversity Ambassador

This book is for the growth-hungry, curious marketer – a reminder to hunt for tension and to overlook 'niche' at your peril. With Helen's unique blend of wit and intellectual horsepower she makes the complex simple and provides us all with a 'how to'. Thank you Helen for this reminder that in such competitive, often homogenous, categories, the marginal can seed the mainstream.

Holly Turner, Vice President EMEA, Johnson and Johnson

From Marginal to Mainstream

*Why tomorrow's brand growth will come from
the fringes – and how to get there first*

Helen Edwards

KoganPage

Publisher's note
Every possible effort has been made to ensure that the information contained in this book is accurate at the time of going to press, and the publishers and authors cannot accept responsibility for any errors or omissions, however caused. No responsibility for loss or damage occasioned to any person acting, or refraining from action, as a result of the material in this publication can be accepted by the editor, the publisher or the author.

First published in Great Britain and the United States in 2023 by Kogan Page Limited

2nd Floor, 45 Gee Street	8 W 38th Street, Suite 902	4737/23 Ansari Road
London	New York, NY 10018	Daryaganj
EC1V 3RS	USA	New Delhi 110002
United Kingdom		India
www.koganpage.com		

Kogan Page books are printed on paper from sustainable forests.

ISBNs

Hardback   978 1 3986 0433 9
Paperback   978 1 3986 0431 5
Ebook   978 1 3986 0434 6

British Library Cataloguing-in-Publication Data

A CIP record for this book is available from the British Library.

Library of Congress Cataloging-in-Publication Data
[to follow]

Typeset by Integra Software Services, Pondicherry
Print production managed by Jellyfish
Printed and bound by CPI Group (UK) Ltd, Croydon CR0 4YY

CONTENTS

LIST OF FIGURES

ACKNOWLEDGEMENTS

This book has been a team effort. I would like to thank the following people for their input and support: Dinah Gray, Derek Day, Leo Day, Amy Sweeting, Jamie Tomkins, Nell Gray Andrews, James Foxall, Will Allen-Mersh, Nils Goller, Pernille Burkhalter. Thanks also to The Nursery research team: Natalie Webb, Lydia Morgan, David Alterman, Pauline McGowan and Emma McHarg and, of course, the editorial team at Kogan Page.

Introduction

This book is aimed principally at marketers, but its arguments will be relevant to business leaders, entrepreneurs, venture capitalists – in fact, anyone with an interest in growth. At its heart is the juxtaposition of a well-rehearsed problem and an utterly counterintuitive solution.

The problem is a stark one: growth has stalled. For industry after industry, sector after sector, brand after brand, meaningful, sustainable growth has become an ideal more often discussed than delivered. Marketers are expected to achieve consistent brand growth for their corporations, yet many spend their professional lives engaged in hand-to-hand combat with competitor brands, scrapping for incremental share gains within categories that are, themselves, static or advancing at a crawl.

There are economic, structural and marketing-specific reasons why this has become the case and why it threatens the future financial performance of brand-owning business – and these are examined in some depth early on in the book.

The majority of the book's pages, though, focus on the solution – or at least, on one promising, potential solution for growth's dispiriting absence. It is this: rather than seek growth in all the usual places – which isn't exactly working right now – seek it in the unusual ones. Instead of looking to the broad mass of consumers for insight and innovation ideas, look to the fringes of society, to the margins, to behaviours and ways of life that are way outside the norms, and way inside the tails, of any societal or behavioural continuum.

Why do that? Why go there?

Because an interesting thing can happen at the margins – and it's one that, as we argue in Part 1 of the book, we will see happening more. The behaviours and ways of life found there can break through and surge in popular uptake. They can go mainstream. And when they do, they can unleash new growth, promote new industries, change the dynamics of the marketplace and create new winners and losers. At its most extreme, this can lead to a phenomenon that we unveil in Chapter 1: consumer-driven disruption.

The simplest, most ready-made, marginal-to-mainstream (M2M) story is the one set out in that opening chapter: the unstoppable rise of veganism, which has unleashed growth across a range of food, beverage, retailing and hospitality sectors, and will continue to exert an influence on others, too. It seemed to come out of the blue, spluttering out from a movement that had been side-lined for decades, with its adherents camped well inside the 1 per cent fringe of adult populations. But 'out of the blue' is too convenient, too defeatist, too lazy. As our analysis shows, there were signs, clues, principles and motifs that could have led entrepreneurial marketers to see the surge before it happened and take action to get ahead of the crowd.

That, in short, is the contention at the heart of the book – that the margins matter and that they can be 'read'. The behaviours and ways of life you find there may seem unpromising, untested, unpleasant, even, but they can point the way to the future. Today's margins are tomorrow's brand growth – if you know where and how to look.

A practical toolkit

So much for theory, what about practice? Well, you will find plenty of practical guidance through both Parts 2 and 3.

The four chapters of Part 2 represent the core of the book, offering marketers a structured, eight-step process for reading and interpreting the margins and identifying M2M journeys before they happen. As well as original tools and frameworks in this section, you'll also see other examples of behaviours and ways of life that broke through – and some that didn't, or haven't, just yet.

Part 3 looks at entrepreneurs who have already started ventures based on marginal behaviours, gaining insights and pointers from their stories, before moving on to a playbook designed to help marketing teams take a more entrepreneurial approach in their own engagement with the margins. Again, the section is rich in tools, techniques, methodologies and frameworks, all set down in a structured, linear process.

Multiple research streams

Two years were spent in the research phase for this book, involving multiple research streams, spanning ethnographic, qualitative, quantitative and modelling methodologies, on a cross-cultural basis.

In all, that research unveiled over 60 candidate marginal behaviours and fringe ways of life, of which 42 are shared and described, either briefly or more fully, in the book. Much of that sharing and description forms part of the main body of the text, but you will also see special panels at the end of each chapter (apart from the final one) entitled 'Notes from the margins'.

These fuller descriptions, often embracing insights from direct, original interviews, take an anthropological approach and simply offer a window into other ways of life. They are not intended to be predictive. As one of our researchers observed, they are like palate cleansers between the main courses of the chapters themselves, and that is not a bad way to view them.

In tandem with our research partner, The Nursery, we also developed a scale methodology designed to rank marginal behaviours in order of their likelihood to go mainstream. You'll find both the methodology and the resulting table in Part 3.

One final observation here. 'Growth' can be interpreted strictly in the financial sense, or in a broader sense, to encompass growth of consciousness, understanding, virtue, respect. As you scroll through the behaviours and fringe ways of life in this book you are likely to be struck, as we were, by how many are rooted in concern for the environment, sustainability, human and animal welfare and respect for life. The margins may point the way not just to the kind of growth that corporations have always sought, but to a fuller, richer, more human kind too.

PART ONE

The margins
and why they matter

01

From 'Does *anyone* do that?' to 'Doesn't everyone do that?'

There are some people who practise transhumanism, but not many. In their ambitions to transcend the limitations of their earthly minds and bodies, transhumanists embrace body augmentation to open doors or enter passwords with the touch of a microchip implanted in their fingers, take performance-enhancing drugs and supplements for their nootropic effects and sign up for cryogenics in the hope of a comeback after death.

Another life choice apt to attract more headlines than followers is freebirthing. The movement dates back to the 1950s but was given a boost of fame in 2012 when a home movie of a woman giving birth in a stream in rural Australia went viral. Freebirthers shun medical intervention and the machinery, pharmacology and process of modern obstetrics. No formal midwifery, either. As an alternative, coaching is offered to 'Radical Birth Keepers', who may attend women at the moment of delivery.

Or take sleep patterns. In adult life there are two prevailing norms: monophasic, where the eight hours or so of sleep happens in one go, and biphasic – the 'siesta' pattern that predominates in hot, traditionally agricultural societies. Coming at things another way are polyphasic sleepers, who get by with a 20-minute nap every four hours, around the clock. Question them as to whether this is really a smart thing to do and they are likely to inform you that the polyphasic rhythm was the preferred sleep routine of Leonardo da Vinci.

What these – and other behaviours that we will encounter through this book – have in common is that they are uncommon. It may be tempting to reach for the descriptor 'minority behaviours' to delineate them but this is misleading, since minorities can be quite large. What we're talking about here are behaviours, choices and ways of life at the extremes of any distribution, well into the tail of the 3 per cent. 'Extreme behaviours' is too loaded, so the term you'll see through the book is 'marginal behaviours': those which, for any given choice frame – like diet or sleep patterns – stand well apart from the repertoire of norms within the 'mainstream'. We'll reserve 'minority' for the space between these two – behaviours that are not exactly common and not exactly rare. (There'll be more on definitions and the three 'Ms' in Chapter 3, but for now these broad brushstrokes will do.)

Sometimes, marginal behaviours amount to a way of life, defining or contributing significantly to the self-image of the people who practise them. The modern homesteading movement in the United States, for example, builds out from an ethos of self-sufficiency to embrace localism in both consumption and political forms – with a belief that current structures of governance in society operate at too lofty a level, and that more meaningful decision making should be transferred to structures at community levels. Homesteaders, like many others for whom 'marginal' is part of a whole way of life, might be relatively small in number, but punch well above their weight in societal and political influence.

Equally, though, marginal behaviours can simply be more of an isolated quirk, the one thing about a person that sets them apart from the norm. Here, there is less scope for group effect, less behaviour-related social cohesion; when a person happens to share a certain marginal behaviour with another, it might well be the only thing they have in common.

Where there is rarity there is curiosity, and TV cameras will often show up to explore why people at the margins choose to do the things they do – or choose not to do things the way the majority goes about it. The British TV documentary maker, Louis Theroux, has pretty much made a living out of this kind of voyeuristic analysis. He delves into the lives and ways of, among others, survivalists, Westerners seeking enlightenment in India, women who legally sell sexual services and people who repeatedly opt for cosmetic surgery, barely completing one procedure before planning the next.

Books have been written, too, both about and by people whose behaviours and life choices put them way outside the mainstream and well into the margins. An ironic example is Fumio Sasaki, who wrote a book extolling the virtues of living without possessions, which became a bestseller, thereby contributing to the sum of humanity's personal possessions.

Marketers, though, for the most part, do not devote much time or budget to the study of the consumers at the fringes of their categories. Marginal behaviour might have its fascinations, but the numbers do not make sense when it comes to targeting, not even for those pursuing a segmentation strategy. 'Size of prize' analysis is something every marketer will be familiar with and the prize at the margins – unless there is some kind of pricing differential involved – is, by definition, small.

Some enlightened marketers will make a foray into the behavioural margins of their category to see if they can gain insights that they wouldn't get in their routine consumer research initiatives – or to borrow some of the intensity that is so often a feature of marginal behaviour to carry back to their mainstream consumers. A German mainstream pain relief brand, for example, turned to the BDSM community for insights into the nature of pain – which led to a more nuanced and spirited positioning that acknowledged that some pain in life can be 'good', that not all pain needed dealing with, and that perhaps only the most tiresome kind required the brand's renowned efficacy.

And marketers with an eye for the zeitgeist, the ones who love to attend trends presentations, will be on the lookout for marginal behaviours that could morph into fads – often to be disappointed. And that's the thing. For all their fascination, for all their intensity, marginal behaviours can perennially fail to engage populations that have become habituated to living life within the accepted norms. Homeopathy, naturism and urophagia – the practice of drinking your own urine – have remained on the marginal/minority cusp for centuries, despite the enthusiastic promulgation of their advocates. Mainstream population reaction to marginal behaviour will often veer from incomprehension to disgust.

Marketers see that. And they see the sense of concentrating their efforts on the mainstream behavioural groupings, where most of their customers are to be found. Why venture to the margins when the rate of take-up for the behaviours that get practised there is close to zero? For busy marketers, charged with growing their brands in fiercely contested sectors, engaged in hand-to-hand combat to win more share, a reasonable heuristic might be: *What happens in the margins stays in the margins.*

Until it doesn't.

Consumer-driven disruption

Sometimes, a marginal behaviour, perhaps one that's been around and overlooked for decades, will burst through and become accepted and embraced by the majority. It will go mainstream. We'll look at one in a moment: the explosive and seemingly unstoppable rise of veganism.

It may not happen often – although we'll be exploring in later chapters the reasons why frequency of breakthrough could dramatically increase. When it does happen, the effect on the categories immediately in the eye of the storm, as well as those in adjacent territory, is profound. It is a kind of disruption. Not the tech-driven disruption that has created colossi like Uber and Airbnb and brought traditional industries to their knees in the process. This time it is *consumer-driven disruption* – but its power to foster new growth, dismantle established barriers and create winners and losers is no less intense.

When consumer-driven disruption is unleashed, the open and free market is no place for the passive. So, businesses, brands and marketers react, with all the alacrity and resources at their disposal, to adjust to and get ahead of the new behavioural reality. Machine lines will be retooled, priorities switched, research hastily scrambled, shelf space reassigned, supply chains culled and new ones opened, regulatory approvals urgently sought, alliances dismantled and fresh partnerships explored.

Marketers will be front and centre in this shifting of priorities – keeping tabs on consumer uptake, monitoring competitor reaction, abruptly clawing back innovation budgets from projects attached to the old paradigm to fund brave initiatives in the new one. They are right to do so. No marketer can afford for the brand to be left on the seashore as the behavioural tide sweeps away.

But perhaps they can do better than that. Better than simply reacting after the storm has broken. Perhaps diligent and perceptive marketers could find ways not just to monitor the change in consumer behaviour as it happens but to predict it way in advance. Perhaps there are signs, clues, principles, motifs that, if accurately interpreted, could take them ahead of competitors. Armed with these projections – these evidence-supported hunches – prescient marketers could make their adjustments before disruption happens, and be at the leading edge when it does. There are risks, of course. It won't be for everyone. But might it not be a better way of unleashing new growth than slogging it out with rivals for the same consumers in the same behavioural space?

And would it be hubristic to go further even than that – to imagine that some marketers, the real frontrunners, could move beyond mere predicting to active facilitating? Could they find ways to look at promising marginal behaviours and play a part in helping create the explosive move to the mainstream in the first place? Making the weather, not merely forecasting it? This would be a view of marketing that sees it as a far more entrepreneurial discipline than it tends to be right now.

The contention at the heart of this book is that both are possible: predictive advantage and entrepreneurial agency. Either way, what is needed is not merely an understanding of the power of consumer-driven disruption but a structured grasp of the underlying currents, forces and circumstances that propel it. In the full-length example and associated analysis that follows, we'll get to grips with both.

'The unstoppable rise of veganism: how a fringe movement went mainstream'

(The Guardian, 1 April 2018)

The British newspaper The Guardian is not the only publication to have marked the ascent of veganism in recent years. Far from it – the phenomenon has been noted, dissected and celebrated in articles both excitable and sober in The Huffington Post, The Independent, The Economist, The Financial Times, Fast Company, and Forbes – which went as far as showcasing 'high-end' vegan dining as its 2013 food trend of the year.[1]

But it was The Guardian's 2018 headline, quoted above, that came closest to capturing not just the explosive growth of this dietary and lifestyle choice but the 'fringe' status of what had preceded it. About halfway down that Guardian piece was a data point that neatly straddled both: a 2016 survey from the Vegan Society, showing how Britain's vegan population had increased from 150,000 to 542,000 in the space of 10 years.[2]

That is a rapid rate of growth – the kind of trajectory that gets noticed by mainstream business, the kind that led, in just a few years, to hundreds of new vegan products in supermarkets and the symbolic arrivals of the McDonald's McVegan Burger and the world's first Michelin-starred vegan restaurant.

On the other hand, look again. Even as recently as 2016, Britain's 'vegan population' represented less than 1 per cent of the total UK population. It was, at that point, what it had been for decades – a behaviour choice confined to the margins.

Some questions cascade from this observation. How did veganism ever get started in the first place? What was it that stopped it spreading more widely? How did it feel to be vegan through the wilderness years? What kept the movement going? And, most crucially, why and how did things begin to change in the mid-2000s, such that growth would accelerate by 350 per cent in a decade,[3] and continue to power away in the years since?

ROOTS: 'THE OTHER HOLOCAUST'

To attempt to pinpoint the inception of a new way of going about life is to be a hostage to fortune. The chances are that the ancients were onto it long before it first seems to pop up on our modern radars. And so it is here: abstinence from all animal flesh and its derivatives was said to have been practised by Pythagoras and his followers around 500 BCE. Who knows, maybe the behaviour goes back even further than that.

But we can get tougher about this. We can ask when 'veganism' first got its name and, alongside it, a definition. This takes us without argument to a room in The Attic Club in London in November 1944. Gathered around a table are Donald Watson, a teacher of woodwork, and five other 'non-dairy vegetarians' whom he has convened for a meeting. The group's aim is to create a new movement based on their trenchant dietary choice and its associated convictions – and to devise a new, 'more concise' term to crystallize it.

Among the options considered are 'dairyban', 'vitan' and 'benevore'. The group settles on 'vegan', a term that Watson, perhaps with a little post-rationalization, later describes as 'the beginning and end of 'vegetarian' – which, literally, it is. Around that table, before the group departs into the night, the world's first Vegan Society is born.[4]

If the process of naming had its random and amateurish moments – which naming in new brand development invariably still does – the uncompromising nature of the beliefs behind it were in no doubt. Watson would later be asked why veganism was founded during the last chapters of the war, when the government's food rationing strictures were at their most severe. He replied: 'Perhaps it seemed to us a fitting antidote to the sickening experience of war, and a reminder that we should be doing more about the other holocaust that goes on all the time'.[5] Veganism was, from its very beginnings, an unyielding activist movement.

An argument could have been mounted that simply refraining from eating meat – vegetarianism – would have had the desired effect of reducing the slaughter of animals. But Watson and the group had long recognized that the benign and bucolic scenes of the popular imagination associated with the production of milk and dairy produce were wide of the mark: milk results from a combination of artificially frequent impregnation and the slaughter of the calf or its premature separation from the cow.

This holistic view of animal welfare was captured in the first definition of veganism, set down by a society member, Leslie J Cross, in 1949: 'To seek an end to the use of animals by man for foods, commodities, work, hunting, vivisection, and all other uses involving exploitation of animal life'.[6] It has been modified since but retains the same core principles and ideals.

RESISTANCE: 'A LOT OF PEOPLE THOUGHT I WOULD DIE'

Markers of progress: by 1946, Vegan News was being distributed to 500 subscribers. The first member of staff was appointed in 1947 at a salary of £205 per year.[7] In 1948 a US vegan society was formed, followed by societies in Germany in 1953 and India in 1957.[8] Between them all, estimated membership was numbered in the low thousands: there were some people who practised veganism, but not many.

The fulcrum of resistance – even for those who shared the movement's concerns for animal welfare – was health. The fear was that eliminating not just meat but dairy produce from the diet would leave vegans seriously deficient in vital nutrients.

There was some truth in this, not that the founding group could have known it at the outset, since it relates to a vitamin discovered only in 1948: B12, which a strict vegan diet does not provide. The solution was to devise a fortified vegan milk – Plamil – and vitamin supplements.[9]

If these helped maintain the nutritional health of the committed, they did little to encourage uptake from those on the outside. The conviction that the diet was innately unhealthy – and the projection of that concern onto those who followed it – would persist for decades, lending veganism a kind of crank, 'other' status, something to be avoided, derided and even feared.

Those few who did become vegan would endure, not merely the practical difficulties of shopping for suitable food or ordering in restaurants, but the patronizing and unsolicited concern of those they knew or encountered.

Imagine a first meeting between two people where one of them confesses – the verb is probably not too strong – to being vegan, perhaps offering the animal-welfare reasons for that choice. The result would be the sympathetic, querying nods of the head that signalled: 'I get that, but…'. The internal, silent 'but' would continue '…there's no way I would ever give up not just burgers and bacon but eggs, cheese and real ice cream'. The voiced, concerned, almost pitying 'but' would go: 'But surely that can't be healthy; surely you must be missing out on proper nutrition'.

As one longstanding vegan put it when talking years later to the US Globe and Mail: 'When I first went vegan, I think a lot of people thought I would die'.[10]

TRACTION: 'IT'S JUST WHAT YOU DID'

Watson had anticipated from the outset that the vegan way of life would meet with disapproval and derision. His reflection on the matter was typically stoic: 'If one is going to be out of step with all the catering that is done for people who are different from oneself, one must accept a certain amount of excommunication, as it were, from the rest of society'.[11]

But things were to get a little more exciting than 'acceptance'. With the baby boomers coming into their teens as the '50s gave way to the '60s, there were suddenly generations of young people for whom being out of step with society was a plus point.

Two countercultural movements were significant in the increased traction that veganism was to enjoy from the mid-60s through to the early '80s. The first was the emergence of the hippies, a 'youthquake' movement that rippled out from San Francisco in 1967's 'summer of love'. As people became attracted to the way hippies looked and lived, they started to adopt behavioural norms that were being established within that subgroup. One was veganism. From California to Cologne, young people would become vegan as a by-product of getting into the hippy rhythms of life.

The second, and more significant, counterculture thrust was punk, which took off in London in the mid-70s. The Anarchist Library reports the 'frequent overlap between punk culture and animal rights'. As one contributor said: 'It's just what you did, which sounds horrible and trendy, but it's true. You became punk, you found out about animal rights and you quit meat'.[12] Even as late as 2006, in a 'Punk Rock Census' published by Last Hours zine, 54.6 per cent of respondents were either vegan or vegetarian.[13]

But if these youth movements were enough to keep veganism from atrophy and irrelevance – helping the term 'vegan' gain its first entry into the Oxford English Dictionary in 1986 – they were ill-equipped to carry it deep into the mainstream, since, by desire, they stood apart from it.

Youth, though, would still be the key to veganism's transformation, when a later generation – just as curious, just as experimental, but a lot less tribal and polarizing – would discover new reasons for turning to a vegan lifestyle and new ways to make it more palatable in every sense.

BREAKTHROUGH: 'MILLENNIALS HAVE BEEN INSTRUMENTAL'

It is a recognized marketing sin to ascribe to entire generations a set of characteristics to which all members conveniently adhere. In that respect, no generation has been more sinned against than the millennials, the cohort born between 1981 and 1996. It is said – often – that they are tech-savvy, socially conscious, collaborative, politically correct, materially unambitious, 'entitled', free-thinking and adaptive to change.

They obviously cannot all be all those things. Regard that statement, please, as a caveat to, and perhaps a mea culpa for, what follows. Because some generalities will be observed about the ways in which this generation has *tended* to be less confrontational in matters of choice and the effects of choice on others: more open, more forgiving, more nuanced. A bit more resourceful, too.

Perhaps that's partly down to the cohering influence of social media, with which millennials grew up – or because previous youth generations had done 'angry', taken that space, and, from the point of view of creating change, had seen little come from it.

Millennials would explore veganism with interest and curiosity, as others had done before them, but would find multiple access points to get into it – not just that of animal welfare. This is not to say that the moral imperative was not evident. It was – promoted by short documentaries about the realities of rearing livestock that were widely shared online, and which exerted a powerful influence. To this seminal ethical consideration, the millennial generation added another: the impact of animal agriculture on the environment, hauntingly evinced in the 2014 crowdfunded documentary film *Cowspiracy*.

But millennials would also alight on other, completely diverse, reasons to reduce reliance on animal produce and move closer to a vegan diet. Principal among them was the very thing that had for so long put people off: health. This 'switchback' reasoning should not be underestimated; it wasn't about discovering that a vegan diet was OK after all – it was about the objective reasons why it actively promoted wellbeing, and why the West's increasingly meat-and-dairy based diets were doing the reverse.

Study after study confirmed the links between meat consumption and mortality or morbidity from cancer and heart disease. For example, a 2016 study by Marco Springmann and colleagues at the University of Oxford found that, globally, a transition to well-balanced vegan diets might result in 8.1m fewer deaths a year.[14]

With 'wellbeing' a constant background media theme during the 2010s, millennials had plenty of reason to experiment with veganism and to inspire others to do the same. Less weighty prompts played a part, too: it was not unknown for 'creative cookery' or 'seasonal eating' to be a route into the culinary genre.

Millennials also brought new ideas to *how* they embraced veganism as well as why. To a large extent, this meant dispensing with the *ism* – to be at ease with the possibility of a more flexible approach to diet, with vegan foods and dairy alternatives mixed in with standard fare in the weekly repertoire. The notion that 'vegan' could be a lunch choice not a life choice probably did as much as anything to help tip its acceptance into the mainstream. Impossible Foods, maker of fake meat products, estimated in 2019 that 95 per cent of its customers were omnivores.[15]

With all that came new language: 'flexitarian' and 'pescatarian', to denote those who followed a meat-free diet only up to a point – and the almost wistful 'plant based', softer both phonetically and perceptually than the harsh sounding 'vegan', which, as a former activist noted, still came with 'f*** you' associations.[16]

This blurring and softening, this reframing and normalizing, would play a significant role in tackling the one remaining hurdle that deterred shoppers from hunting down non-meat and non-dairy alternatives: the difficulty of finding them. Supermarkets and manufacturers would now succumb to the positive arguments and angles that millennials would come armed with. As Technavio Insights observed in 2016, 'Millennials have been instrumental in propelling the growth of the packaged vegan foods market over the last few years'.[17]

Accelerators of a more sinister kind also played a role. The 2013 horsemeat scandal in the UK and Europe, where equine-derived meat was found in products marketed as beef, jolted people out of their inertia about complex food supply chains and made them question why they were eating meat in the first place. Meanwhile, in East Asia, consumers have increasingly explored alternative sources of protein and healthy oils since becoming wary of fish after the 2011 Fukushima nuclear power plant accident in Japan.

Veganism's 21st-century rise was multifactorial – steady until about 2017, and more rapid since, as these datapoints attest:

- One in 10 adult Americans consider themselves vegetarian or vegan[18]

- In a 2020 survey in Canada, more than 60 per cent of respondents showed interest in or intention to cut down on meat[19]

- The UK market for plant-based milks is valued at $320.6 million and is projected to more than double by 2025[20]

- In 2020, German companies produced almost 39 per cent more meat alternatives, increasing the value of the meat alternative market by 37 per cent[21]

- In 2021, the Swedish oat milk brand Oatly floated on the Nasdaq with a valuation of $13 billion[22]

- It is predicted that meat and dairy alternatives will be worth €7.5 billion in Europe in 2025, up from €4.4 billion in 2019[23]
- One in four food products launched in the UK in 2019 were labelled 'vegan'[24]

The 'vegan population', though, has yet to encompass more than a modest minority. Those who report sticking rigidly to a vegan diet reached 4.4 per cent in the UK in 2019 according to Statista.[25] Equivalent figures for the United States and China were 3.8 per cent and 2.1 per cent respectively. Across Europe – even though Germany was something of an outlier at 6.9 per cent – the average was just 1 per cent.[26]

In the end, it is majority acceptance not minority adherence that made the most difference to veganism's growth – and that broadly-spread, now-and-then behavioural norm is what gives plant-based, vegan-compliant foods, drinks, medicines and even fashions potential for further growth in the future.

POSTSCRIPT

Watson died in 2005, living long enough to witness the first glimmers of the vegan awakening but not its later, enthusiastic, almost fashionable, embrace.

What he didn't get to see were the queues outside vegan butchers in Boston, London, and Amsterdam, the vegan menus at the BAFTAs, the mass uptake of 'Veganuary', nor the sight of big-brand owners in diverse categories scrambling to make their products vegan friendly, so as not to be caught on the wrong side of the popular tide. The most piquant example of that has to be Guinness, which, in 2017, removed the requirement for fish bladders in its hitherto unchanged, 300-year-old recipe.[27] It is hard to imagine that it took this particular 'exploitation of animal life' to make a stout, but apparently it did. Until it didn't.

Lighting the pathway: an introduction to the beacons

The point of a full-length example is similar to the idea behind the case methodology taught in business schools: it is to live vicariously through the complexities, twists and tangents of what otherwise might seem a unidirectional, 'just so' narrative. Real life isn't neat. Outcomes aren't inevitable. You have to make your predictions and judgements about where the phenomenon may be heading within a messy, and often contradictory, societal and commercial matrix. The ascent of veganism – like any other marginal-to-mainstream

(M2M) journey – was not preordained and would have looked unlikely for most of the period since the movement's inception.

Nevertheless, we can point to signs, clues, principles and motifs at certain stages in the narrative that would have given guidance about the direction in which things were moving. Some of these might have been glimpsed relatively early in the journey; others only much later. Some would have been faintly predictive of veganism's growth; others much more strongly so. Combined, as a reward for the attentive, they might have led to the commercial advantage that stems from seeing things more clearly than, and some way ahead of, competitors.

Signs, clues, principles and motifs, you'll agree, is a bit of a mouthful. It cries out for an overarching term that embraces them all – especially as sometimes we'll be talking about a combination of two or more at any single step of the journey: a sign that gives way to a principle, for example.

So, the collective term you'll see from here on in is 'Beacons' – chosen because they light the pathway along the journey from marginal to main-stream behaviour. There are eight M2M beacons in all. (See Figures 1 and 2). We'll take a first look at them now, linking each back to the veganism narrative – and we'll be returning to each more fully as we move through the central chapters of this book. Because the point is this: the beacons can be extrapolated beyond a single example to all M2M journeys. When you're looking at a marginal behaviour and wondering whether it has the potential to break free from its constraints, and tip into consumer-driven disruption, probing for the presence – or absence – of the beacons will give you a struc-tured way to go about it.

FIGURE 1.1 The four constituent elements of a beacon

SIGNS

CLUES

PRINCIPLES

MOTIFS

BEACON

*A single beacon comprises one or more of the elements
above: signs, clues, principles or motifs (repeated patterns).
There are eight M2M beacons in all, and each will display its
own combination of these elements.*

FIGURE 1.2 The M2M beacons

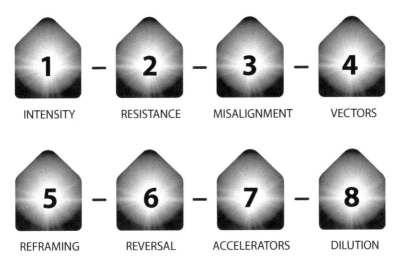

The eight beacons help marketers discern which marginal behaviours are most likely to break through and go mainstream, perhaps leading to consumer-derived disruption. They will tend to be manifested in the order shown above. Where all or most are observed for a given marginal behaviour, its likelihood of breaking through is higher. Where only the first two or three are observed, the behaviour is likely to remain at the margins (practised by fewer than 3 per cent of the population), or even to fade.

The eight M2M beacons

1. INTENSITY

A sense of intensity – of impassioned commitment – is a tell-tale motif of marginal behavioural choices. It was evident from the outset in the vegan narrative, with Watson's stark reference to 'the other holocaust' – and has been a recurring theme since, with the often-violent demonstrations and protests that committed vegans have unleashed.

But intensity – or at the very least a quiet determination to go your own way – is a natural component of marginal behaviour even where idealism or ethics are less of a driving force. Marginal choices are usually hard to maintain – less convenient, less socially comfortable, frequently more expensive, than going with the flow. A certain force of will has to be there just to persevere with behaviours and life choices that are way out in the tails.

Perversely, though, that intensity can be off-putting at the moment when a wider population is ready to consider the behaviour, and perhaps take first steps to adopt it. If the behaviour has to come with all the emotional fervour that gets attached to it, that can be too much for what is often a simple quotidian decision. Veganism got going when millennials found a way to take some of the heat and confrontation out of it. This is an important concept that is developed further in the final beacon, 'dilution', below.

2. RESISTANCE

Resistance is the counterforce that keeps marginal behaviours marginal. It is the push-back against intensity, the mass wall of defiance that says, 'Well, maybe for you, but not for us'.

There can be many forms of resistance, some of them simply practical, but a common well from which the most stubborn are drawn is fear. Fear of what? The strange, the 'other', the uncomfortably challenging, at the general level – and at the specific, something tangible about the behaviour in question, like the fear of malnutrition with veganism.

What makes fear-based resistance so potent is that it results in something more robust than a little meek anxiety or timid unwillingness to try when advocates and doubters collide. What is breathed in by the doubters may be fear but what gets breathed out is revulsion, disdain or – worse – pity.

It is axiomatic that for any marginal behaviour to start its journey towards acceptance into the mainstream, resistance must be overcome. When it is, opportunities cascade. But as we'll see next, there is an important nuance to that.

3. MISALIGNMENT

Intensity and resistance are the elemental forces of marginal behaviour. The two can be held in balance for decades, as we saw with veganism, but this is not to suggest that they are always directly opposed. It is not always the case that proponents of the behaviour believe X, while the majority who resist believe Not-X. Reasons for and reasons against can exist on different planes: they are misaligned.

What happens in practice is that the two sides talk past each other. Veganism wasn't resisted within the mainstream because the broad mass of people felt that the slaughter and exploitation of animals was perfectly OK. The resistance emanated from a pervasive fear that the strictures of a vegan diet were innately unhealthy. Yet the vegan movement's response to the lack of uptake of their cause was to double down on their own ethically driven reasons for adhering to it.

Misalignment fosters an opportunity to come between two sides and change the conversation through new emphasis and new evidence. Whereas two antagonists going head-to-head in direct disagreement presents little opportunity for reconciliation, since one or other must back down for the status to change, misalignment presents a crack that can be infiltrated.

4. VECTORS

When people come to join an identifiable tribal group, they tend to adopt the incidental behaviours that come along with it – including marginal ones.

In that sense, anyone who becomes involved with the group can be a vector, with the potential to carry the behaviour to other sectors of society.

In the veganism narrative, the hippy and punk tribes were vectors. Young people would become involved with these movements, discover the veganism that was part of their culture, and adopt it as a secondary imperative.

The potential of vectors to carry a marginal behaviour into the mainstream will depend on the extent to which the vector group is socially isolated or embedded. Hippies and punks were countercultural movements, so the direct effect was limited. Indirectly, though, they helped keep veganism to the fore and stopped its slide into irrelevance.

5. REFRAMING

Reframing starts as a verbal adjustment, develops as a mental reassessment, leads to an emotional rapprochement and culminates in a shift in behaviour.

For many in the mainstream, the term 'vegan' was off-putting. It didn't just signify a dietary and lifestyle choice, it evoked images of activism, confrontation and violence. The term 'plant based', which became increasingly used from around 2016 onwards, is an elegant example of reframing: gentler, softer, more descriptive, innocent of 'f*** you' associations and unattached to any doctrinaire *ism*.

Reframing is an established concept in marketing and can be used at the level of an individual brand – to overcome a barrier to purchase relating to that brand or its category. Oatly employed the technique brilliantly to counter the mental model that its product was not the real thing – not real milk – with witty ads that reframed 'alternative' as a more rational choice for humans than something that had passed through the body of a member of another species. In that sense, it also reframed the norm, making it feel like the odd thing to do. (There'll be more on the Oatly approach in later chapters.)

6. REVERSAL

We saw earlier (in Beacon 2) that before a marginal behaviour can make progress towards the mainstream, resistance needs to be overcome. If the reason for resistance fades away, the resulting neutral state allows people to reconsider the behaviour and perhaps adopt it.

Sometimes, though, resistance doesn't just fade, or even disappear – it goes into reverse: the reason for the initial resistance makes a $180°$ turn and becomes a positive reason for uptake. That sudden 'switchback' can make for rapid change: it's like the difference between cycling laboriously uphill (gravity providing resistance), then freewheeling dizzily down (that same gravity working for you).

In the vegan narrative, health was that gravitational force. For many decades it provided resistance, as the diet was felt to predispose adherents to malnutrition and morbidity. But new research in the early 2010s turned that on its head; the vegan diet was shown to be good for you and the meat-and-dairy habit was the one that now came with the health warnings.[28] Resistance didn't just fade, it flipped into reverse, and the gravitational force now worked in veganism's favour: health became the predominant reason for seeking out vegan options.

Reversal is one of two beacons that help explain the two-speed movement characteristic of M2M journeys: gradual then sudden. The second one is coming up next.

7. ACCELERATORS

An accelerator is an event or a new factor in the wider societal, geopolitical or economic environment that serves to turbocharge the speed of uptake of a marginal behaviour. The Covid pandemic has been a massively significant accelerator of pre-existing behavioural trends, especially in workplace practices.

Two accelerators were important in the veganism narrative. In Asia, the 2011 nuclear power plant accident in Fukushima, Japan, prompted millions of consumers to seek alternatives to fish as a source of protein and healthy oils. Two years later, the 2013 horsemeat scandal prompted European populations to think twice about their animal-derived consumption.

As the name suggests, accelerators apply when something is already moving. They are usually insufficient, alone, to kickstart progress when the brakes are firmly on; a powerful accelerator might give an inert marginal behaviour a shunt, but it will invariably shudder to a halt again.

But if you are observing a behaviour that is already slowly in motion, and you sense or reason that conditions for an accelerator are propitious, then you are at a pivotal diagnostic point – with the prospect that speed of uptake could suddenly surge and gain unstoppable momentum.

8. DILUTION

Dilution is more exciting than it sounds. It marks the final phase of the diffusion of a marginal behaviour into the mainstream and, with it, the potential for consumer-driven disruption.

Dilution starts with acceptance – a recognition that the behaviour is a reasonable thing to do, even by those not quite ready to try it themselves. As we saw in the veganism example, that acceptance was for decades sorely lacking, as doubters worried on behalf of vegans that their dietary choice was unhealthy – dangerous even.

But even when the acceptance hurdle is cleared, it does not usually lead to the mass adoption of the behaviour in its full, committed form. Instead, it will tend to be tried flexibly, in dilute form – a bit here, a bit there, in a kind of dance with the prevailing behavioural norm. With veganism, that meant casually combining plant-based and meat-and-dairy options within the weekly repertoire – going flexitarian, perhaps, and certainly doing away with all the ferocity and dogma associated with hardcore vegan ideology.

Dilution is a phase of significant growth – because *majority acceptance counts for more than minority adherence*. Imagine, for example, that the market for vegan options was restricted to 2 per cent of the population who bought vegan 100 per cent of the time. That's not nothing, but neither is it huge – a specialist, niche market. But if 50 per cent of the population choose vegan just 20 per cent of the time you have a market that is now five times bigger – with considerable potential for further growth. Marketers familiar with Professor Byron Sharp's work on brand growth will recognize this as a version of the importance of penetration over loyalty.[29]

This is not to say that dilution is always welcomed by the diehards. The idea of 'vegan lite' has gained a mixed response, sometimes verging on hostility, from those who still regard their ideology as a way of life – all or nothing. True vegans will insist that the avoidance of animal exploitation inhabits all corners of human agency, proscribing choices in everything from makeup to shoes. They term themselves 'lifestyle vegans', in contrast to mere 'dietary vegans', who dabble with only one aspect of the practice.

The effect, though, is to solidify the sense that the hybrid is now a norm, by providing a new 'outlier' – the fully committed version – on the behavioural fringe.

Upstream versus downstream

Two factors that aren't in the beacons, and you might find yourself wondering why: the influence of celebrity and the network effect of digital media.

Numerous commentators have cited the uptake of veganism by the famous as a key influence in its more general ascent. Images of Beyoncé and Jay-Z embarking on a 22-day 'vegan challenge' in 2013[30] were widely reshared by way of illustration.

But this is to confuse effect with cause. Why was it veganism they were embracing and not other marginal dietary choices like, say, rawism or the consumption of insects and larvae? The answer is that a groundswell movement towards plant-based eating was already in play. Veganism didn't get going because A-listers embraced it; it was the other way around. This is not to say that celebrity is without influence; it will help the movement along, for sure. It's just that it is a downstream influence, when the dam of resistance has long since been breached.

Digital connectedness is also offered as an explanation for the explosive uptake of veganism through the late 2010s. Does that analysis hold up? Yes and no. At a meta level – as we'll see in later chapters – instant, networked, digital communications are a contextual factor that can rapidly foster the spread of any emergent behavioural trend. But that contextual backdrop does not offer an explanation why it should be this trend, this emergent behaviour, rather than that.

You can think of digital communications like a city with a wonderful metro network. In theory, it is always possible for a huge number of people to converge rapidly on a given destination at a given time. The transport network facilitates that human swarm. But it does not help you predict precisely where or when it will happen. Similarly, the global digital network is out there, ripe and ready for sudden convergence around an idea; but thousands of ideas compete for attention and sharing. The reasons why one powers through ahead of others will have been shaped upstream, much earlier in the process.

Certainly, if the first time you glimpse an unusual but promising behaviour is when you notice that somebody famous has adopted it, or when you see a surge of digital communication devoted to it, you are coming to it late. The point of the beacons, conversely, is to help you see that behaviour change, and perhaps directly engage with it, much earlier in the journey: upstream, not downstream – and certainly well ahead of the phenomenon's emergence into the mainstream.

A note on 'Notes from the margins'

At the end of each of the chapters from here on (aside from the final one), you'll see a panel under the title 'Notes from the margins'. Each one will get under the skin of a marginal behaviour or way of life that has been researched as part of the background for this book – often including highlights from interviews with people who practise, advocate for and perhaps have themselves written about the behaviour in question.

The aim of these panels is not to be predictive – not to suggest that each is poised for an explosion into mainstream life. In fact, there is nothing judgemental intended at all. It is more to come at things from an anthropological angle – to get closer to an answer to the dispassionate observer's classic question: what's going on?

The point is that marginal behaviours, choices and ways of life can be eye-openers in their own right, even where they are likely to remain at the fringes – a nuance we'll be exploring further in Part 3 of the book. For mainstream marketers and business leaders, there are myriad ways in which a glimpse into the margins can be a source of insight, revelation and inspiration.

Because one thing is for sure. Meaningful growth is unlikely to be the outcome of plodding on with the same tired thinking within the same, me-too, 'sideways' innovation groove into which mainstream business seems to be ever more firmly stuck – a reality that we'll confront full-on in the chapter coming up next.

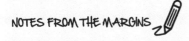

NOTES FROM THE MARGINS

Biohacking

Biohacking sounds thrillingly futuristic, given its devotees strive to become cybernetic organisms – *cyborgs* – by implanting technological devices into their bodies. We've all heard of wearable tech like Fitbits; this extreme body modification goes a whole lot deeper, quite literally, in its aim to improve the human condition.

Rather disappointingly though, embedding technology through biohacking isn't as sci-fi as it sounds at first. After all we've worn contact lenses for decades, can easily and safely implant hearing aids, stents and pacemakers and attach prosthetic limbs. The contraceptive implant was taken up by 1.4 million women in Britain in its first decade after licence in 1999. Why wouldn't we harness tech advances to make our bodies work more efficiently?

Millions of dogs are micro chipped with ownership details, to allow them to be identified if they get lost. It's not a huge leap to imagine storing vital information on ourselves too rather than carrying it around with us on paper or stored on phones that can be lost or stolen. US self-identified *transhumanist* Winter Mraz, for example, has several cyber implants in her body, including an NFC chip which typically contains her business card, so she can easily transfer her contact details. (NFC – Near-Field Communication – transmits data when activated at very close range, so is now widely embedded in phones or smartwatches to be used for Apple Pay, travel cards etc).

However, when Winter travels, she also uploads to that chip a link to all her medical information. "I have an autoimmune disease, so I'm allergic to a lot of things, and it's way too much to put on a medical alert bracelet. So instead I've got all of the information like what I'm allergic to, what medication I can't have, what type of EpiPen I use, on there".[31]

For more everyday uses, US tech firm Three Square Market gave employees the option of a microchip implant which allows them to unlock doors, log into computers and pay for snacks in their offices. And while it's useful for the able-bodied and their lunch queues, it could be truly life-changing for those with disabilities. Anyone with dexterity or mobility issues, for example, could embed a chip and very simply install an Radio Frequency Identification-powered lock which would allow them in and out of their homes without having to fumble with keys.

So far, perhaps it's not much more than a novelty to carry a travel pass, bank card or house keys on something the size of a grain of rice, inserted under the fleshy skin between your thumb and forefinger. But this could just be the beginning.

As microchips get smaller and cheaper, and the DIY-bio movement and its open-source intel gains ground, what started as a niche interest begins to nudge its way into the mainstream. Biohacker, scientist and *Shark Tank* entrepreneur Ryan Bethencourt believes it "could change the world as we know it".[32] And where big brains and big names are investing big money, the rest of us are likely to feel its impact before too long.

02

Why modern mainstream marketing is a low-growth zone

The number one job of marketing is growth. In big, brand-owning corporations, marketers are charged with the sustainable and profitable growth of market share – or the invention of new markets altogether – with the objective of increasing the dollar value of the brand assets on the balance sheet.

Marketers may pursue interim metrics as part of their day-to-day practice – prompted and unprompted awareness, net promoter score, customer acquisition and retention rates – but they are aware that brand-growth outperformance is the only currency that counts when defending budgets in the boardroom.

Growth is not merely celebrated but fetishized when businesses open up about their brand portfolio strategies or when marketers come together to debate the current state and the future shape of their discipline.

The highly respected Marc Pritchard, Chief Brand Officer at Procter & Gamble (P&G), describes the corporation's marketing endeavour as a 'force for good and a force for growth'.[1] In 2021 he announced a new internal programme – GrowthWorks – to help promote the cultural entrepreneurialism that would achieve that ideal.

In a 2019 interview with Marketing Week, Linda Boff, Chief Marketing Officer (CMO) of GE, declared that 'marketing leaders need to be growth hunters'[2] – a nugget adopted later by the CMO Club, as the theme for one of its European 'summits'.

And marketing leaders are increasingly given to inserting the word 'growth' into their job titles. At Walgreens Boots Alliance, Vineet Mehra's title was Global CMO. When he moved to Good Eggs Grocery Delivery, he ensured that it was changed to Chief Growth and Customer Officer. Since he is also chair of the Worldwide Effies – an award scheme that recognizes advertising effectiveness – this is not an insignificant intervention.

Meanwhile, on both sides of the Atlantic, the biggest marketing conventions have rounded on growth as the higher-order discourse theme. For the US-based Association of National Advertisers (ANA), which holds its annual, 3500-delegate Masters of Marketing conference in Orlando, Florida, growth has been the headline theme every year since inauguration in 1981. In London, Europe's lead event, the multi-stage Festival of Marketing, kicks off its Day 1 programme under the title 'Powering growth'. If you work in marketing, you are under no illusion what your overriding objective must be: growth, growth, growth.

And yet.

For many of the world's estimated 10.6 million marketers – probably for the majority – the reality falls some way short of the rhetoric. That reality will often consist in endless scrapping for incremental share gains – nudging them up a point or two, striving to stop them sliding back down – within categories which, themselves, are static or in decline. In mature, mainstream markets, runaway growth is an ideal rarely realized, falling at the hurdle of breakthrough innovation that rarely transpires.

The US haircare market is an example. The sector is dominated by three big players – L'Oréal, Unilever and P&G – with 60 per cent of the market between them and shares that remain stable within a one-to-two percentage range year on year.[3] The brand product portfolios are virtually interchangeable, innovations are slight and easily copied, and there is considerable crossover even in the way the luscious, cascading hair is captured in publicity stills and moving images. Consumers, for their part, switch brands readily; they are 'promiscuous', to use the industry term. Meanwhile, the category overall is in long-term stasis, with predicted annual value growth at just over 1 per cent.[4]

This anaemic rate of growth is by no means atypical in consumer-packaged goods (CPG) sectors. According to industry data, total CPG unit sales growth in the United States hovered at around 1 per cent in the 2016–19 period.[5]

Nor are things any easier in the world of business-to-business (B2B) brands. An example is professional wound care – dressings and devices to help clinicians manage wounds that arise from surgery, trauma or systemic illness. Since the category is worth some $9 billion globally and since the demands on health systems will only get tougher as populations age, you would think the sector ripe for innovation. Yet the most recent significant innovation – negative pressure wound therapy – is over 25 years old. Today, so-called 'advanced dressings' still account for more than 54 per cent of revenue sales, with Smith & Nephew and 3M dominating the market.[6]

As for growth, the only meaningful kind has arisen from acquisition or merger. Simply maintaining share in this kind of complex, multi-influencer market, requires a dogged salesforce covering multiple call points where many have a veto and few have direct authority to buy. Marketers try to provide air cover by commissioning expensive randomized controlled trials (RCTs) to show why their dressing has superiority on one key dimension over a rival's. Overall, although the sector is growing in volume sales as populations get older and sicker, value sales are depressed, through the downward pressures of commoditization and procurement nous. It is a picture that will be familiar to marketers in diverse B2B sectors: the need to keep one eye on competitors, the other on commoditizers and discounters, all the while parrying canny procurement professionals who play everyone off against each other.

The three growth blockers

If brands in multiple sectors are failing to achieve the kind of soaraway growth that shareholders seek, it isn't for lack of desire on the part of marketers. The concept of the game-changing innovation and repositioning that powers surging, sustained growth, eclipsing rivals and leaving them gasping in its wake, occupies a space in the marketing psyche as potent as that of the 'scoop' in the psyche of the journalist. Sadly, it is about as rare.

Why should this be? What are the forces that contribute to the suppression of unequivocal brand growth in 21st-century business? There will be a host of reasons for that, dependent on the specific sector involved (and, of course, some sectors will defy the trend altogether, at least for a while, when things are going their way). At the heart of mainstream marketing's crisis of stasis, though, it is possible to discern three pernicious underlying factors:

1 Convergence. The tendency for brands to cluster around sector points of parity, with little meaningful differentiation that would see one power ahead of the others, to ignite category growth

2 Lateral innovation. The tendency for marketers to devote resources to 'sideways' range extensions, or alternative routes to market, rather than to bold innovations that would propel a leap forward

3 Invention famine. The present and predicted dearth of high-order technological breakthroughs (like those of the past, from refrigeration to the microchip) on which flourishing marketing categories depend and from which all are downstream

We'll take these in order as we look at each in more detail now.

The curse of convergence

In early 2021, the UK-based clothing-to-food retailer Marks & Spencer (M&S) embarked upon a bitter and very public legal dispute with the German-owned discount retailer Aldi. The lawsuit raised eyebrows for two reasons. First, because this kind of gladiatorial struggle seemed out of character with the bland, 'British-safe' traditions of the M&S brand. And second, because the dispute centred on a cake in the shape of a caterpillar, with the unlikely sub-brand name of Colin.

This gooey confection was one of the M&S Food division's bestselling lines. But Aldi had copied it – copied it faithfully, right down to the colour of the icing that made the caterpillar's smile. They'd even given it a similarly deadpan alliterative name: Cuthbert. Since M&S believed they enjoyed patent protection on their caterpillar concept, which they'd launched in 1996, they took their case to the high court for a judge to preside.

Colin v Cuthbert gave British news headline writers and their readers a bit of levity in the depths of a grim Covid winter. For marketers, though, the story serves as a reminder of the insanely tight, zero-sum-game markets which they increasingly inhabit – and the attendant failure of imagination that can sometimes beset the discipline.

Look at things first from the Aldi perspective. Managers could have noted a gap in their portfolio for novelty cakes and designed one in the shape of a bridge or a famous building. Or they might have determined that resembling some kind of animal was the key to consumer appeal and created a cake in the shape of a dolphin, say, or a stretched-out koala. Or they might have narrowed it down still further, reckoning the secret was to mimic some kind of friendly bug, and gone for a cake in the shape of a ladybird. At least that would have provided a little consumer choice. Instead, they opted for total convergence.

Now switch sides and take the M&S point of view. Was legal action the only recourse? Perhaps they could have risen above the fray and observed that, while others might copy the design, they would never match the famed quality of M&S ingredients. Or they might have moved the design on, and come up with a cake, symbolically, in the shape of a butterfly. Or perhaps changed the dynamics of the market altogether, moving away from fattening, layered cream sponges to produce a fruit-based cake with healthier credentials. Consumers would be the winners here, gaining the benefits of meaningful choice – and the M&S brand would have gained, too, with a nod towards nutritional modernity.

As it was, the only winners were the lawyers.

This is an example, an extreme one, admittedly, of *deliberate convergence* – where managers display a cynical absence of pride to get as close as they dare to the detail of a rival's offer. For the managers of the more successful brand that ends up getting copied, the emotional reaction is normally a mixture of frustration and flattery. A part of business life.

But far more troubling is *insidious convergence* – where near-perfect overlap is the outcome even where marketers and business managers are doing everything in their power to differentiate their brand from the competition. They will decamp to workshops and brainstorms with fire in their veins and determination in their souls to 'take the brand to another level' and 'bust category norms'.

But norms are stubborn things. Norms fight back, in that asymmetrical-warfare way that saps the spirit and suffocates aggression. Gradually, without noticing at first, ground is given by those workshop attendees, and their brave new brands start to conform to the contours of the competitive landscape. There are reasons why this happens – some more within the control of marketing teams than others – and it's worth exploring them to see where opportunities for new ways of thinking might lie.

REGULATIONS AND LEGISLATION

The regulatory environment is like a wind tunnel in reverse: it determines a consistent shape for everything that enters inside it – but one that makes everything less, not more, streamlined. A marketing team for a lean, challenger bank might devise a beautifully simple account-opening process, getting it down to just a couple of clicks – only to be thwarted by anti-money-laundering regulations that compel it to adopt the same byzantine procedures as the most bloated of its legacy competitors.

It's trickier still for managers of global brands, since regulations can differ wildly by geography. In a workshop, a team might determine that the time is right for its skincare brand to go 100 per cent natural, using hitherto unexplored, efficacious active ingredients. Not so fast. In the United States or Europe, health and safety approvals might take up to three years. In Brazil, there are multiple agencies from which approval would need to be sought and numerous regional and city bodies are entitled to ask for additional evidence at any time. Pretty much every other market around the world would contrive to do things differently. It would take extraordinary determination for the brand team not to slide back to some combination of natural actives already in use and approved – which would in turn bring the brand closer to its competitors.

SUPPLY CHAIN CONCENTRATION

There are hundreds of beauty brands out there: mass, premium, 'masstige', midmarket, niche. Yet the product ingredients come from a handful of suppliers. In fragrance, there are just three big supplier firms, with the largest claiming to silently serve four billion customers a day.[7]

Or flip across to a category at the other end of the spectrum – cars – and witness the same 'funnelling' effect, where a breadth of marques relies on a narrow set of original equipment manufacturers. Auto marketers do their best to differentiate shared technologies through distinctive names and promises that reflect the brand positioning. So, Audi calls its automated emergency braking (AEB) system Pre Sense Plus; Ford calls it Active City Stop; Peugeot opts for Active Safety Brake. But it is the same piece of kit, outsourced from the same supplier.

Clearly, where brands share key suppliers with dozens of competitors, the prospects for wholly owned breakthrough innovation are slim. Equally clearly, although marketers may have a tangential influence on supply chain decisions, it is not an aspect of business over which they have control. Coming up, though, are three convergence-inducing factors in which marketers are very much central, since each relates in some way to the relationship between the business and its consumers.

DIDACTIC RESEARCHERS

Any marketing leader seeking to invest in long-term brand building – whether through positioning, communications or innovation – is likely to need to defend that decision to senior directors who may well have a preference for short-term, promotional initiatives. To bolster their recommendation, marketing leaders will invariably present research showing that the messages, positioning and product or service improvements resonate with consumers, and are worthy of investment. It would normally be impossible to gain acceptance without that backup.

This gives consumer research companies considerable influence at the highest level in brand-owning corporations, even if they never get to directly present their findings in the boardroom. Senior directors will often place extraordinary trust in the pronouncements of the researchers, neatly captured in the CMO's PowerPoint charts.

Meanwhile, the research industry itself has seen consolidation over recent years. The upshot is that a big research agency turning up at a briefing will have considerable background experience in the sector. Researchers will be forthcoming in their advice on what 'works' and what doesn't – based on aggregated previous findings with thousands of consumers.

This can sometimes be helpful, but it also constitutes an ingoing bias. For the marketing leader determined to do things differently, the first hurdle can be getting the research agency to approach the proposals with an open mind, and recognize that there is a value to iconoclasm, even though it runs counter to known category 'rules'.

In communications, some research companies have gone further, to openly declare a bias irrespective of category. They claim to have evidence that 'emotional' advertising is more effective than other kinds such as humour or reason – and they seek to steer brand teams in that direction. This doesn't actually have to be wrong to be problematic. There may well be some behavioural science behind the 'emotional/effective' claim. But if researchers are dispensing the same advice to anyone who will listen, then convergence must be the outcome – which will negate the supposed advantage of creating the 'right' kind of communications work.

Marketing leaders are not powerless over didactic researchers – marketers are the clients, after all – but it can take unusual strength of spirit to counter the pronouncements of those who have become only too accustomed to speaking with self-perceived unassailable authority.

THE UBIQUITOUS METRIC

Marketers employ a bewildering array of metrics to monitor the progress of their brands and to assess the performance of their marketing endeavour. Some of these will be sector-specific; others are chosen according to previously agreed priorities or simply based on what each individual marketer deems most illuminating.

But there is one metric that has attained near-ubiquity among brands in all sectors, one that is tracked and assiduously monitored not just by marketers but increasingly by chief executives too: Net Promoter Score (NPS).

The seduction of NPS arises from a combination of its methodological simplicity and its ability to provide a single number that can be easily compared across category and over time. Devised by management consultancy Bain in 2003, NPS works by asking customers a pivotal question: *On a scale of 0–10, how likely would you be to recommend this product or service to a friend or colleague?* Customers who give a score of 9–10 are called promoters; those who go low with a 0–6 are detractors; in between you have the passives. The NPS score is arrived at by subtracting the percentage of the detractors from that of the promoters, with the passives acting as inert ballast between the two.

Since a metric is of only limited use if it doesn't tell you how to improve, the methodology bequeathed by Bain to the world also involves a follow-up customer question: *What could we do better?*

NPS is a useful and logical metric but it serves to exacerbate the problem of convergence between rival brands in two ways – both of which derive from the fact that it focuses exclusively on customers.

First, note that in most categories, customers overlap – they will be customers of multiple brands. This means that many of the same consumers will be answering that second, 'improvement' question across competing brands. If two brands are perceived to be falling short in a similar way, then both will receive the same directive to improve. The question will also serve to iron out asymmetry between brands. If brand A is strong on product quality and relatively weak on service delivery, and brand B is the other way around, then both will receive customer advice to improve their weaknesses, and convergence is the likely result.

From the consumer's point of view, this is no bad thing, but looked at from the viewpoint of the brand, deliberate asymmetry might be preferable to neat conformity since it is a way to stand out – to be known for one big thing that the brand does exceptionally well, even if at the expense of a relative weakness elsewhere.

The exclusive NPS focus on customers also precludes engagement with those who might have something more original to offer: people who, for whatever reason, do not use the brand or even the category. These are voices that marketers routinely ignore, and yet they can often be the key to breakthrough thinking, since they frequently have startlingly unexpected insights to share.

LEVITT CONSUMER CENTRICITY

Perversely, the most significant contributor by far to brand convergence is the very principle that underpins the discipline of marketing: consumer centricity. Embedded in that two-word concept is not just the fundamental marketing practice of working backwards from consumer needs and desires but the whole panoply of consumer research techniques that accompanies it: focus groups, depth interviews, video diaries, friendship pairs, accompanied shopping trips, ethnography – and the newer, more tech-based neurological probing methodologies.

At the level of a single brand the aim is to understand consumers better, to prise open deeper insights into their lives, emotions and psyches so that they can be better served with a more apt combination of product, service and brand meaning – ideally one that will attract them in higher numbers, for greater lengths of time at more profitable prices.

To modern marketers, it is second nature to work this way. Other exigencies count of course – the wider cultural and competitive environment, the needs of the people inside the workplace – but it is a rare marketing department that does not openly and vociferously put the consumer at the heart of everything.

It wasn't always like that. Midway through the last century the consumer was somebody to be sold to – the dutiful recipient of the bounty that big business had become ever more adept at providing. Detroit rolled out huge cars because it could, and was inclined to, not through any evidence that a living room on wheels was what people were crying out for. Marketing, back then, was a fancy word for sales.

It took a sharp and courageous mind to change that. It belonged not to a member of the commercial caste but to an academic – Theodore Levitt, a professor at Harvard. His seminal 1960 paper, *Marketing Myopia*, opened eyes to the growing gulf between what people wanted and what business wanted them to want. In a tightly argued treatise that spared not even the biggest and most powerful of US sectors, Levitt expounded his central tenet that business needed to completely reverse its approach to market – putting customers first, not last, and working back from there. The paper had an immediate and stunning impact, with corporations falling over themselves to become – as many would express it – 'obsessive about the customer'. With that academic contribution, Levitt created modern marketing.

What was revelatory then is routine now. Ask, learn, offer. What modern marketer doesn't work this way? Yet mingled with the self-evident good sense of the Levitt doctrine is a glaring problem: the consumer will unveil similar glimpses into their souls irrespective of who happens to be asking. Those research methodologies are available to all with the means to deploy them. What consumers reveal to one brand in the sector, or subsector, they will reveal just as candidly to its competitors. Convergence is built into the Levitt consumer-centric system because consumers are not interested in helping marketers achieve distinction between brands; they are interested in getting what they want.

Or what they think they want – which brings us to a second flaw in the marketers' quest for research-led understanding: consumers can be a poor guide to consumers. They might have a vaguely reliable feel for what matters to them today but often a wayward one for what they would be willing to try tomorrow. Brands, by tethering their innovation feats to the limits of consumer imagination, rein the possibilities in.

Look at electric cars, for example. In theory, the switch from internal combustion technologies to electric should allow designers to question just about everything about a car's makeup and build. Yet the shape and design aesthetic of electric cars differs barely at all from its internal combustion predecessors, because consumers report themselves to be uncomfortable with change. Electric cars do not need a long hood, because the engine takes up so much less space – yet invariably they have one. And since electric cars don't require a radiator, manufacturers could do away with the grille entirely. Yet the all-electric Jaguar I-PACE still has a grille, in common with all other Jaguar models, because it is a feature that conforms to consumer expectations of the brand.

What we see here is that the reliance on consumer research intelligence fosters convergence not just horizontally, across rival brands within the same market space, but longitudinally, across time, so that today's offerings end up insufficiently differentiated from yesterday's. Either way, the effect is a kind of stultification, where competitors gather around sector points of parity that evolve painfully slowly, in line with conservative consumer diktat.

For any brand with an ambition to do things differently from its rivals, and take a leap away from where they doggedly cluster, a trenchant principle needs to be acknowledged:

UNLESS YOU'RE AHEAD OF THE CONSUMER, YOU CAN'T BE AHEAD OF THE COMPETITION

Easier said than done, because anticipating what consumers might be willing to consider even as they tell you 'no way' requires extraordinary intuition; and betting big on your hunch when the board is asking for consumer research evidence to back it up takes extraordinary courage.

One who had both was the late Steve Jobs. A natural marketer, Jobs took the view that 'it is not the consumer's job to know what they want'. His most famous manifestation of that publicly declared mantra was the launch of the iPad in 2010. Consumers didn't recognize the need for something between their smartphones and their laptops. Analysts predicted disaster. Yet almost 500 million units later, it seems consumers have worked out what they needed it for all along.

It is often said of Jobs that he refused to commission consumer research. It is interesting – and, from the viewpoint of this book's subject, relevant – that the truth is not as simple as that. The cohort that Jobs would often turn to for views, reactions and insights about prospective innovation was the internal one – Apple's own employees – since, as he put it, 'they are consumers, too'. Talking about the inspiration behind the iPod around the turn of the century, he recalled that Apple staff would go jogging back then with the latest Sony Walkman and muse on 'how cool it would be to have something smaller, maybe even credit card size, that would hold all your music in one place'.

This casual inference from a serendipitous 'respondent' pool would run afoul of today's 'best practice' research recruitment principles because those Apple insiders – young, tech-savvy, Californian, cool – were then unrepresentative of the mass-affluent market at whom the technology would eventually be aimed. But it was a benign bias; they were not so much unrepresentative as ahead. What they would buy today, others would buy tomorrow – and a 'tomorrow' that was not so far off. This is an example of *doing the wrong thing* that is resonant with the approach explored in this book – of looking to the margins for clues about tomorrow's mainstream.

A new lens on Levitt

Convergence is a curse because it blunts the distinction between brands, robs the category of its dynamism and makes it easy for commoditizers and discounters to settle in. From that point, a kind of low-risk truce takes hold. Share defence becomes the imperative and growth is constrained. Since consumer centricity, as currently practised, is the principal cause of convergence, does that mean it is time to part ways with the Levitt paradigm?

Not necessarily. What will be argued over the coming chapters is that marketers could do worse than divert their gaze from the same mainstream customers – profitable though these may be – and spend more time and resource coming at things obliquely. It is Levitt through a new lens: still about understanding consumers – but tomorrow's, not today's. Still about observing human behaviour – but broadening out to include groups and behaviours that do not seem remotely relevant now and asking whether they could soon inspire a breath-taking change in the cultural and commercial landscape.

With marketing imagination, brands can start to slip loose from the ties of consumer-derived sameness. If the resultant innovation programmes offer the potential for massive gains, then, with the whole organization pulling together – not just marketers alone – perhaps those other convergence-inducing challenges such as regulations and supply chain concentration can be overcome too. It is a tempting prospect.

Convergence, though, was just one of the three growth blockers identified earlier in this chapter. Let's now turn our attention to the remaining two.

21st-century marketing: a great leap sideways

Today's marketers spend considerable time and energy bringing to market what they call NPIs – new product innovations. Only rarely are these worthy of the name. Only occasionally will they be breakthroughs that surprise consumers and wrongfoot competitors. What they will mostly be instead are the tweaks, enhancements and fillers of marketers who are not so much looking forwards as sideways. We're talking here about *lateral innovation*: brand extensions, new variants and signature specials intended to make a noise in the sector, even though they might make little real difference.

So, a cough remedy brand might devise a variant based on a specific usage occasion, such as evening, using almost the same cocktail of ingredients as its core range; a gaming brand might bring out a repackaging of last year's big success; and brands in categories from cars to confectionery will dabble with time-limited special-edition lines.

Often these routine NPIs will not even be designed with the consumer principally in mind. The real focus will be the retail customer. In physical retail, shelf space is prime real estate, and if the addition of new lines can help a brand increase its facings, it stands a chance of out-muscling less endowed competitors. In online retail, products that come to the party with a bit of 'news' will often get prioritized for visibility.

Up to a point, sideways NPI tactics make sense for marketers with nothing of substance to announce. Lateral innovation can keep the brand front of mind, impart the feel of activity and help in the struggle for distribution. Yes, some proportion of any sales gain will come at the expense of existing variants in the portfolio, but if the overall outcome is to keep share erosion at bay, the investment can be justified.

The downside is that marketing resource is finite. If the constant quest for minor innovation consumes a disproportionate chunk of that resource, there is a risk that streams of activity aimed at high-growth innovation will remain undernourished.

A more insidious risk is when marketing teams believe they are exploring something truly forward-looking and innovative that turns out to be a sideways step after all. Nowhere is this more likely to occur than when they find themselves tempted by what has become the Big Idea in 21st-century marketing. So, it is worth devoting a few paragraphs now to the paradox that is DTC.

THE LURE OF DOING A GLOSSIER

If you gather marketing teams together in a workshop devoted to breakthrough innovation it will not be long before somebody exclaims 'Let's create a DTC brand'. The initials stand for 'direct to consumer' and the inspiration that will have got teams excited will be the stories of how Dollar Shave Club and Glossier carved out juicy shares in the shaving and beauty sectors respectively by challenging the hegemony of established brands with a different way of coming to market.

DTC brands have emerged in an impressive range of niches, but the shape of the offer is always the same. The product focus will be very narrow. These are sniper brands, devoted to a single, tightly defined customer need. Beltology is just belts. Eve is just mattresses. Ohne is just tampons. Niches don't come much narrower than that.

The reason for the focus is related to the reliance on the digital interface through which DTC brands engage, seduce and sell. DTC brands need to impart a sense of specialist expertise, since this is the key to both credibility and profitability. If they broaden out their offer too widely, they become just another e-tailer and run headlong up against Amazon.

But that bespoke, specialist allure is often more image than substance, mediated through a characteristic visual and verbal vernacular: sans serif fonts, minimalist backgrounds and a kind of cool-wit, boutique charm.

Although some DTC brands get hands-on and manufacture – Harry's Razors bought an old German razor factory, for example – most opt for the production stacks in a system known as 'supply chain as a service' (SCaaS). The merchandise will tend to feel more exclusive than it actually is. In theory, anybody can alight on a DTC niche without the remotest experience or expertise in the sector. In practice, many have.

Looking at the phenomenon of DTCs and asking to what extent they have contributed to growth results in a conundrum. From the viewpoint of the entrepreneurs who have founded DTC winners like Warby Parker (eyeware), Bonobos (clothing) and Hims (men's wellness), their personal stock has certainly grown. They started with little more than a vision and created a viable brand. That said, the route will not have been simple even for the successful: in DTC the cost of customer acquisition is high; it is not unusual to take a decade to break even and the pathway around you is strewn with those that didn't make it.

Conversely, take a helicopter view and look down at market sectors as a whole, and it becomes clear that a new way of selling essentially the same thing is not true market growth. For mainstream marketers who already sell through established retail outlets, the process of adding another sales channel – no matter how sexy it might seem in the workshop – is less like innovating than shuffling.

And to complete the enigma, notice how many DTC brands have come full circle and moved across into physical retail. Away (luggage), Heist Studios (hosiery) and Glossier have opened stores in high-end locations from London to Los Angeles. It would be absurd for brands already with a physical retail presence to establish a DTC alternative, only to see it eventually veer back to physical retail again. Not so much sideways as circular.

Bottom line: for a handful of true entrepreneurs, DTC has been a route to riches, exploiting the complacency of legacy incumbents. For mainstream marketers it is probably a distraction. Bigger prizes hide elsewhere – and the contention of this book is that the margins constitute a more promising, more inspiring, and more original place to look. That said, there is nothing wrong with marketers emulating the audacity and entrepreneurship of DTC founders, even if they do not follow their chosen route. Those who wish to venture to fringes to reinvigorate their brands are going to need it.

Let's move on now to the final of our three growth blockers – the 'famine' in upstream invention.

Marketing in the age of stagnation

The Great Stagnation is the title of a 2011 book by Professor Tyler Cowen of George Mason University. As often with business books, it is the subtitle that does the real enticing: 'How America ate all the low hanging fruit of modern history, got sick and will (eventually) feel better'. The 'low hanging fruit' amounts to the extraordinary litany of breakthrough inventions of the past three centuries, from the steam engine and the automobile, through to electricity, refrigeration, pharmaceuticals, aircraft and television, and on to the computing advances of the mid and late 20th century. To this Cowen adds the windfall benefits that once came with free land and cheap immigrant labour.[8]

The argument is that this was a one-off period of extraordinary economic bounty that will not be replicated. Inventions of this scale are unique opportunities that just cannot keep coming. We have reached, as Cowen puts it, a 'technological plateau' and advancements will be scarcer and smaller from here.

The theme was developed in 2015 by Professor Robert Gordon, an economic historian at Northwestern University, with his weighty, almost magisterial, book, *The Rise and Fall of American Growth*. Gordon argues for a narrower period of one-off technological progress – the 100 years between 1870 and 1970 – describing it as 'a revolutionary century when, through a set of miracles... the modern world was created'.[9] Across 16 chapters, Gordon shines a light on those 'miracles' one by one, showing the transformative effect each had not just on economic growth but on everyday lives – the difference between having a flush toilet and an outside latrine, for example.

But in a bare two chapters at the end of the book, the same conclusion is reached as that of Cowen: the party is over. Economic data document the decline in growth (measured by a combination of metrics including total GDP and output per person) since 1970, notwithstanding the entry of digital communications into the mix, which has prompted upward blips but not a steady rise.

The significance for business and the marketers who work in the world's great corporations is that the pipeline that once provided a source of expansion no matter what is spluttering. It is not something that marketers routinely think about, but all commercial categories that exist today are downstream from one or more of those higher-order inventions. There would be no frozen foods or chilled goods without the invention of refrigeration. No cars, vans, trucks, motorbikes, dealerships or gas stations without the breakthrough of the internal combustion engine. And no search or social media giants without the coming of the microchip and the internet.

Whole sectors get birthed every time a new technology lands, and those sectors wouldn't exist if it hadn't. It might not be top of mind for a marketer striving to devise the right format for a new business class airline cabin to whisper a quiet word of recognition to the Wright brothers, but the arc of dependence is there, nonetheless.

If the first two blockers of growth identified earlier in this chapter are part of the marketing world and amenable to marketer agency, the invention famine is an extraneous reality. The dearth might dampen expansion, but what can marketers do about it?

The answer to that might be teed up by the counterarguments of some heavyweight critics of the 'growth pessimist' school – which has not had things all its own way. Pre-eminent among those who incline to a more optimistic view of the future are the Nobel Prize winning economist Paul Krugman and Microsoft founder Bill Gates.

Instructive is *why* they are optimistic. It is not that they deny the central pessimist contention that the pace of great technological breakthroughs has slowed – though both argue that technology has some way to go yet – but that there is huge untapped potential in what already exists, and limitless human ingenuity ready to find new ways to deploy it, solve problems and ignite growth.

Another who remains determinedly optimistic is Deirdre McCloskey, professor of economics and history at the University of Illinois. Her argument – vividly expounded across a trilogy of virtuoso macroeconomics books – is that the ultimate source of prosperity is *ideas,* which may or may not be attached to technology, and which will never run dry in liberated societies.

Ideas are a marketer's stock in trade – or should be. But marketers and business leaders will need to reach far deeper into their reserves of human ingenuity than they do right now if they are to discover new growth opportunities sufficient to compensate for the slowing of upstream technological invention. Where might they look for inspiration to help them achieve that vigorous shift in gears?

Tomorrow's brand growth

This has been a chapter on where growth is *not* going to come from. It will not come from the 'mainstream inhibition' that sees brands stick so rigidly to consumer research feedback that they end up clustering around sector points of parity with near-perfect convergence. It will not come from the insipid outputs of lateral innovation – a form of endless tinkering while waiting for something of substance to turn up. And nor can great technological inventions – 'miracles' – be relied upon to keep coming and conveniently grow the sky while corporations cruise.

If modern mainstream marketing is to become a high-growth zone, something more daring will need to be tried. The next chapter rounds on what that 'something' might be. It argues the need to break through mainstream inhibition and turn attention to the margins – to confront, evaluate and embrace the strangeness of behaviours, ideas and ways of life at the fringes. They may be unpromising, untested, weird, even sometimes repulsive – yet they can point the way to new innovation, new routes to disruption and exciting new category creation. Today's margins are tomorrow's brand growth – if you know where and how to look.

 NOTES FROM THE MARGINS

Insect protein

Do you get a warm glow of smugness when you do 'the right thing' and pick a veggie dish from the menu? Opting for a bean burger over a hamburger feels like an eco-aware choice, as the environmental issues relating to industrial meat production and the health issues of a heavy meat-based diet become clearer.

However, environmental teaching fellow Professor Tilly Collins at Imperial College suggests choosing an <u>insect</u> burger would be even better for the planet. Since plant-based diets often come with substantial carbon mileage and their harvesting and production involves massive use of fresh water, efficiently farming insects is far preferable from an environmental point of view.[10]

Could our palates stomach the idea of eating insects? What seems like a strange choice now could be commonplace in a decade, much as oat milk or Quorn were niche products when they were developed, and are now sold in corner shops. Times change and so do our tastes – even lobster and oysters were once considered peasant food (in the early days of the United States, the lobsters which washed up plentifully on the Atlantic coast were only deemed fit for feeding to prisoners and slaves).

As Giovanni Sogari, a social researcher at the University of Parma, puts it: 'There are cognitive reasons derived from our social and cultural experiences, the so-called "yuck factor", that make the thought of eating insects repellent to many Europeans. With time and exposure such attitudes can change'.[11]

And though insect ingredients might sound strange to Western ears, they are already used broadly in diets around the world. Grubs are commonplace in New Guinea and in aboriginal Australia; cicadas and ants are often roasted into traditional Latin American dishes and termites are used in bread and with porridge across different nations from Ghana to South Africa.

Elsewhere, the exposure that Giovanni Sogari mentioned in his research is still fairly small-scale, but it's there. Until Brexit meant the UK Food Standards Agency decided to re-regulate the serving of edible insects, the Grub Kitchen was dishing up cumin and mealworm hummus, mixed insect pakora and bug burgers for visitors to Dr Beynon's Bug Farm, a quirky tourist attraction in Wales.

EatGrub have 12,000 social media followers and position themselves firmly alongside active, healthy and eco-aware people; their list of ambassadors is packed with triathletes and extreme adventurers who swear by their edible crunchy roasted crickets and insect protein powder.[12] Similarly, FoodyBug is also building business in the margins, with their hero product being Crickolate spread, a 21st-century insect-based take on Nutella. Their Instagram feed features attractive young Italians enthusing about its taste alongside messaging on climate change.[13]

Ento Kitchen are another early adopter, who developed their offer from mealworm-based pet food to market edible insects for humans in snack and powder form.[14] (The insects are farmed in Europe but marketed from their base in northern England). Their bright graphics push the sustainability story; insects breed more quickly, grow more quickly and deliver protein more efficiently than farm animals. 80 per cent of a cricket is edible, compared to just 40 per cent of a cow.

All Ento Kitchen's numbers are pretty convincing; their buffalo worm powder, for example, is 59 per cent protein, compared to 20 per cent protein in a regular three-ounce hamburger.[15] Alongside the environmental consequences of meat production (from overuse of land and greenhouse gas emissions) that's a pretty efficient way for humans to consume protein – and these companies want you to feel good about doing so.

A change is afoot. The smart money is already twitching its nose at the edible insects industry, which could one day be the new normal; by 2027 the market is projected to reach £3.36 billion ($4.63 billion).[16]

03

Going for growth:
Why the margins? And why now?

The simplest answer to the first of the two questions in the chapter heading is the one that's baked in, the one that's obvious when you think about it: if you're looking for high growth, don't start with something that's already grown. Don't start, in other words, from the mass – because growth from here will tend to be slow and incremental. Start, instead, from something small, marginal, promising – and see if you can achieve the spectacular.

It was telling that at the 2019 ANA Masters of Marketing conference in Orlando – the last live 'Masters' event before the Covid pandemic – the only presentation with jaw-dropping growth figures was the one from Mike Messersmith, General Manager of Oatly US. While other speakers talked of 'overcoming the odds' or 'building from purpose', Messersmith was able to cut straight to the chase and report 1600 per cent value growth in 18 months.[1] But he had an advantage: the concept of oat milk had barely existed in the United States when the brand launched in 2017, and even alternative milk as a category was only just beginning to flicker. The chances of failure were high, of course, but the prospects for momentum from that low base were considerable – with effort, talent and luck. In the event, Oatly managed to both ride and drive the behavioural shift towards non-dairy, plant-based nutrition.

What happened next is that the growth kept coming – doubling and redoubling – and Oatly floated on the Nasdaq in 2021 for $13 billion. Let's take a reality check here, though. It would be misguided to read this as an overnight M2M journey. Although the brand was relatively new in the United States, it had existed in Europe for some 15 years, the first ten of which were confined to serving a super-marginal cohort who chose non-dairy milk on the basis of dietary need, lifestyle or beliefs.

Marketers will be looking for faster turnaround than that, if they are to take the risks attendant with committing resource to the margins – and this chapter will give them reasons for optimism on that front. It will also offer up more marginal behaviours to stimulate the imagination. First, though, let's aim for some clarity about what is meant by those two words, 'marginal behaviour'.

A WORKING DEFINITION

What does 'marginal' mean, when we're looking at human behaviour through a marketing lens? How small are we going? What makes the cut and what doesn't? There are reasons for imprecision here, not least of which is the difficulty of finding accurate numbers for behaviours and ways of life which have often not been formally categorized and analysed before. But we do need to have some idea of where the boundaries between 'marginal', 'minority' and 'mainstream' lie.

Taking a marketing perspective, the principle to work from is that a *marginal behaviour* needs to be big enough to be able to appear on your radar – so not atomized among a few dozen individuals within a population of 50 million – yet small enough that it is not already something that numerous competitors are likely to be actively probing and exploring. That will probably put it at 3 per cent or less of the adult population.

Moving beyond that, we alight on *minority behaviours* – ones big enough to be more recognized and perhaps have niche brands attached. These would be somewhere between that 3 per cent and 12 per cent.

Then come the behaviours that are clustered within the *mainstream* – anything above that 12 per cent. (See Figure 3.1.)

If we think back to the veganism example and look at UK 2016 figures (before things really took off) those who claimed to be vegan were fewer than 1 per cent – so very much a marginal behaviour back then. Vegetarians were reported at 5.5 per cent – so a minority behaviour. The mainstream was all the rest – composed of omnivores of different stripes.

The word 'behaviour' also merits a little ringfencing. For the purposes of this book, it will be framed as follows:

- A behaviour or life choice entered into voluntarily and repeated or maintained over time – so not just a one-off trial of something novel
- Not based solely on religion or politics
- Not a reflection of mental disorder or anything that would obviously harm self or others

- Could be enhanced by technology but not technologically driven – in other words, not a behaviour that required a technological leap to get it started
- Not simply a single habitual consumption choice, but a rounded human behavioural pattern that might prompt multiple consumption decisions – or have no obvious consumption relevance at all

Working from that definition, what kinds of interesting marginal behaviours might be thrown up? There will be literally hundreds of possibilities. That's the wonderful thing about the fringes: they are a constantly renewable source of new ways of thinking, doing and being. Here are some marginal behaviours that are happening right now (working, in some cases, from best-guess estimates of sizes of adherent populations):

FIGURE 3.1   Definitions: the three Ms

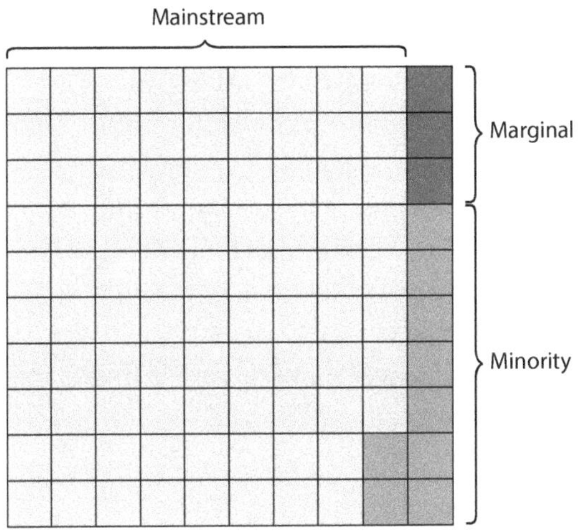

Marginal: a behaviour practised by <3 per cent of the population
Minority: a behaviour practised by 3–12 per cent of the population
Mainstream: behaviours practised by >12 per cent of the population

UNIFORM WARDROBE
People who wear the same outfit every day. Not the same actual items – but having found a look they like they buy multiple copies and take the strain out of wondering what to wear. Think Steve Jobs, with his Issey Miyake black turtleneck and Levi 501s.[2]

Barack Obama had his own slightly extended version, with only blue or grey suits in the same cut. 'I'm trying to pare down decisions', he explained in a 2012 Vanity Fair piece. 'I don't want to make decisions about what I'm eating or wearing. Because I have too many other decisions to make.'[3]

Psychologists call it decision fatigue, and the more complex and prosperous contemporary lives become, the more of it there will be.

NO-SOAPERS

People who don't use soap when they wash. Advocates rinse and wash themselves with water but reject detergents – which is what much of modern soap and shower gel amounts to. They believe that the skin microbiome is as important as the gut microbiome and has a similar need for friendly microbes – particularly the ammonia-oxidizing bacteria that are found in dirt.

The key is getting the balance right – so that the dirt that causes odour is naturally broken down. Advocates cite the example that the reason horses roll about in mud and dust is to correct the microbiome on their skin. Their contention is that modern humans have become unhealthily clean.[4]

POLYAMORY

This is the practice of having intimate relationships with more than one partner, with the informed consent of all partners involved. The term was first coined in the 1990s in Morning Glory Zell-Ravenheart's article on the subject, *A Bouquet of Lovers,* and is also sometimes known as CNM, or consensual non-monogamy.[5]

There is a full-length write-up on polyamory in 'Notes from the margins' at the end of Chapter 4.

COSPLAY

Cosplayers wear costumes, make-up and accessories to portray characters they love from comic books, video games, television and movies – especially science fiction. It's a colourful part of popular culture in Japan where the name was coined and the phenomenon started in the 1980s, but cosplay is now widespread at fan conventions around the world.

ICE SHOWER CONVERTS

A daily ice-cold shower is a growing wellbeing/lifestyle choice. The advocates' playbook is *The Wim Hof Method*, devised and written by a Dutch extreme adventurer whose amazing physical feats, he claims, are down to breath control and exposure to increasingly cold water.[6]

Enthusiasts cite studies showing a range of wellbeing benefits. Due to the high density of cold receptors in the skin, an ice-cold shower sends an overwhelming number of electrical impulses from peripheral nerve endings to the brain, which can result in an anti-depressive effect; exposure to cold is also known to activate the sympathetic nervous system and trigger a beneficial anti-inflammatory norepinephrine release.

There may even be a productivity pay-off: a Dutch study of 3,000 people found that those who took a 30–90-second cold shower for 30 days were 29 per cent less absent than their colleagues.[7]

NEO-LUDDITES

The epicentre of the movement is Pocahontas County, West Virginia – a tech desert with no Wi-Fi, no TV, no mobiles, no microwave ovens. There it's the law, and rules have been in place since the 1950s, when astronomical telescopes were erected in the area which couldn't function with any electrical interference. The locals simply learned to live with it. Then came newer additions to the population of 8,000 who moved there deliberately, seeing what looks like a downside to most people as a massive plus, and reframing the county as a refuge from the modern world.[8]

Neo-Luddites even have airtime in the United States. Steve Hilton (British Prime Minister David Cameron's one-time adviser) now lives in California and hosts a regular show on Fox. His anti-tech views mean he hasn't owned a mobile phone for years and evangelizes that others should do the same. 'It's not enough to just manage your use of tech devices. You have to give up.' He compares the negative impacts of mobile phones to tobacco, claiming that one day we will come to view them with the same scorn that we direct at cigarettes.[9]

As you trawl through fascinating marginal behaviours like these, and discover other secret tribes of your own, it can take a feat of imagination to envisage how they might erupt into the mainstream and what the commercial implications might be. The beacons are there to help, of course, but to liberate the mind and bolster your resolve, it can also help to reflect on a behaviour that was once marginal, but which grew and developed and went on to spawn an entire market category today. Here is one to think about:

The mindfulness journey

Mindfulness started life as meditation. It was a form of the millennia-old Zen Buddhist meditative technique reinterpreted for the West by Jon Kabat-Zinn, a New York born practitioner who founded a clinic for stress in the late 1970s.

Awareness of meditation was high back then – the transcendental form had been made famous by the Beatles – but few practised it in Western societies. It was something slightly esoteric and 'fringe', a trope of the rich or those, like the hippies, with time on their hands, who could make the journey to India or Korea to learn the practice and devote themselves to it once they got home. But – in a kind of reframing effect – Kabat-Zinn's 'mindful meditation' and then more simply 'mindfulness' succeeded in drawing in people from across the social spectrum.

Interest in mindfulness grew towards the turn of the millennium – fuelled in part by Deepak Chopra's 1993 book, *Ageless Body, Timeless Mind*, which sold 137,000 copies in a single day after an interview with Oprah.[10] Scientific exploration into its positive effects also increased dramatically from a low base. In the period 1995–97, there was just one randomized controlled trial involving mindfulness; by the period 2004–06 that had grown to 11; jump to 2013–15, and there were over two hundred.[11]

At its simplest, the practice of mindfulness involves being still and present in the moment, without evaluation or interpretation. It can be practised with no artefacts whatsoever, beyond perhaps a chair. Nevertheless – and to the disapproval of some – the discipline has inspired a thriving and multifaceted commercial sector, valued at over $3.5 billion in 2020 and growing annually by more than 11 per cent.[12]

On the experiential side, the concept has been taken back to its meditation roots. Studios such as MNDFL in New York opened with classes titled 'breath' or 'movement', run by 'spiritual leaders', with the objective of making practice more accessible and less intimidating. But technology is where the real growth is happening. Mindfulness-based apps such as Headspace and Calm have been downloaded in the tens of millions, with Calm now celebrated as a 'mental health unicorn', valued in 2020 at over $2 billion. As one analyst observed in a piece in The Atlantic, 'It has monetized sitting doing nothing.'[13]

Beyond that core, though, are the more tangential but flourishing spin-offs that are associated with the mindfulness state: scented candles, bath oils, weighted blankets, specialist teas and even adult colouring books, which claim to still the chattering mind. Perhaps the recent uptake of knitting, with its low-stakes, repetitive rhythms, is based on a similar need.

Mindfulness is a concept with further room to develop because it essentially feels good and taps into the concerns of the age. In the UK, it has even received a kind of governmental endorsement. In 2015 the UK Mindfulness All-Party Parliamentary Group published a paper entitled *UK Mindful Nation*, which sought to 'address mental and physical health concerns... through the application of mindfulness-based interventions'.[14]

There was no commercial 'mindfulness category' 20 years ago. There was traditional meditation, practised by relatively few, and there was mindfulness as concept and practice, offering a more accessible entry point into one form of meditation for a broader spectrum of people. Today, there exists a whole suite of access points for many, supported by a fast-growing mindfulness sector giving brands in multiple categories new ways to enhance the lives of their customers.

The principle at play here is to not dismiss something practised deep inside the margins as too insubstantial for consideration. Growth can come from unlikely places. And in today's world, it is apt to spring up more readily from those places, for reasons we will look at more closely now.

Why growth from the fringes is happening faster

Marginal behaviours have always been with us. There have always been those who, in one or more aspects of their lives, have done things a little differently – sometimes very differently – from the people around them. And there is nothing new in the phenomenon of diffusion, where some of these behaviours practised at the fringes break through to capture the imaginations of others and become widespread.

Look at tattoos, for example. The first body painting examples were brought to the West in 1769 by sailors returning from Tahiti (the word tattoo derives from the Tahitian 'tattau'). Uptake shifted around a cluster of very different marginal cohorts on the long journey to the mainstream. They were first adopted by aristocracy. Then taken up by servicemen to demonstrate patriotism, right through until just after the Second World War. From there, they became a marker of the underclass, with convicts overrepresented. Then out of fashion until new, more customized designs increased appeal and demand. In the 1990s they began to be taken up by the middle classes, and from around 2000 it became more common for women to get tattooed. Now, tattoos are almost ubiquitous in the UK, Europe and United States (though still very much taboo in Japan).

The *shape* of M2M journeys for today's marginal behaviours is destined to be similar – moving among different cohorts, evolving, hitting pivot points, gaining traction, breaking through in some cultures but not all. But two aspects will be different: the *number* of marginal behaviours that go mainstream will be greater, and the *speed* of that change will be swifter. We are entering an age of 'faster from the fringes'. Why?

There are three structural and cultural factors that underpin the more prolific diffusion of marginal behaviours into mainstream lives – with the third also acting as a 'jump start' for increased economic activity relating to them. They are:

1 Content and connectivity

2 'Gen-yes' demographics

3 Diversity inside and out

We'll look at each of them in more detail now.

Supercharged awareness: the first outcome of connectivity

All marketers understand the seminal importance of awareness in consumption decisions. Consumers are not going to seek out products, brands or experiences that they haven't even heard of. Yes, some may come across them serendipitously and give them a try on the off chance, but that is a very slow way to grow a brand. For marketers who want millions to get to the point of consideration and then, with luck, to trial, the first step along the way is simple awareness. It is why the metrics of awareness are such vital tools in the marketer's kit-box.

A similar principle is at play with the uptake of human behaviour – even though there is no 'marketer' driving things along. Awareness is the start point for anything that comes next. If the behaviour is marginal and kicks up a lot of resistance then awareness will not automatically prompt consideration, let alone trial. But without mass awareness, the potential spread of the behaviour is stunted from the start.

As with consumption, it is possible for people to discover a marginal behaviour serendipitously, without knowledge that others are engaged in it. A person might become an 'ice-shower convert', for example, through accident or experiment. But for growth in the behaviour to happen at scale, many need to arrive at the step of registering it and knowing that others are doing it – ideally with some idea of why. In the M2M journey, awareness is almost like a meta beacon, lighting up the pathway from the start and exerting its influence all the way along.

How do people become aware of unusual behaviours practised out there by some (but not many) of their fellow citizens? Classically, this would happen by chance – knowing or meeting somebody who practises the behaviour – or by word of mouth, or through some form of media, such as a magazine article or TV programme.

These routes to awareness have long been there – but what has been amplified in very recent years is the third: the disseminating power of media, which has grown exponentially in less than a decade and shows all signs of evolving further from here. If people once accessed strands of media content as a function of considered momentary decisions, now they are more or less bathed in it, within an organic, fluid, and ever-present media milieu.

One effect of this contemporary media context – with social, streamed, user-generated and on-demand aspects overlapping and playing off one another – is to bring people up close and personal with facets of human behaviour that they might otherwise not have encountered.

THE GROWTH AND INFLUENCE OF SVOD

Let's start by looking at a relatively simple media phenomenon: the recent runaway growth of subscription video on demand (SVOD) services. Using 2021 data, the total number of SVOD subscriptions globally was 1.06 billion, a rise of 17 per cent on the previous year. You can get a feel for how much content is made available for people – at any time, on any device – by looking at just the biggest provider, Netflix, which brings to its 213 million subscribers a constant, streaming menu of over 6,000 films or TV shows.

In the past few years, numerous providers have joined the party, notably Disney+ and AppleTV (both launched in 2019), with an estimated 160m subscribers between them. These are commercial players but in countries with public service TV channels – such as the UK's BBC – richly endowed streaming services have been made available to entire populations without additional charges.

Either way, those who manage SVOD services face two interrelated challenges. First, the constant and bottomless requirement for affordable content. And second, the need for an audience – for viewers to willingly subscribe and watch. In both, real-life, human stories, including those about people who make marginal behaviour choices, have a built-in advantage.

Compared with some other genres, human interest, documentary-style production is relatively inexpensive. A small crew can spend a couple of days following and interviewing, say, extreme hoarders in suburbia, and put together a watchable 60-minute show for about one twelfth of the cost of a scripted, professionally acted drama.

But that would be of no great significance if the resulting content did not attract an audience. Here, the second advantage of real-life observation kicks in. It is inherently fascinating. In 2020, *Tiger King,* featuring the voluble Joe Exotic, became one of Netflix's biggest-ever original shows, reaching a US TV audience of 34.3 million unique viewers in its first 10 days.[15]

The upshot is that there now exists a wealth of content lifting the lid on marginal behaviours and eccentric life choices made instantly available to tens of millions of people who might otherwise never have come across them.

Some of these behaviours have entire series devoted to them. *Extreme Cheapskates,* for example, follows families living so frugally that they spend next to nothing, with each episode showing how a different family makes it work. *Sister Wives* is a long-running series exploring polygamy – delving into the lives and complications of a single family with 18 children. Off-grid living is particularly well endowed, with popular shows originating either side of the Atlantic. In the UK, Ben Fogle's *New Lives in the Wild* visits a different remote, off-grid eccentric each time. In the United States, *Homestead Rescue* fronts a survivalist dropping in on newbie homesteaders to help them fix their mistakes, while *Mountain Men* has spent ten series (and counting) doing what its title suggests – living alongside men who have built their lives in remote and hostile mountain locations.

Of course, awareness is still spread by the printed or spoken word and non-moving imagery, in newspapers, magazines, books, posts and podcasts. But there is something about video that puts the receiver right there in the action, making the experience of marginal behaviours and ways of life more vivid, visceral and memorable. Marketers who have witnessed the difference in impact and brand awareness uplift generated by a TV ad blitz versus a print campaign will immediately recognize the point.

Video is an extraordinarily effective conduit for heightened awareness of lives lived differently, and SVOD is instrumental in driving that. Nevertheless, dynamic as the trajectory of professionally produced streaming content may be, it represents only a fraction of the video that cascades into people's consciousness every day. The far bigger proportion comes not from the pros, but the everyday amateurs.

THE PEOPLE POWER OF USER-GENERATED VIDEO

Every minute of every day, 500 hours of user-generated video content is uploaded onto YouTube.[16] Of TikTok's one billion active users, 83 per cent have uploaded at least one video.[17] Some have uploaded thousands. The destiny of much of this content is to attract only very small viewing numbers – or to be ignored. Being easily shareable does not automatically equate to being widely shared.

But again, marginal behaviour lifestyles – this time observed from the inside, by those actually doing them – have a curiosity and fascination advantage. People tend to reshare what they do not encounter routinely. This is a version of the atavistic human impulse to focus on what is novel in the environment, to take that in, and to absorb its significance. 'Note the new' is a wired-in heuristic. So, the less a phenomenon is observed in everyday life, the more likely it is that it will be viewed on a screen.

For those who have uploaded homemade video content reflecting their unusual life choices – even though it may be rudimentary, fragmentary and artlessly filmed on a smartphone – viewer numbers can sometimes get very high very fast.

You'll recall that early in Chapter 1 we touched on the freebirth movement – where women shun all medical intervention associated with pregnancy and childbirth – and how it got a boost after a woman who was filmed giving birth in a stream shared the video online.

That new mother was Simone Thurber, whose daughter Perouze was born safely in 2012 in a remote rainforest location in Queensland, Australia. 'I'm not a hippy drippy mum but I wanted my fourth child to be born away from beeping machines in a hospital environment', was how she framed her choice at the time.

In 2013 Thurber posted the 22-minute video on YouTube, on her daughter's first birthday, as a present to her partner, who had done the filming and editing. When it clocked up 50 views, she was hit by the realization that 'all my friends have seen me really naked'. When it rolled past the 500 mark, she professed herself 'shocked'.[18]

To date, that original video has registered 119 million views.[19] That is a phenomenal awareness contribution to the ideals and tenets of this alternative behavioural approach to childbirth. And much of that awareness will be concentrated on the most relevant recipients – pregnant women – because birth stories are eagerly sought and devoured by mothers-to-be and the system of tagging facilitates easy searching.

As already observed, awareness alone does not lead to mass adoption of marginal behaviours, because resistance tends to intervene – in this case, the resistance of fear, based on the perceived risks of shunning medical help, which (for most) trumps the innate desire to keep birth as natural as possible. But that high awareness of the freebirth alternative is like the force of a body of water on a dam, exerting a pressure that could become critical should something in the risk profile change.

In 2020, it did. More women began to question the sense of giving birth in hospitals where Covid infections were perceived to be rife. According to an October 2021 analysis in *The Guardian*, it wasn't just the hospital birth itself that was seen with sudden alarm but the process leading up to it, with many expectant parents choosing to opt out of scans and to decline antenatal care.

That does not imply that a new generation of women are about to give birth in local streams; the full freebirth experience is still a long way from mass acceptance. But it signals perhaps that more will challenge the mainstream childbirth norms and resist the coercion of the obstetrics discipline to trust everything to the hospital machine. One indicator of that is the increased online search for 'homebirth' – up by 53 per cent in the UK and 239 per cent in the United States in 2021, relative to pre-pandemic norms.[20]

As an incidental point, note how this story demonstrates three of the later M2M beacons in action: Accelerators (the Covid pandemic), Reversal ('safety' switching sides, from reason to resist to reason to accept), and Dilution (the likelihood of increased experimentation with a weaker form of the behaviour). At the root of it all, though, is the underlying awareness of a behavioural alternative that surged beyond all previous norms thanks to a simple, candid, socially shared homemade video.

SOCIAL: FROM AWARENESS TO COHESION
Everyday engagement with social media does not only bring awareness of marginal behaviours to those who have not yet tried them, but acts as a

locus of cohesion for those who have. Instead of adherents remaining atomized, pursuing their fringe ways of life alone or in small, unconnected clusters, they group together as an online nexus, fostering a powerful sense of community that helps the behaviour take roots and imbues it with a substance beyond its size.

The tendency to seek cohesion, and the endorsement of others, when adhering to a behaviour well outside the mainstream norms pre-dates digital media. In earlier times it would have been manifested in the profusion of societies and clubs devoted to the various behaviours in question. No doubt those early vegans in the late 1940s and 1950s looked forward to the arrival through the post of that quarter's Vegan News, and perhaps occasionally contributed their points of view to its letters page. And that sense of cohesion, though sparse and sporadic, might well have encouraged some to stay with the cause where the fatigue of pursuing it alone might otherwise have beaten them.

The US social scientists Albert Muniz and Thomas O'Guinn, in a seminal 2001 paper on 'brand communities' (similar to the passionate devotees of Harley Davidson), identified three characteristics that define the notion of community achieved through shared habits and attitudes rather than simple locality. First is a 'consciousness of kind', which they express as a shared 'knowing of belonging'. Second is the presence of shared rituals and traditions. The third one is tougher, but if it applies to communities joined only by a brand choice it would apply with even greater force to those joined by a shared marginal behaviour: a sense of duty or responsibility to the community as a whole, to the extent that it would fuel collective action if the community were seen to be under threat. [21]

If the need for community, and the reinforcing power of cohesion, are nothing new, the speed and breadth of the contemporary version take them to a different level. The aspects that are intensified are those of immediacy and reach. Where once it might have taken years, or even decades, for a community to crystallize and grow around a fringe behaviour or way of life, now it can be a matter of months or weeks. And whereas clubs and societies would typically exert influence at a local, regional or at best national level, the social media version basically recruits and draws together like-minded souls from every corner of the world. The effects are orders of magnitude stronger.

An example is Wicca. This modern-day witchcraft movement, with its roots in paganism, has captured the imaginations of (mostly) young women in societies from Mexico to Norway. The practice goes back to the 1940s and has fluctuated in popularity since – though witchcraft itself obviously long predates that. Today's version is a rich mix that takes on many elements of the zeitgeist – aesthetics, magic, mindfulness, solidarity, purpose and power: 'A feminist form of spirituality'[22] is how it is described by Sissel Undheim, Professor of Theology at the University of Bergen.

The reasons for the dramatic recent rise of Wicca are varied, and include the effects of the Covid lockdown, which both gave people time and took away autonomy. As one practitioner put it in an interview with USA Today, 'All you can control is what you think is truth in this world'.[23]

What is clear, though, is that social media has given modern-day witchcraft a massively cohesive centripetal force. The ten most popular Witches of Instagram influencers have three million followers between them. But the real eye-opener is WitchTok – a niche section of TikTok – which has racked up over 24 billion views. Interactive sessions are especially valued, involving tarot readings, pendulum board divination and crystal meditation. You need not spend long on these platforms to observe all three of Muniz and O'Guinn's characteristics at play.

For all that, modern-day witchcraft is not, as some have claimed, a social media phenomenon. It is its own phenomenon, created and coloured by its adherents' own palette of needs, desires, values and concerns. If Wicca was due for a resurgence, based on the circumstances and mood of the times, it would have happened anyway. But more slowly, more patchily and with less gravitational pull. Social media has not created the movement – but it has broadened, deepened and hastened the sense of belonging and community of those who have come to it.

Potential, not prediction

Given that there are hundreds of marginal behaviours out there, and given that new fringe ideas and new ways to be human are springing up all the time, the presence of contemporary digital media does not automatically mean that any given behaviour can be predicted to take off. Many will remain low key, or quietly wither away, despite all the pizzazz and awareness modern connectivity can bring.

But if a behaviour carries within it elements of appeal that could take it to another level in the right circumstances – if it broadly follows the trajectory of the beacons – it is not hard to see how digital connectivity can spectacularly amplify that uptake. This is the big difference between now and a decade or two ago.

What is harder to envision is that 'now' is an early waystation on the digital journey. The ascent of connectivity has been rapid but has far further to go. And it will combine and interact with the second of our three structural and cultural reasons for the faster diffusion of marginal behaviours: 'gen-yes' demographics, coming up next.

Demographics: the wide-open world of Gen Z

Some things about Gen Z can be asserted as statements of fact. It is the biggest single generation in human history, comprising 2.47 billion people, born between 1996 and 2010, constituting 32 per cent of the global population. In the United States it is the first generation where 50 per cent are from the ethnic minorities.[24]

Beyond that we move to observations and generalizations regarding the tendencies, traits and characteristics that can be reasonably ascribed to this body of people. So, we are no longer in the realm of fact but nor is it pure conjecture either. Anyone who has conducted original research with members of this cohort is likely to have been struck by a harmony of attitudes and ways of being, founded on the notes of openness, curiosity and a seemingly intuitive desire not to pre-judge – often signalled by a noticeable pause between question and answer. Not all of these tendencies are markedly different from those of the millennials who preceded them, but where they are analogous, they are taken further, practised with more considered conviction.

As with the millennials, the lives, ways and views of Gen Z have attracted considerable media commentary. In 2020 The Times opined that they are 'all about diversity and gender fluidity yet obsessed by TikTok likes'. The WSJ, in a 2021 feature, rounded on 'tolerance' as a seminal marker, especially in racial issues and sexual orientations. Meanwhile, McKinsey, in an influential 2018 report, concluded that 'Gen Z behaviours are all anchored in one element: this generation's search for truth'.[25]

But let's get more hands-on here. As part of the original research for this book, two cross-cultural studies were conducted involving different age cohorts in Europe and the United States. Both (one quantitative, one qualitative) will be reviewed in detail in the next section of this book – but, since light is shone on the attitudinal palette of Gen Z in that research, let's take a brief, relevant foray into some of the findings now. Let's have this generation speak for itself, by quoting representative verbatims from the qualitative fieldwork:

> *'Nothing is strange anymore, it's all normal.'*
> *'I don't feel comfortable labelling people.'*
> *'We put an emphasis on respecting others.'*
> *'We are more publicly questioning of things that were taught to us as givens.'*
> *'You go out and explore and don't have a fixed mindset.'*
> *'We challenge societal norms a lot more.'*
> *'Our generation is open to a lot more stuff that's looked down on by the older generations.'*

Given this openness and reluctance to 'label', you would feel safe to judge that this generation is likely to approach marginal behaviours with a greater spirit of exploration and acceptance than generations that preceded them. In both the qualitative and quantitative phases of our original research, it was instructive to see that borne out.

As the core element of both methodologies, a range of marginal behaviours was outlined and described, ranging from the relatively mild, at one end – such as veganism and uniform wardrobe – to the more contentious at the other – such as polyamory and urophagia. We were interested in learning whether respondents had heard of them, would consider them, would be willing to know more about them, or would flat out reject them, feeling them wrong for both self and others.

When it came to Gen Z, in both methodologies, three significant themes could be determined.

First, they were consistently more aware of the behaviours – even the more arcane ones – prior to seeing the full stimulus. This corresponds with their greater familiarity with digital media in all its forms, corroborating the points made in the prior section on connectivity. When asked how they had heard of the behaviours, the answer was invariably 'social media' or 'internet'.

Second, they were more able to see themselves experimenting with behaviours outside the usual repertoires than the older generations. Where even millennials had trouble imagining existence outside 'the system' – living without money, for example – Gen Z respondents could see it as something really positive, and worth working at to experience.

Third, they were far more reluctant to reject out of hand, or to judge others for engaging with a challenging or contentious behaviour. Where a majority of respondents in the oldest groups felt polyamory to be simply 'wrong', this younger, Gen Z cohort was ready to find out more. Even with urophagia – deliberately seeded to probe where the boundaries of acceptance might lie – there was a curiosity to learn more about its antiquity and claimed health benefits. Older groups could not get beyond their disgust.

In body-language terms it is like the difference between arms defiantly folded across the chest, and an inquiring leaning forward to listen. The significance is not so much about a willingness to try these behaviours personally, but the establishment of a climate of acceptance for those who do – for those who choose to live differently. The considered openness of Gen Z helps take the 'weird' out of 'marginal', and takes the brakes off the progress of even the most unlikely behaviours.

NB: A summary of the objectives, methodologies and sample sizes for these strands of original research can be found in the research overview to Part 2 of this book, just ahead of Chapter 4.

Gen Z is 'gen-yes'. And it is the future: 2028 is the date for the coming-of-age of its youngest members. This generation is not just big but prosperous, with direct spending power estimated at $140 billion[26] in the United States alone. Should it collectively seize upon hitherto marginal behaviours in the way that the millennials did with veganism, it has the economic firepower to fuel consumer-driven disruption and create entire new mega markets. Overall, it represents an attitudinal, demographic and commercial combination that no marketer would wish to ignore.

We now move on to the final of our three structural and cultural reasons for the more marked proliferation of marginal behaviours into the mainstream: the underlying heartbeat of diversity.

Diversity and inclusion: the irresistible force inside

In 1984 Apple launched one of the most famous TV commercials ever made. It depicted a dystopian, regimented organizational space, with workers hunched over their stations, all dressed the same, all looking the same, all controlled like zombies by a master on a giant screen. All except one – a lone female who charges down the aisles with a sledgehammer and smashes the screen, liberating everyone.

Apple's most famous tagline, 'Think different', would come later, but its seed was sown right there. It was a breath-taking spot celebrating the spirit of individualism and defiance in the face of organizational conformity, and inviting those with an inner uniqueness to express it. In theory, that is pretty much everyone. In practice, in those days, 'thinking different' within organizations that were only too homogenous – and especially daring to openly express that difference and risk being the one person out of line – was extraordinarily exposing.

One of the great achievements of the diversity and inclusion discipline since then is to quieten the crushing background hum of homogeneity within the modern workplace. It's not hard to see that different ways of thinking and expression will arise more naturally when 'difference' is part of the very fabric of the organization – with the active inclusion of people of diverse ethnicity, gender, background and sexuality.

Today, the most enlightened organizations are taking things further to explicitly prioritize 'diversity of thought'. This might emanate from people's divergence of background or life experience, but also through 'neurodiversity', reflecting different innate patterns of mental processing – including, for example, people with ADHD or people on the autistic spectrum.

The combination of 'diversities' now beginning to enrich the workplace gives the promotion of marginal behaviours a thrust from the inside – from the corporate world out. The more people differ in their ethnicity, gender, background, age and sexuality, the greater the likelihood that they will have encountered different marginal behaviours and life choices. Combine that with a declared celebration of diversity of thought and you will get people speaking up for those marginal behaviours in corporate decisions: innovation programmes, new product development, new market categories, new routes to growth. This enhanced diversity on the inside is one of the reasons we will see more ways to satisfy the extraordinary behavioural diversity that exists – hitherto often unrecognized – in contemporary society.

In a sense, then, there is a circularity to this final structural and cultural factor. One of the prime reasons for businesses to commit resources to the margins is that other businesses are already doing it. The enlightened ones. The future-facing ones. The ones that have shaken off their mainstream homogeneity of thought. Maybe not yours. Not yet. But one of the reasons for this chapter – for this book – is to change that. And who better than marketers to lead the charge?

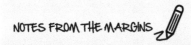
NOTES FROM THE MARGINS

Freebirthing

When Leonie Rainbird Savin was pregnant for the first time, she told a midwife at her 13-week antenatal check that she could feel her baby moving. The midwife told her flatly that she was wrong. This blunt dismissal – whether correct or not, that wasn't the point – was the first of many controlling slights which led Leonie, some months later, to opt out of the system altogether and freebirth her child in a tent in her in-laws' back garden.

It wasn't always her plan. In fact, Leonie remembers having a rather romantic view of packing her bag for the hospital, having the case ready by the front door. However, as her pregnancy continued, she began to consider a midwife-supported home birth instead, until again being disheartened by the idea of regulated 15-minute internal checks and monitoring throughout the labour. After a lot of research and planning, what Leonie felt she wanted was a safe space that was private, dark and undisturbed, where she could welcome her baby without time pressure or interruption. Her husband was supportive of the idea; they had both been inspired by a video of a freebirth, and hoped for the same feeling of privacy and control.

The couple rented a large bell tent and heaters – it was November, in England, after all – and settled in to wait for nature to do its thing. After a nine-hour labour the baby was born; the couple and the new baby stayed warm and quiet in the tent for five further days, until the umbilical cord dried and broke off naturally from the placenta (what's known as a lotus birth). They found the whole thing profoundly moving: 'Nothing could have prepared us for how wonderful it was. It was incredible. Earth-shattering'.

Leonie is now a mother of three young children, all of whom were born without medical attendants, and uses Instagram to share her experiences and knowledge in an effort to destigmatize freebirth. The calm and thoughtful thirtysomething philosophy graduate is aware of her privilege too; after all, not everyone has the time, money and family support to make these choices.

She believes the interest in freebirth is a millennial thing; unlike their mothers and grandmothers, women of her generation are comfortable talking about their feelings and bodies, confident enough to unpick what's necessary and what's not, and assertive enough to openly question 'the system'.

East London-based Anna Clarkson agrees that freebirthing is a growing trend. Anna runs birthing classes for local women, wherever they plan to deliver. 'It's about getting back to basics. Regaining control. You're not legally obliged to give birth in hospital or do what a doctor tells you, even though it feels as though once your pregnancy is confirmed, you get sucked into the system and then have to follow someone else's medical timetable. It might be going back to basics, like the trends for organic food or rewilding, it might be the huge amount of inspirational real-life stories that are out there on social media. Either way women's confidence, and the desire to have control over their own bodies and their own births, is growing.'

Kinship has swelled around these desires, for example in the Freebirth Society, who have built a community of women against what they call the institutional harm caused by the obstetric system and formal midwifery. Paid membership is kept private, but they have 78,000 followers on their Instagram page (@freebirthsociety). Leaders Emilee Saldaya and Yolande Norris-Clark even offer coaching to become 'Radical Birth Keepers' and attend women in freebirth, in their efforts to push back against one-size-fits-all birth plans.

These radical views have a less woo-woo iteration in women simply feeling they want to have a say with their own bodies and experiences. It does seem extraordinary that something that's been happening for 200,000 years, something on which all future human life depends, could be seen as a niche concept. But deciding to give birth without medical assistance is undoubtedly an extreme choice in the 21st century developed world. It's entirely legal to do so[27] – but maternity groups and medical experts rarely support it.

Also known as 'unassisted childbirth', it's not about early or unexpected labour, or a taxi driver delivering a passenger's baby in the back of their cab (that's known in the trade as BBA, or Born Before Arrival). Right now, freebirthing is about a small number of women making deliberate choices to sidestep the medical locations and support that the vast majority find reassuring.

That small number, however, seems to be getting bigger.

PART TWO

How to read the margins

Research overview for Part 2

Part 2 looks at the eight M2M beacons in more detail, taking them in themed pairs across four chapters. Throughout this section, insights, themes and findings were informed by two types of original research that were commissioned specifically for this book.

1. QUANTITATIVE SURVEY IN THE UK AND THE UNITED STATES

In partnership with The Nursery, a consumer research company based in London, online quantitative surveys were conducted with nationally representative samples (age, gender, region) across the UK and US. The aim was to explore awareness of, and attitudes towards, a total of 21 marginal behaviours plus two behaviours already considered mainstream, to be used as a benchmark.

Two studies were completed in the UK, with a sample of 1,037 in the first round, evaluating 11 marginal behaviours, and 1,030 in the second, also evaluating 11 marginal behaviours, of which 10 were new.

In the United States, data was collected for 1,019 respondents in a single study across a slightly reduced set of the behaviours used in the UK studies (19 in total).

On either side of the Atlantic, the surveys included measures on: current knowledge of the behaviours; attitudes towards them (eg personal and perceived third-party emotional responses, practicality); willingness to try; personality factors on risk aversion; and general demographics.

The behaviours tested and how they were described:

Insect protein
What: eating protein derived from insects instead of animal meat.
Why: sustainable, cheap and environmentally friendly as well as delivering more protein and less fat.

Polyphasic sleeping
What: sleeping in short bursts throughout each 24 hours.
Why: mimicking animal sleep patterns helps some people who struggle with night-time sleep to function better and more productively.

Polyamory

What: committed emotional and/or sexual relationships with more than one person.

Why: polyamorists feel able to love more than one person deeply, so live openly in non-monogamous relationships.

Urophagia

What: the ancient practice of drinking your own urine.

Why: believed to support a healthy body and immune system.

Home burial

What: burials in gardens, back yards and on private land.

Why: to keep your loved ones close, and lay them to rest in a place they loved.

Freebirthing

What: giving birth without any medical intervention.

Why: to deliver new human life in the most natural way possible, whether at home or even outdoors.

Microdosing

What: taking daily minuscule doses of psychoactive drugs.

Why: at very low intake levels, psychoactive drugs like LSD or psilocybin (magic mushrooms) boost mood and sharpen senses without making the user high.

Living without money

What: avoiding the use of cash or money.

Why: sidestepping problems related to having too much or too little money by minimizing consumption, bartering or working for necessities and dramatically simplifying lifestyle.

Quantified self

What: daily measuring and recording of personal metrics.

Why: self-improvement by intense focus on oneself; by visualizing their lifestyle in numbers and on graphs, users highlight problems and can be encouraged by small improvements.

New nomads

What: living permanently in motor homes.

Why: a cheaper way to live for those nearing retirement age without pension arrangements.

Living off the sea

What: harvesting and eating the ocean plant kelp, which grows in coastal waters.

Why: sustainable and tasty source of non-meat protein, with less impact on the environment than any other superfood.

Veganism:

What: abstaining from the use/consumption of animal products – particularly when it comes to diet.

Why: ethical, health or environmental reasons.

Neo-Luddites

What: people who reject technology and live without Wi-Fi, mobile phones or computers.

Why: to find refuge from the overwhelming barrage of communications from the outside world.

Extreme frugalism

What: spending the bare minimum on living expenses and saving up to 40 per cent of income.

Why: to build up cash reserves while working in order to retire young.

Naturism

What: going without clothes when weather (and public decency) allows.

Why: to enjoy the liberating back-to-nature feeling, and boost mental health.

Wicca

What: modern-day witchcraft rooted in paganism involving potions, crystal meditation and a spiritual connection with elemental forces.

Why: a sense of control and empowerment based on rituals inspired by nature, the moon and the sun.

Biohacking

What: embedding tech such as microchips into human bodies to create cyborg capabilities.

Why: to improve able-bodied and disabled lives with easy access to tech, security, speed.

Voluntary celibacy

What: people purposefully choosing not to have any sexual relationships.

Why: to avoid poor decisions and their consequences, to develop meaningful relationships and boost their own self-awareness.

Raising children gender-neutral

What: not categorizing children by gender in their infancy, giving neutral names, pronouns, clothes and toys.

Why: to avoid defining or even limiting their prospects by pigeonholing children at an early age.

Ayahuasca

What: a powerful psychoactive drug harvested in the jungles of South America and administered at retreats by shamans.

Why: to search for enlightenment and the meaning of life – participants are evangelical about its life-changing properties.

Neo-tribalism

What: singles, couples and families living communally, often with a guiding principle in common.

Why: wanting to live a simpler, more fulfilling life with like-minded people.

2. QUALITATIVE FOCUS GROUPS IN THE UK AND THE UNITED STATES

A total of 10 focus groups were conducted: four in the UK and six in the United States. The groups included a mix of ages, genders, ethnicities and backgrounds. The aim was to understand more about prior awareness to marginal behaviours, how respondents came to hear about them, and their attitudes and feelings towards them.

Across groups, following open-ended discussion about marginal behaviours in general, the moderator revealed specially-prepared stimulus relating to a total of eight marginal behaviours to be probed more deeply, chosen to give a representative arc in terms of rarity, practicality and surprise. The eight were: microdosing; uniform wardrobe; freebirthing; polyphasic sleeping; polyamory; insect eating; living without money; and home burial.

By gradually revealing new information about the behaviours, we were able to get a feel for which kind of factors might encourage people to reassess their initial reactions.

04

A smouldering fire in the fringes: the elemental beacons

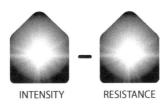

INTENSITY   RESISTANCE

Intensity and resistance are the elemental beacons – two oppositional forces that constitute the thrust and parry of behaviours that reside at the fringes. They are elemental because without the presence of both, a given behaviour would not be marginal – at least, not for long. Without intensity, the behaviour would fade away in the face of the difficulties of pursuing it; without resistance, there would be nothing to stop it filtering through unimpeded to the mainstream. It is the combination that characterizes the presence of a marginal behaviour or way of life, and where marketers discover a new one, they will be witness to the dynamic tension between these two defining forces.

Intensity can present as an impassioned advocacy for the beliefs behind the behaviour or merely a dogged determination to do things a certain way in spite of the impediments involved. Certainly, some kind of thrust, or zeal, or inner strength, is needed to counter the inconveniences, higher costs, social awkwardness and sometimes even hardships of going against the prevailing norms – what we will call *frictions* from here on in.

These frictions are real, and can be underestimated or overlooked by those comfortably inside the behavioural norm. Until relatively recently, to be a committed vegetarian, let alone a vegan, would mean frustration when ordering in restaurants – combatting the disdain of unhelpful waiters and trying to cobble something together from the vegetable accompaniments to the 'proper' meals. A person who believes in the efficacy of alternative medicine might need to accept that treatments are not reimbursed by the health system, so would be more expensive. Choosing to live as a neo-Luddite becomes ever tougher in a world where digital efficiency is prioritized and everything from banking to medical diagnosis is increasingly mediated online.

True, if your marginal way of life happens to be that of an ice-shower convert, the cold water is as plentiful as the warm and the cost is, if anything, lower. But there is still the business of standing under the freezing stream for minutes on a heartless midwinter morning: a friction of a more somatic kind. There has to be some kind of emotional or psychological intensity coming the other way to keep going beyond about day three.

And all that is before the resistance of others comes into play – which, if the behaviour is marginal, it will. As with intensity, there can be varying shades to resistance, from the 'hot', like fear, disgust or disapproval, through to the disdainfully 'cool', like ridicule, pity or even the 'you do you' declaration of a Gen Z-er who is clearly not up for personal inclusion this time. In the face of both friction and resistance, then, intensity is what keeps a marginal behaviour alive. It is a kind of heat that requires energy to maintain, to ensure that convention is not the crusher of difference. Even for those who claim to enjoy being at odds with others, whose sense of self derives from standing outside the mainstream tent, some form of energy has to be committed to ensure that behavioural intensity is actively maintained.

It is an interesting dynamic. Resistance doesn't blunt intensity; if anything it hones it. If resistance were to fade to mere indifference, then the behaviour would gradually seep into the mass population and the intensity associated with it would likewise fade. Being confined by resistance to the margins is what keeps the flame of intensity alive.

This is why those who look at the fringes and perceive the behaviours side-lined there for years to be somehow inert are misreading the reality. It is the opposite: a smouldering fire that threatens to break free, bulwarked by an impassive defiance that keeps it contained. Sometimes that stand-off can exist for decades – centuries, even. But look closer, and you see that it is not inert. There will be periods when one force seems to gain against the other – only to be beaten back again. But while that fire in the fringes continues to burn, there is always a chance a breakthrough will come.

We'll delve more deeply into each of these elemental beacons further down the chapter, using some of the findings of our original research as reference points. First, though, let's look at a two-century case that will help to illuminate both.

Homeopathy: the 200-year tussle between sceptics and believers

Among the luminaries who have expressed a firm belief in homeopathy down the years – a list that includes Anton Chekov, Mark Twain, Sir Arthur Conan Doyle, Tina Turner, Cher, Mahatma Gandhi and King Charles – the most frequently quoted is the British rock musician and national treasure Sir Paul McCartney. 'I can't manage without homeopathy', he is reported to have said. 'I never go anywhere without homeopathic remedies. I often make use of them.'

McCartney is wealthy, knowledgeable and well-connected. He has access to the best medical minds out there, and the means to pursue whatever remedies and healthcare approaches he feels best for him and his family. That he chooses so vociferously to align with the 1 per cent of UK citizens [1] who regularly take homeopathic treatments is not an insignificant endorsement.

Every bit as significant, though, is the battery of resistance that comes the other way, much of it from the great and the good within the medical establishment, who dismiss homeopathy as pseudoscience, quackery or a kind of elaborate scam.

In 2017, announcing plans to make homeopathic medicines unavailable on prescription, Simon Stevens, Chief Executive of NHS England, described homeopathy as 'at best a placebo and a misuse of scarce NHS funds'. In 2019, he and Stephen Powis, NHS England Medical Director, in a letter urging for the delisting of the Society of Homeopaths from the official register of professional organizations, wrote: 'Anything that gives homeopathy a veneer of credibility risks chancers being able to con more people into parting with their hard-earned cash in return for bogus treatments'.[2] Meanwhile, Edzard Ernst, Emeritus Professor of Complementary Medicine at the University of Exeter, has frequently hit out at the enthusiasm of the then Prince Charles, in his role as Patron of the Faculty of Homeopathy, labelling him 'a snake oil salesman', among other graphic insults.[3]

This is a kind of 'gatekeeper' resistance, a tough-love attempt to deter lesser mortals from traversing the homeopathic portals through which McCartney, Charles and so many other famous people have already publicly passed. The language is charged with vitriol and derision; yet it is not sufficient to deter the dedicated, nor to prevent homeopathy gaining most traction in the more highly educated cohorts – an interesting feature of the typical user base across multiple cultures. And devotees are not afraid to hit back, sometimes allowing intensity to spill over to aggression. When Natalie

Grams, a former practitioner turned critic, published a book dismissing the scientific basis of the homeopathic doctrine, she reported receiving hate mail and death threats.[4]

A TRENCHANT CHALLENGE: HOMEOPATHY'S BEGINNINGS

The twin themes of intensity and resistance have accompanied the discipline of homeopathy ever since its origins in the early 19th century. The practice and its governing principles were first set down in 1810 by a German physician, Samuel Hahnemann, who had made an interesting discovery from his prior work with his patients.[5] He noted that certain diseases could be ameliorated with substances that caused the same symptoms: so cholera, for example, would be improved by tiny doses of arsenic – which would in higher dilutions cause the classic symptoms of cholera.

Hahnemann was courageous enough to imbibe many of these substances himself, to a degree that caused toxic effects, and stubborn enough to ignore those who questioned his methods. Eventually, after a 20-year period of one-man pharmacological experimentation that included diverse plants, poisons, metals and minerals, he was ready to codify his 'rational medicine' with the publication of the first of five editions of similarly titled 'Organon' tomes between 1810 and 1842.[6]

Hahnemann's new school of medicine centred on two principles. The first was the 'law of similar' – or the edict that like cures like. (The derivation of 'homeopathy' traces back to the Greek words for 'same' and 'suffering'.) This notion had been experimented with since classical times and was not without substance. For example, if you were to consume copious amounts of the bark of cinchona – and Hahnemann duly did – it would produce the sweating and fever characteristic of malaria. Within the bark (though unknown at the time) is the alkaloid quinine, which is still used to treat malaria today.

The second of Hahnemann's principles was more contentious: that of the 'minimum dose' – where 'minimum' is indistinguishable from 'absent'. Anxious not to actively cause illness through treatment of it, Hahnemann gradually experimented with compounds that were more and more dilute, in a process of vigorous shaking and reduction called 'succussion'. This dilution was sometimes so extreme that, by the time the patient took the remedy, there was not one molecule of the originating active ingredient left in it. Nevertheless, Hahnemann argued that 'vital energy' was transmitted to the water during the dilution phase – a phenomenon that modern homeopaths refer to as 'water memory'.

The audacity of this argument did not prevent homeopathy rapidly becoming popular, and by the 1830s it was practised in all the leading economies of Europe, across the United States and in parts of Asia. Some early homeopaths saw it as a viable complementary treatment to run alongside conventional medicine, but Hahnemann did not; he called those who practised even minor deviations from his methods 'apostates' and 'traitors'.[7] Intensity – a purity of vision from which no diversion was countenanced – was part of the very foundation of the system.

A BLISTERING RESPONSE: HOMEOPATHY'S 'SCIENCE' PROBLEM

Resistance came early on in the form of a challenge from the outraged Medical Officer of Health for Nuremberg, Friedrich Wilhelm Von Hoven, who was dismayed to see something so irrational adopted wholesale by the aristocracy in his own hometown. Von Hoven published a scathing criticism of homeopathy which in turn provoked the ire of local leading homeopaths and eventually led to the establishment of a medical trial – the Nuremberg Salt Trials of 1835, which were to become famous as the first ever randomized double blind test.[8]

The results were inconclusive – with the phials containing the homeopathic tincture dissolved in melted snow eliciting slightly more claimed effect among recipients than those containing just the melted snow, but with the vast majority of the recipients of either reporting no effect at all. Hahnemann ignored them. For Von Hoven it was vindication of his judgement that homeopathy was without scientific foundation.

That will resonate with those of a scientific mindset today – but a little context is appropriate here. The 'medical science' of the 1830s revolved around the four humours, bloodletting and leeches. In France, 42 million leeches were imported in 1833 alone.[9] Serious interventions such as surgery were performed in unclean conditions, since this predates the discovery of the infectious role of invisible pathogens. Homeopathy at least could claim, truthfully, to do no harm. How could it, when it consisted solely of diluent – aka water? Without knowing why, those who opted for homeopathy rather than the alarmingly dangerous methods of the day were in fact making the more rational choice.

This counterplay with conventional medicine must surely be part of the explanation for the persistence of homoeopathy through the decades between then and now, even as its efficacy has been subject to relentless challenge. Conventional medicine may have improved beyond recognition since the early 19th century, but the awakening of scientific understanding has come at the expense of individual patient nurture and consultation time. Modern medical practice has about it an almost industrial feel. Homeopathy, conversely, has always stressed a balance within the whole body and mind rather than a reductive focus on singular disease, and patient engagement with practitioners involves detailed reflection on all aspects of a patient's life, work, relationships and emotions.

If conventional medicine has an Achilles heel it is its tendency to see the problem with ever greater specificity and yet be blind to the patient who presents it. Homeopathy's Achilles heel, meanwhile – maybe bigger than a heel – is the sheer implausibility of its key tenet of the curative effect of tinctures in almost total dilution. As the US physician and poet Oliver Wendell Holmes quipped as far back as 1842, you'd need to drink 'the waters of 10,000 Adriatic Seas' to get a single dose.[10]

AN UNEASY TRUCE: HOMEOPATHY TODAY

Homeopathy has been a great deal more popular than it is now. In the first half of the 20th century, it could claim a sizeable following in continental Europe and, within the United States, a system of 22 homeopathic colleges and over 100 homeopathic hospitals.[11] In the UK it was the preferred medical choice of generations of the Royal Family and had four great hospitals devoted to it. Today there are none on either side of the Atlantic.

Homeopathy may be down, but it is not out. The sizeable variation in user prevalence by geography, gender and educational status adds further impetus to the notion of a dynamic narrative still very much in play. According to a meta-analysis study by Sheffield University, while user prevalence languishes at 1 per cent or less in the UK, Ireland and Scandinavian countries, it is well over 10 per cent in Germany, France and Switzerland. Women and those with a college education are significantly over-represented.[12]

The debate rages. While those on the intensity side cite concerns over the indiscriminate prescription of pharmaceuticals and claim to have experienced health benefits beyond placebo, those on the resister wing either simply fret about the lack of scientific evidence of efficacy, or actively agitate against the whole edifice of this almost mystical alternative medicine that refuses to lie down and die. You get the feeling of two sides talking past each other – which is why we will pick up the story again in the next chapter, when we look at the beacons of misalignment and reframing.

For now, though, we round on the beacons of intensity and resistance as separate subjects, to help marketers gain a richer understanding of the fascinating, swirling dynamics of both.

Understanding intensity: the fuel of difference

In a classic psychological experiment, a volunteer would be shown into a room with a row of eight chairs and asked to sit at one end. Others would gradually file in and occupy the other chairs, and the experimenter would ask the group to perform a simple, repeated task.

For each round, the group was shown two cards. On one was a single straight line, while the other showed three lines of varying length – only one of which corresponded with the length of the line on the first card (as depicted in Figure 4.1). Starting at the far end of the row, the group had to call out one by one which it was: a), b) or c).

FIGURE 4.1 The Asch conformity experiment

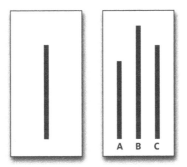

Participants were asked to choose which of the three lines on the comparison card (right) matched the line on the reference card (left). Stooges would call out the wrong answer and genuine volunteers would follow the crowd.

To our volunteer, the task seemed absurdly easy: it was obvious which line was the same length – corroborated when all the others ahead called it out. But then something disturbing would happen. For subsequent rounds – when the choice was equally obvious – the others ahead would call out a different line. So, for example, when it seemed clear the answer was c), they would all agree on a).

And so it would go on. About three-quarters of the time, those calling ahead would all agree on a bafflingly different choice. Each time that happened, our volunteer would be presented with a dilemma: say what they thought or fall in with all the rest.

Those others were stooges. Our volunteer was the patsy. While a few such volunteers stood their ground throughout – about 25 per cent overall – many would settle into a pattern of passive concurrence and most would align with the wrong calls of the others at least once. In a control group, where there were no fake actors, calls were accurate over 99 per cent of the time, so the only explanation for the wrong calls made by the genuine volunteers in the stage-managed version was group effect.

This was known as the Asch conformity experiment, devised in 1951 by the Polish American social psychologist Solomon Asch[13], to investigate the role of peer pressure in decision making and to explore how uncomfortable solus non-alignment would feel, even when respondents knew they were right.

And it is uncomfortable. Those 25 per cent who stuck to their guns would probably have been aware of mildly disturbing physiological signs while doing so: perhaps their pulse would rise a little or they might sweat, reflecting the release of cortisol into the bloodstream, which happens in situations of stress. It would have required a certain strength of character to get through to the end without taking the easier option of falling in line with the others.

The instinct to conform is part of the atavistic human wiring passed down from man's savannah past, when to be the outsider in the tribe was not merely uncomfortable but dangerous. For all our talk of individualism in modern life, it still exerts a pull. Try standing up and clapping at the end of a show when everyone else in the audience has remained sitting down. Try staying sat down when everyone else has stood up.

People who decide to pursue behaviours and ways of life way outside the mainstream norms are also confronting that wrench away from the atavistic comfort of conformity. They may not have been ambushed by wily psychologists, but their free and open choice to be different still requires a little intensity if it is to overcome conformity's gravitational pull.

There are two broad ways in which that intensity can be directed – two base stratagems to defuse the sense of exposure of going against the flow. One is to seek to bring others with you – to recruit from the mainstream and draw supporters to your cause. The other way is to ignore the mainstream crowd but do all you can to bolster your own personal sense of resolve.

Within each of these broad stratagems there are variations that we'll call hot and cool, so that we can create a simple two-by-two grid that maps out the overall territory of intensity. (See Figure 4.2.) So, the 'mainstream recruitment' option can be hot – with confrontation, activism and even aggression deployed to convince others that your way is the better road to travel. Or it can be cool, with lower-octane promulgation, persuasion and charm deployed to attract others to your chosen way of life.

Similarly, there are warm and cool variants for the stratagem that focuses on personal resolve. The hot version is all about out-group solidarity, orienting towards (or creating) a community that clearly stands apart from the mainstream, but which gives huge encouragement to its members. The cool version is simply to develop and manifest a quiet inner determination to follow your chosen path irrespective of anybody else, whether part of the mainstream or otherwise.

FIGURE 4.2 Typology of intensity

	Engaged with mainstream	**Disengaged with mainstream**
Hot	Confrontation	Mutual encouragement
Cool	Persuasion	Solus determination

The characteristics of emotional and psychological intensity that accompany marginal behaviours can be plotted in a simple, four-quadrant grid. In the two quadrants on the left, adherents seek to recruit people from the mainstream to their cause or way of life. The actions they take to achieve this can be grouped as 'hot' (such as confrontation) or 'cool' (such as persuasion). In the two quadrants on the right, adherents ignore the mainstream, but seek ways to bolster their choice to be different. Again, solutions can be 'hot' (such as seeking mutual encouragement within an 'out group') or 'cool', with a reliance on personal determination.

Behaviours and quadrants

Within the long tail of marginal behaviours out there, some show a tendency to be more associated with a particular intensity type than others. We'll take a look at a few examples now. As part of that journey, we'll revisit behaviours we have already encountered, such as veganism in its pre-popularity days, and modern-day witchcraft, along with behaviours that we'll be meeting for the first time, like extreme carnivorism – veganism's polar opposite – and the naked world of naturism.

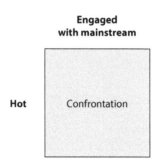

This is where we find veganism, in the long years before it became trendy. There were times when the intensity of its believers reached the extreme of violence, and undoubtedly did more harm than good to the cause. In the UK, balaclava-clad activists have blocked lorries carrying livestock, smashed windscreens, logged the names of the drivers and threatened to locate and set fire to their homes.[14] In France in 2019, activists were imprisoned for attacking restaurants and butchers' shops. Windows had been smashed, graffiti daubed.[15]

As part of the original research for this book, we conducted qualitative groups with longstanding vegans to get a sense for how things have changed for them more recently, now that vegan choices have gone mainstream. The first point to note was just how socially difficult their commitment was beforehand, as recently as five or six years ago. As one respondent put it, 'I played a lot of rugby then, did a lot of sport. To admit to being vegan was like saying you were the antichrist'.

Although the group welcomed some of the more recent changes, they were still scathing of those who were less committed to the animal welfare cause. There was much talk of 'dirty vegans' – a reference to those who occasionally opt for products that resemble meat. The extremes of intensity may have faded in line with veganism's recent mainstream drift – and will continue to do so – but it is clear that, for the committed, this once marginal behaviour will always have something of an edge.

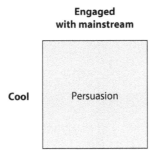

The image of a naturist – standing naked except perhaps for a pair of Birkenstocks – using violent confrontation to draw others to the cause is sufficiently implausible to prompt a certain cognitive dissonance. It's not going to happen. Yet, though the methods are different, naturism, too, exhibits a yearning to proselytize and recruit. Naturists often report feeling misunderstood and many are passionate about the goal of 'normalizing nudity'.

Naturism used to be called nudism. Its origins as a social movement date to 1903 in Germany, with the first nudist club opening near Hamburg as a rejection of the repressive prudishness of the 19th century. Nudism in the United States got going in the 1930s after the establishment of the American League of Physical Culture in 1929. Its locus today is a 15-mile stretch in Pasco County, Florida, just inland of Tampa Bay, which has been dubbed the 'nudity capital' of the United States.[16]

Like homeopathy, naturism is a behaviour that has oscillated between the margins and the minority. In France, for example, it is estimated to be practised by about 2 per cent of the adult population and in a 2015 survey only 15 per cent said they would consider giving it a try, with 83 per cent rejecting outright.[17]

What might change that? Traditionally, the elements of persuasion have centred on the virtues of bodily vigour and open air. More recently, naturists have begun to reference more internal, emotional themes. Writing in The Spectator in 2021 about his attendance at a 'naked dining club', the UK journalist Cosmo Landesman observed how the naked 'airline pilot, former police superintendent, nurse and business analyst', he spoke to would extol the joys of feeling 'liberated and empowered' when the clothes came off. 'Back in the 1930s', Landesman wrote, 'nudism used to be all about health and getting back to nature; now it speaks the language of personal growth and social liberalisation'.[18]

Marketers will recognise these themes as the more sophisticated persuasive tools of the trade. Naturists – already a reframing from the more polarizing 'nudists' – are clearly serious about taking the mainstream with them.

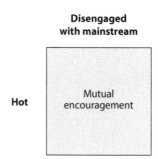

This quadrant is not about recruitment but solidarity, where people aim for the sweet spot of standing apart from the mainstream but being part of a discrete community.

Modern-day witchcraft fits here. There are an estimated 1.5 million witches in the United States,[19] but their remit is not to draw in more from the byways of everyday life. Witches have always been society's ultimate outsiders. But as we saw in Chapter 3, with the Wicca communities, there is tremendous internal support and encouragement for those who have chosen to follow this path. And it is not all mediated online. In New York, an all-women's co-working and networking space called The Wing describes itself as a 'coven' – a verbal encapsulation of the paradox of insider and outsider status at once.

It is interesting to see extreme carnivorism – veganism's polar opposite – orient towards this space. Adherents follow a super-restrictive diet that includes only meat, fish, and other animal foods such as eggs. No fruits, vege-tables, legumes, grains, nuts or seeds. For drinks the options are strictly water or bone broth, and certainly nothing that was once a plant, like coffee or tea.

There is a philosophy behind the movement – that this was the natural diet of man's ancestral past – but devotees tend not to proselytize. Encouragement of a distinctly macho kind is meted out in closed-group forums, often involving a chiding of those who have strayed even briefly from the rigours of the diet – understandable given the frictions involved, which include high costs and loose bowels.

The US social psychologist Dr Marilynn Brewer has published extensively on the tension in contemporary society between the desire to express
individuality and the ancient human need to belong. Those who orient to
behaviours that settle in this intensity quadrant, whether consciously or not,
could well be on a quest to reconcile both.

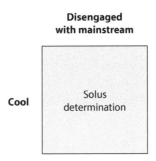

This is the quadrant where we see the simplest and most private expression of
intensity: personal determination, inner resolve. It most naturally accompanies
behaviours where frictions are high, such as polyphasic sleeping. It was revealing from both our quantitative and qualitative research work that the notion
of sleeping often through the day, for relatively brief periods, was an attractive
thought to many – but was dismissed by virtually all as impractical. Those
who carry on regardless must clearly have to draw on some inner force of will.

But that quiet resolve might also be the crutch when practical frictions
are low but prospects for social awkwardness are raised. Uniform wardrobe
is an example. Anecdotally, one of our research team had once worked in a
New York advertising agency where an art director had decided she couldn't
face the daily decision of what to wear – so opted to always dress in exactly
the same combination of black jeans, black blazer and white shirt.

She became famous within the industry for doing so – but not only was
it a notoriety she had never craved, it was a source of embarrassment.
Explaining to others became the hardest part of her marginal behaviour
choice. Inner resolve was the only way through.

A marketing take on intensity

Many marketers – perhaps the majority – work in categories where consumers are anything but intense. There is a lot of 'so what' out there – it's just

a detergent, or a van, or an app or a can of corn. Nice, but nothing to get worked up about. In focus groups you can almost feel moderators trying to whip up some fervour among indifferent respondents: 'So why does *that* matter?' you will hear them repeatedly ask. Often, if we're honest, it doesn't.

It would be natural, then, for marketers to welcome some consumer intensity into their professional lives, perhaps by venturing to the fringes to ignite it. Some pointers from our original qualitative research might be instructive here – drawing on the groups with mainstream consumers who didn't engage with any of marginal behaviours, commenting on the intensity of those who did. There were positive and negative themes.

On the positive side, the commitment, single-mindedness and determination of marginal behaviour devotees was recognized and admired, especially for their role in creating change. 'You need the crazy people to get things going', said one respondent. Others recognized the courage of pioneers and expressed the lack of it as a failing in themselves: 'I would love to be able to do something like this but wouldn't have the confidence to do it.'

But on the negative side, intensity can be off-putting. One respondent commenting on 'old-school vegans' resented the fact that they would 'shove it down your throat'. Others, even if tempted by a marginal behaviour, would be wary if they thought that they, too, would be required to be as single-minded and committed when engaging with it.

Insistency, as expressed at the behavioural fringe, is two-edged. It needs to be there to keep the behaviour alive in the face of everything railed against it but can get too much just at the moment the mainstream is ready to relinquish its resistance and give things a try.

If it ever does. Because, as we'll see next, resistance, too, is a doughty, deep-seated and surprisingly mercurial counterforce.

Understanding resistance: keeping outsiders out

An insight into the psychology of resistance can be glimpsed from the negative undertones of the words humanity reserves for those who stand apart from the main group. 'Extremists', 'outsiders', 'loners', 'weirdos' – even 'marginals'. When people talk of a 'fringe group' they are often deliberately trying to signal a distaste for the values that its members espouse. Even slightly more affectionate terms such as 'oddball' or 'eccentric' carry within them the cargo of otherness, abnormality or 'something not quite right'.

Social psychologists and anthropologists are in agreement that, as Marilynn Brewer phrases it, 'the human species is highly adapted to group living and not well equipped to survive outside a group context'.[20] This is a system of thriving that reflects the realities of both a hunter-gatherer past and the long dependency of infants, each of which made co-operation and cohesion within the tribe advantageous on a risk-benefit basis.

Ways of being, social norms, behavioural codes and ethics were therefore powerful signals of a defining sense of 'us' – the people whose sharing of biology and culture permitted the sharing of tasks and food. Interestingly, for many ancient tribes, the name by which they called themselves was the same as the name for 'humans' in that language. To be an outsider was, in a sense, to be not properly human.

Given this behavioural imprint it is not hard to see that, just as it is uncomfortable to be the one person who dares to be different, so it is uncomfortable – threatening even – for members of the main group to be confronted with new ways of behaviour that contravene the societal norms. Curiosity may be piqued, but one or more of a slew of negative emotions will inevitably cascade in short order: revulsion, disgust, contempt, disdain, disapproval, ridicule, bemusement.

We are a long way from hunter-gatherer days, but that instinctive resistance to 'otherness' is still enmeshed within us. It was instructive to see that borne out in the qualitative phase of our research initiative, conducted with a range of age cohorts in the UK and the United States.

For this research respondents were first shown simple descriptions of eight marginal behaviours, chosen to give a representative arc in terms of rarity, practicality and surprise. The eight were: microdosing (magic mushrooms and LSD); uniform wardrobe; freebirthing; polyphasic sleeping; polyamory; insect eating – where people gain the bulk of their protein from the consumption of insects and bugs; living without money – where people rely on a system of barter rather than monetary payment; and home burial – where families choose to intern the remains of recently deceased loved ones within the confines of their own properties.

What was revelatory across all groups – but particularly the ones outside the Gen Z cohort – was the instant, visceral reaction when the stimulus board capturing these behaviours was first unveiled. Accompanied by screwed-up faces, shaking heads, eyes that would look askance and arms that would remain defiantly folded, these are the verbal fragments that would come up in that first, involuntary, almost primal rejection:

> *'This is insane!'*
> *'This is just weird to me'*
> *'Wrong on all levels'*
> *'Abnormal'*
> *'It's alien'*
> *'Weirdos – it's baffling my head'*
> *'Just wrong'*
> *'Bonkers'*
> *'Ridiculous'*
> *'Grim'*

But these were just initial reactions. What would happen when the behaviours were probed a little more closely, one by one, with a bit more detail on aspects such as their history or places where they are more commonly practised? It soon became clear that the phenomenon of resistance is far more nuanced than a reading of those first visceral reactions would indicate – and that some responses are far more emotional and intractable than others.

A spectrum of resistance

An important finding from this work – corroborated by the quantitative phase, which looked at 21 behaviours – is that resistance can be plotted on a spectrum from highly emotional and closed at one end, through to less emotional and more open at the other. (See Figure 4.3.) The headers inside the spectrum capture the centre of gravity of responses at each point along the way, working down the emotional gradient from left to right. So, a behaviour could be perceived as: Dangerous (most emotional); Disgusting; Weird; Idealistic or Impractical (least emotional). Inevitably, there is the prospect of a certain degree of overlap here, as some behaviours tend to straddle two points or pop up in different places according to the makeup of the respondent group. Nevertheless, the principle at work is:

THE FURTHER TO THE LEFT, THE MORE INTRACTABLE
THE RESISTANCE

Let's take a closer look at the waystations along that spectrum, and the behaviours that tended most to be associated with them.

FIGURE 4.3   The spectrum of resistance

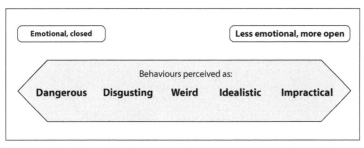

The 'emotional charge' of mainstream resistance to marginal behaviours and ways of life can be plotted on a spectrum – with reactions carrying a higher emotional charge to the left, through to lower emotional charge on the right. The higher the emotional charge, the more closed people are to considering the behaviour. The characteristic responses at each locus on the spectrum are captured in five 'centre of gravity' headers.

DANGEROUS

The prevailing emotion at this early point in the spectrum is fear, expressed as an overriding focus on the perceived risks – even threat to life – of the behaviour for both self and others.

Freebirthing often found itself here in our research groups, with comments such as 'You don't roll the dice with this stuff', or, more blankly, 'Back in the day, women used to die'. There was little-concealed disdain for people who would practise it: 'I just don't get it; why would people go for this?' (Interestingly, though, freebirthing was the most polarizing of the behaviours explored, with some – more women than men – deeming it desirable but simply impractical.)

One marker of whether people would soften on their initial reaction to a behaviour was the extent to which their curiosity was aroused. If it was, the process of discovering more would sometimes modify their view, and they would become more open. With behaviours at this 'dangerous' point on the spectrum, though, curiosity was absent. Respondents didn't wish to know more. They just wanted to reject.

DISGUSTING

Even where respondents felt a behaviour to carry low objective risk, they could be repulsed by it, disgusted at the thought of engaging with it, and prey to misgivings about those who did. Eating insects tended to come up as the most common exemplar of this point on the spectrum, with many using the word 'dirty' to describe it: 'Dirty, I wouldn't even try it.'

Polyamory was also here, with shades of strong disapproval most prevalent in the more religious United States. There was also a deft verbal tendency to dissociate self from others who practise, as in this unforgettable nugget: 'Well, I don't know any [polyamorists] in Philadelphia but there are probably certain states where it's popular.'

Curiosity was more in evidence here than at the most extreme emotional locus on the spectrum, especially in younger cohorts. As one Gen Z respondent put it, 'I see life as one big experiment and on something like this, I'm my own test subject.'

WEIRD

Around this marker came the behaviours that made people feel uncomfortable for simply being out of the ordinary, with comments often preceded by a smirk, giggles or face-pulling. Respondents felt challenged, often without really knowing why, as with this comment on home burial: 'We still laugh about the woman who buried her husband in the back garden, joking around, because it's not normal, is it?'

This sense of weirdness and abnormality could often be defused once people got to probe more deeply into the behaviour and articulate for themselves why it was not so strange after all. Groups, through their own deliberations, might get to the conclusion that what is weird today will be accepted tomorrow. The emotional content of 'weird' responses is hence more brittle than those further to the left of the spectrum. They can be strongly declarative at first, but crumble later.

IDEALISTIC

There was a paternalistic element to responses at this locus, reflecting a sense that people who indulged in certain behaviours were well-intentioned but naïve. Living without money came up here ('I feel it's slightly irresponsible'), as did microdosing ('They think it makes them more interesting, but it's not interesting, it's silly'). Sometimes concern would morph into something akin to pity for those perceived as haplessly pushing against the flow to maintain their idealized way of life: 'Well, I guess it's her choice, and I suppose she's doing no harm' (about uniform wardrobe).

Overall, though, these reactions amount to a relatively mild form of personal resistance, and one that could flip when respondents began to see why perhaps it might be worth the effort after all. Here, for example, is a respondent reaction to living without money: 'I want to know more about their life, it seems tranquil, stress free, the key to ultimate freedom'.

Whenever respondents felt they could see themselves flirting with one of the behaviours, though, there was inevitably a further tug of resistance: impracticality, coming up last.

IMPRACTICAL

For some of the behaviours, during the initial discussion when respondents would tend to voice their immediate negative reactions, there would be respondents who would remain quiet, looking on more thoughtfully. Often, when probed for their thoughts, they would be guardedly positive.

Polyphasic sleeping – the notion of taking multiple shorter naps throughout the day – appealed to a significant minority of the respondents. Freebirthing, though viewed as dangerous by most, would sometimes capture the imagination of a (usually female) respondent: 'A beautiful experience, something to consider'.

Inevitably, though, the sheer impracticality of pursuing these behaviours with the world as it is formed a barrier, and respondents would wonder how devotees managed to achieve it: 'It would require a complete societal restructuring, which we won't see' (polyphasic sleeping). 'Well, I can't bury my dad on the balcony' (home burial).

But now we are in the territory of rational, rather than emotional response. At this point, people are in effect recognizing the reality of frictions, and, unlike true adherents, do not have the inner intensity to overcome them.

This is probably the point at which entrepreneurial marketers can make the simplest difference: finding ways to remove or reduce frictions for behaviours that otherwise have the potential to broaden their appeal. We will look at that more closely when we get to the later beacons and in the chapter on entrepreneurs, further on in the book.

Plotting behaviours on the spectrum

From this qualitative work, with some cross-referencing from the quantitative findings, it was possible to plot the eight behaviours (plus 'naturism', which came up spontaneously in several groups) along the spectrum of resistance, as shown in Figure 4.4. It is not neat and tidy and fixed, of course. There is overlap and dual positioning in some cases. But it gives marketers a glimpse at which kinds of behaviours are more amenable to influence and serves to illuminate the nuances of what at first might seem overwhelming, blanket rejection.

There is a second gradient to be aware of – one that we touched on in Chapter 3: age. Almost without exception, the younger the cohort, the more likely respondents were to allow curiosity to overcome initial visceral

FIGURE 4.4   Spectrum of resistance with behaviour placement

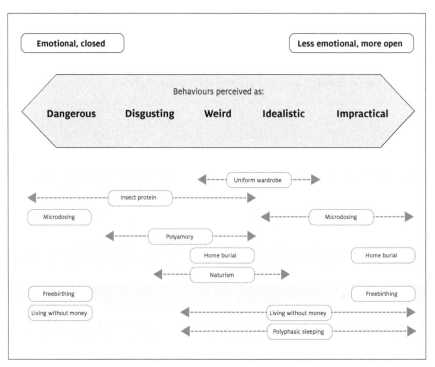

The eight researched behaviours plus naturism, which came up spontaneously in groups, can be plotted along the spectrum of resistance – so those towards the extreme left generated greater emotional rejection than those towards the centre or right. Some behaviours straddled more than one locus on the spectrum, while others (notably Freebirthing) occupied two distinctly different points.

doubts. In the Gen Z groups, you could almost see this inner dilemma being resolved, with pauses before speaking and circumlocutions along the lines of 'Well, obviously many people would find this dangerous/disgusting/weird, but I'm open minded, so…'

And so, we have the first indications of a 'sweet spot' for marginal behaviours that might more readily burst into the mainstream: those to the right of the spectrum, with most relevance to the younger cohorts.

A marketing take on resistance

The negativity of resistance, unlike the positive thrust of intensity, is something with which most marketers will be all too familiar. It will often show its face as a 'barrier to purchase', where consumers cannot get to focus on the benefit of a product or service because there is something else putting them off. It can famously show itself in new product development, when consumers can sometimes almost fall over themselves to reject unexpected innovation.

And what seemed like a communications breakthrough in the ad agency meeting can often raise the hackles of resistance in focus groups, as consumers tear the work to pieces in front of the chastened eyes of those looking in through the one-way mirror.

Marketers, when faced with the hostility of consumer resistance, tend to capitulate and regroup. Understandably. They have researchers on one shoulder whispering 'we told you this wouldn't work' and board members on the other looking only for unequivocally positive proof.

But any marketer venturing to the fringes to make a breakthrough will need to be both more courageous and more determined than that. They will need to look past initial resistance to see the more nuanced contours and patterns underneath. And they will need imagination to project that what is summarily dismissed today could be bursting through to the mainstream tomorrow.

By way of encouragement, they could do worse than reflect that there is something to be welcomed about this force of active resistance: that it is, indeed, a force. It is not inert. Not neutral. Not flat. Yes, it is a force coming at you, often with a crazy look on its face. But that makes it a more thrilling prospect to work with. As with the principles of the martial arts, with technique, that opposing force can be turned around, and put to work in your favour. The next three chapters, on the remaining six beacons, will offer insight on when and how that turnaround can be best achieved.

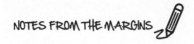

NOTES FROM THE MARGINS

Polyamory

'When you have a child you love with all your heart, and then later have a second child, you don't just lose your love for the first. Romantic love works the same way; I can love more than one person at a time.' That's the simple starting point that polyamorist Mary Crumpton gives to explain her unconventional lifestyle in Manchester, where she lives with her two 'husbands', Tim and John.

Therapist and life coach Mary is out and proud about her polyamory, which for her is a simple rejection of the received social norm that requires you to fall in love with one person at a time. She speaks openly and passionately about it, determined to shift lazy assumptions about orgies or sex parties, and help people understand her view that love isn't a limited resource. Mary's transparency about her emotional, romantic and sexual life triggers wildly different reactions. She's been spat at by strangers and called a slut in the street; at the same time she's had messages from strangers thanking her for her honest stand, which has enabled them to 'come out' to their own families, and received kind letters acknowledging that her calm eloquence has helped the writers relate to something they couldn't previously understand. Death threats posted through her door were frightening, but made her even more determined to carry on talking about it even if 'the worst were to happen'... this is a hill she is actually willing to die on.

It might be worth having a dictionary moment. Polygamy is probably familiar, from the Greek meaning 'many marriages', and legal in around 50 nation states across north Africa, the Middle East and parts of Asia. Though illegal in the United States since the 1850s, where the Mormons are particularly associated with it, the authorities tend to turn a blind eye – so much so that in February 2020 the punishment for polygamy was reduced to the same legal status as a speeding ticket.

Polygyny is the state of a man having many wives, and polyandry refers to a woman having multiple husbands (very rare, and seems only to be legally allowed in Gabon). A polycule describes the connected network of a polyamorous group. Triads and throuples are three-person relationships.

Polyamory was first coined in the 1990s in Morning Glory Zell-Ravenheart's article on the subject, *A Bouquet of Lovers*[21], and is also sometimes known as CNM, or consensual non-monogamy. This rejection of monogamy is key for Mary, who thinks more people should be truthful about their emotions: 'most people, if they're honest, have developed feelings for someone else even if they haven't kissed or even had sex'.

Mary married Tim seven years ago in Manchester. A year later she met John and after convincing Tim that he posed no threat to their marriage, John moved in too; later Tim even accompanied her up the aisle at her second unofficial 'wedding' which Mary hopes could one day become legal. The three live happily together and the two men are friends; there's even a term for the warm feeling that polyamorous people experience when seeing their partners with someone else: compersion, as in: 'I feel compersion when I see my husband come home happy from spending time with his girlfriend. His happiness brings me happiness,' This feelgood factor is a reaction to what many polyamorists feel about monogamy as being stifling or oppressive.

You couldn't find a stat to prove there are more polyamorists than ever before, or whether we're just hearing more about them. As with so much in 21st-century life, social media and the internet have lifted the lid on this marginal behaviour, allowing the poly-curious to explore the idea, realize they're not alone and then connect with other like-minded people. It's certainly no longer just the stuff of extreme film festival documentaries, and advocates of this niche lifestyle choice feel validated by having a specific term for it: polyamory. They're not just sleeping around or having open marriages, but striving to build strong and long-lasting romantic attachments. As Mary says: 'It's not about sex – I've never had a one-night-stand in my life! It's very much about love.'

Voluntary celibacy

You?! Not having sex?! That's how Emma Smith's friends reacted to her announcement that she was going to dive into voluntary celibacy – vol-cel – and deliberately and purposefully not engage in any sexual activity.

For the bright, glamorous and highly libidinous Emma, the next three months were torture.

She'd climbed onto the emotional rollercoaster of online dating in its infancy – 15 years ago, and after a short-lived marriage – and she'd become addicted. At first the fun and excitement of the messaging, the online chats, the dates and the sex were thrilling; at times, not so much, but it took years for her to change her behaviour and attitude to it. Occasionally, after a particularly bad date or poor treatment by a man, Emma would delete all her dating apps – only to re-install them within days.

It was actually a positive experience that prompted her deliberate vol-cel experiment, not a negative one. Emma met a guy. A nice guy, who was warm and kind, who had a good job, who she got on well with, but realizing that even this nice guy wasn't going to be 'the one', she decided to remove herself from the pool. She'd heard about vol-cel before, but was the first person she knew to actually take the plunge.

Pop star Justin Bieber is probably the most famous proponent, talking openly about his pre-marriage period of celibacy[22]. 'Sometimes people have sex because they don't feel good enough, because they lack self-worth. I think sex can cause a lot of pain.' With 175 million followers on Instagram, Bieber is what social media influencing is all about. Just to be clear, the key word in voluntary celibacy is voluntary. Like Bieber, this small but significant number of young people aren't not having sex because they can't find anyone to have sex with – they're not having sex because they find it improves their wellbeing.

At first Emma wasn't sure whether wellbeing was worth giving up sex for. Likening it to an alcoholic going cold turkey, she deleted the dating apps she'd used for years, didn't reply to messages and blocked booty calls from what she calls the boomerangs (the dates who would go quiet and then re-appear again). She told all her friends what she was doing and declared confidently she was at the start of three months being voluntarily celibate, so there'd be no going back. No-one was more surprised than Emma that at the end of the three months, she realized she didn't want to.

She was beginning to feel the benefits of vol-cel, so decided to continue for a further three months. At the end of the six months, she opted to do another six. Her friends were supportive though a little dismayed, missing the jaw-dropping stories she shared about her dating mishaps and sexual shenanigans – but Emma knew it was just what she needed (those stories won't be wasted; she is now shaping the best and worst into a one-woman show).

A year in, she was finding some freedom from the drama of dating, the let-downs and being on the receiving end of some very unpleasant male behaviour. She had more time on her hands than ever before, spent quality time with her friends and was finding new and enriching things to do – and as the pandemic took hold, she embarked on a further year vol-cel. Online dating was an emotional rollercoaster which she'd managed to jump from, at least for a while. The reboot worked.

In the last few months Emma has returned to dating, but feels that the strength and headspace she gained from her two years vol-cel has been invaluable, even now she's having sex again. She's less obsessive about it, much calmer, and closes down poor behaviour immediately.

For her, going vol-cel has been the best thing she's ever done for herself, and she'd recommend a period of it to everybody. And as Emma says, with her high sex drive, if she can do it, anyone can.

05

What's hidden, what's there and what could be: the revelatory beacons

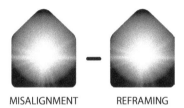

MISALIGNMENT   REFRAMING

Misalignment and reframing crop up at slightly different points along the M2M pathway – Beacons 3 and 5 – but have a yin-and-yang relationship with one another because both are about different ways of perceiving. It would be too simplistic to regard one as a problem and the other as the solution but there is, nonetheless, an element of negative and positive about these two powerful features along the faultline of marginal and mainstream interaction. In any case, from the entrepreneurial marketer's point of view, both should be viewed through an opportunistic lens, since both offer scope for intervention.

Misalignment is a recognition that the forces of intensity and resistance do not always go head-to-head. As so often in the sphere of human discourse, two sides talk past each other, without really internalizing what the other side is banging on about or engaging with what's actually being said. It's as though they perceive arguments through a filter, and then, rather than respond to the actuality, simply shout their own viewpoint louder.

If you paraphrased and condensed this kind of miscued dialogue, it would look a little like this:

'We engage in this behaviour because we believe that issue A is fundamentally important.'

'Yes, but adopting that behaviour would make us worried about problem X.'
'But issue A! Look how crucial issue A is!'

One side has a point to make, the other has an objection that doesn't directly relate to that point, and the first side simply restates its original argument with greater force. This *doubling down* that tends to be seen within the marginal group is an important motif within the beacon of misalignment because it works to ossify the discourse in two ways: first, by raising the defences of the mainstream mass, and second by acting as a feedback mechanism within the marginal group itself.

The original argument, in other words, becomes reinforced and more deeply ingrained within those promoting it through its very declaration and repetition. If you think back to the early vegan days, this pattern was evident. Vegans wanted the mainstream to embrace the animal welfare cause, the mainstream was concerned about the perceived nutritional shortcomings of a vegan diet, the vegan response was to double down and that encouraged a 'committed vegan' mindset that became ever more closed and obdurate about animal rights. Neither side could see past their own concerns to engage with the other's viewpoint.

This would appear a daunting tension to surmount, but the more symmetrical situation of direct disagreement is actually harder. If one group fervently believes X and the other just as fervently believes Not-X, then mediation is made tougher by the need for one of them to give ground, since one argument cannot gain unless the other recedes. But where there is asymmetry of disagreement, there is a chink for a third party – or voices within one of the two engaged parties – to infiltrate and help the two sides understand one another, without either having to give way. An important principle is:

WHERE THERE IS ASYMMETRY THERE IS OPPORTUNITY

Often though, if the discourse has been misfiring for years, the very language and terminology associated with it will have become charged with confusion and negativity. The empathetic go-between will want to defuse that, to get people to think about things afresh without bringing along all their preconceptions. One way to do that is with the help of reframing.

For something so simple, the act of reframing an established concept in people's minds can have a profound effect. Typically, the process involves no more than presenting the same information in a different way, using a different overall start point, to help people see it through a more positive mental lens. The key point is that nothing of substance is changed. The entity in question – behaviour, product, proposal, tax, law, medical intervention – remains intact. It is the altered cognitive framing that does the work.

A classic study from the behavioural economists Daniel Kahneman and Amos Tversky showed the marked difference when the same basic question is given a positive or negative framing.[1] Participants were asked to imagine 600 people with a fatal disease and choose between two treatment options. Treatment A was predicted to result in 400 deaths, while Treatment B offered a 33 per cent chance that nobody would die but a 66 per cent chance that all would die. This combination of options was presented to participants in two ways:

Positive
Treatment A: saves 200 lives. Treatment B: a 33 per cent chance of saving all 600 people, a 66 per cent possibility of saving no-one.

Negative
Treatment A: 400 people will die. Treatment B: a 33 per cent chance that no-one will die, a 66 per cent probability that all 600 will die.

Treatment A was chosen by 72 per cent of respondents with positive framing, but that plummeted to 22 per cent when framed negatively. Yet the fundamentals are unaltered.

Within the marketing industry, UK author and ad-man Rory Sutherland has long extolled the value of carefully framing experiences so that what might be seen as an issue gets interpreted as a bonus. He cites the welcome procedure at UK Japanese casual dining chain, Wagamama, as an example.

What's unusual about Wagamama is that dishes can arrive haphazardly, in a different order from the one you might have expected, and at slightly different times for everyone in your party. With this kind of rice- and noodle-based food, it suits the kitchens to work this way. If that seemingly random timing came as a surprise it might look like shoddy procedures. So, as guests are led to one of the long trestle tables when they first arrive, the host explains that, according to kaizen principles, all dishes are cooked fresh and served the moment they are ready, whenever that may be. The unusualness of the arrangement helps add to the experience and make it memorable. The 'problem' of mistiming has been reframed as a benefit.

When plotting a behaviour along the M2M Pathway, the significance of reframing is not just its yin-yang relationship with misalignment but as an important possibility wherever some kind of negative mental model prevents a marginal behaviour from gaining traction. The act of reframing could come from within the marginal group itself (like the switch from 'nudism' to the less voyeuristic 'naturism') or from would-be sympathizers within the mainstream, deterred by current unwanted associations (as in the verbal shift from 'vegan' to 'plant based'). These are important diagnostic cues for marketers to be aware of, since they can precede a consumer re-evaluation and lead to more widespread adoption of the behaviour.

But of course, reframing could also be attempted by those with a commercial interest in seeing a behaviour leap forward – with entrepreneurs, business leaders and marketers in the vanguard. This is a beacon, then, that straddles both assessment and agency. It is both a marker of the likelihood of a behaviour going mainstream and a tool for the entrepreneurial marketer to help it on its way.

We will take a deeper look at these 'revelatory' beacons further down the chapter, when we consider each of them separately. But first we revisit and conclude the homeopathy story, looking at how misalignment blights the discourse today and how reframing might possibly help resolve that tomorrow.

Homeopathy revisited: two sides without a language in common

The discourse faultline between the homeopathic few and the mainstream many is the one that separates anecdote and science. It is not that the anecdotes are to be breezily dismissed, since many relate to profound personal experiences of the transformative effect of homeopathic remedies on incapacitating ailments that have persisted for years and resisted conventional treatments.

Those of a more scientific leaning cannot simply deem that these personal experiences are to be disbelieved. Instead, they argue that there can be no credible scientific explanation for them, since there is no plausible mode of action by which substances that have been diluted out of material existence can have a medicinal effect within the body. If you were to paraphrase and condense these oft-repeated exchanges it would run like this:

'It works.'

'Then show us *how* it works.'

'It works – what more do you need?'

This is a classic misalignment and one that could conceivably simply persist, with homeopathy sticking with the marginal or minority territory that it holds now, and the scientific community sticking with its derision.

But homeopaths have occasionally, if never convincingly, striven to rise to the scientific challenge and seek to offer proof to the sceptics. You can see why. These days, to extol but not explain is to be judged as *anti-science,* which is as close as we get to blasphemy in the modern world. When the Oxford-educated UK Minister for Health, Jeremy Hunt, passed along homeopathic case studies to the heads of the NHS for consideration in 2012, he was pilloried by the publication New Scientist as the Government 'minister for magic'.[2]

But in homeopathy's patchy engagement with science, neither the will nor the language has really been there. That the will is wanting can be inferred from the reluctance of homeopaths to engage in randomized controlled trials, since it is argued that it is impossible to isolate the effect of just one element from the patient-practitioner-remedy 'tangle'. As for language, you only have to look at some of the diagnostic questions that homeopaths ask their patients – 'Do you feel sad when you hear piano music?', 'Are you excessively tidy?' – and compare that with norms in conventional practice, to get the measure of two sides that talk way past each other.

Homeopathy comes across as something akin to medicine by metaphor, speaking a language that is closer to poetry than the taut, desiccated certainties of scientism's would-be enforcers. You can see this unembarrassed evocation at work when it engages in its own internal 'proofs' – documented comparisons of the effects of homeopathic remedies.

Here, for example, is a fragment from a comparison between a preparation of ozone diluted 10 to the power of 60 times, and another called *Haliaeetus leucocephalus sanguinaria*. Both, according to the database, 'share themes of 'upward', floating sensations, such as feeling light and free, feelings of elation and euphoria and dreams of being high up in the mountains'.[3]

Since ozone is heavier than air and therefore sinks, it is hard to see how it prompts any kind of uplifting. *Haliaeetus leucocephalus sanguinaria,* meanwhile, is a remedy prepared from the blood of the American bald eagle and is thereby somehow supposed to elicit this mountainous mood.

Whatever is at work here, it clearly isn't science, and is apt to prompt a 'We rest our case' response from the established medical community. But life isn't that simple. There is much about accepted clinical practice that is not yet understood but is applied nonetheless because it works. Pain control is one area. It is still not known how anaesthetics work. Within everyday analgesics, the mode of action of acetaminophen/paracetamol is still a mystery. More difficult yet for the science side, it has been shown that branded painkillers, with their garish colours, punchy logos and assertive, targets-and-arrows iconography, relieve pain better than exactly the same generic pharmaceutical actives in unbranded packs.[4] Is that 'magic' too?

No, comes the answer, it is the placebo effect – a crust that is thrown by the medical establishment to homeopathy but not caught. Neither side seems in a hurry to own this 'dummy' treatment phenomenon, and perhaps, in refusing to do so, both miss an opportunity.

COULD HOMEOPATHY BENEFIT FROM REFRAMING?

It is difficult to see how homeopathy might gain more widespread acceptance without some kind of substantive or perceptual intervention to help. Of the alternative therapies out there, it is by far the most polarizing, galvanizing supporters but attracting far greater mainstream hostility than, say, acupuncture or ayurveda.

One option for reframing might be to drop the contentious references to 'medicine' and opt for a description such as 'adjuvant therapy'. But just as Hahnemann would countenance no such support-act role for homeopathy 200 years ago, so modern homeopaths like to insist on its status as a prime mover in mankind's fight against pathology.

Up to a point, a kind of reframing has been undertaken in the UK, with the repurposing of the former homeopathic hospitals as centres of 'integrative medicine'. But this option, ironically, dilutes the influence of homeopathy as a standalone therapy, since integrative medicine is defined as 'any treatment option that takes account of the whole person, including all aspects of lifestyle', and embraces regimes as diverse as traditional Chinese medicine and aromatherapy.

If there is one part of the puzzle that is ripe for reframing, though, it is the concept of the placebo effect, which is so often proffered as an explanation for homeopathy's successes. If placebo has a bad rep, it is perhaps because of the associations with its role as the 'dummy' or 'sham' alternative in medical trials – with the implication that the recipient is somehow being fooled. Or perhaps its value is downgraded through the perception that any old substance would do the trick – plain water or a sugar pill.

That is not strictly true. There is more science and more complexity around placebo than that. One theory gaining ground is that a convincing placebo encourages the body to invest more in immune response – which otherwise remains muted much of the time since it is expensive to maintain. The immune system cannot be consciously willed to fire up – but the subconscious could be primed to intervene given a sufficiently compelling stimulus. And studies have shown that the more elaborate the placebo concoction, the more marked the alleviation effect.[5] That favours homeopathy since both its diagnostic procedures and its modes of production are so very rococo and ritualistic.

If 'placebo' could be reframed in a less passive, less 'dummy' way – 'active integration', say, or 'the stimulus effect' – perhaps homeopaths would be more willing to embrace it as an explanation for positive outcomes, and be less vulnerable to the hostile ordnance of scientism. But the orthodox side has something to gain, too, if the power of placebo, suitably reframed, is allowed to be further recognized, explored and enhanced. In his 2019 book, *Alchemy*, Rory Sutherland declares himself at a loss to understand why health system investment in placebo research is not a number one priority.[6]

The subtitle of Sutherland's book is 'The surprising power of ideas that don't make sense', and that is as apt a note as any on which to conclude this four-beacon analysis of homeopathy and its prospects for expansion. Homeopathy clearly does not make sense. Whether sufficient numbers of people might nonetheless decide that it contains surprising power, and carry it into the mainstream, it is a 200-year question that, for now, remains in the balance.

We now turn our attention to the beacons of misalignment and reframing as separate entities, to help marketers gain a richer insight into their roles in the dissemination of marginal behaviours and ways of life away from the fringes and into the mainstream mass.

Understanding misalignment: an all-too-human flaw

There is a technique used by psychotherapists and development coaches to help people resolve a persisting disagreement or conflict – often in a work or organizational setting. The principle behind it is that before a conflict can be resolved, each side must understand what it really is – and often, as becomes obvious, their interpretations differ.

The moderated session starts with one side telling the other how they see the problem. But not the whole story – just the first sentence or two. The other side will of course be allowed to respond. But before they can do that, they must repeat back to the first person what they have just said. Not necessarily verbatim, but enough to show that they have accurately listened to the point that was actually made. If they somehow misrepresent it, the moderator will intervene. Once they have achieved this face-to-face repetition, they can make their own point back.

The first person then does the same – repeats what the other has said before moving on to address it or make another point in return. And so the dialogue continues – repetition, point; repetition, point – until some kind of resolution, or at least better mutual understanding of the issues, has come to fruition.

The technique is called reflective listening and was developed in the 1950s by the US psychotherapist Carl Rogers as a therapeutic tool for use by therapists to reflect client experience but not be insincere. The problem he was seeking to solve derived from the then current practice of offering an immediate *interpretive* response to the client, which could often be way off what had been intended, with the result that clients would get defensive and clam up. The technique became adopted by professionals in conflict management and negotiation and was neatly summed up by the US author and educator Dr Stephen R. Covey, as, 'Seek first to understand, then to be understood'.[7]

If you have ever been an active party to reflective listening – sometimes called echoing or parroting back – you will doubtlessly have been struck by two things. First, it slows the dialogue down, which is no bad thing; the emotions cannot kick in as fast, owing to the need to concentrate on what is being said and then repeat it. And second, it reveals totally new contours to what had in the past seemed an unnavigable conflict landscape. You realize that you had been talking at cross purposes all along. You had been misinterpreting. You were misaligned. From that realization, genuine dialogue could begin.

What is true of individuals is truer still between groups, for reasons we'll come onto later. The two sides become more and more bent on being understood and devote too few resources to understanding. In our original research we found numerous examples of this misaligned, misfiring pattern of exchange. One of the most striking was the disagreement on whether it might be a neat idea for more of us to start eating insects.

The cerebral pros and visceral cons of insect protein

In the quantitative phase of our original research, during which 21 marginal behaviours were explored, the question design was always the same. Each of the behaviours was set down in a what/why format – briefly capturing what the behaviour entailed, followed by a single sentence summary of why people engaged with it, based on the typical declarations of the advocates themselves. Here's how that looked for insect protein:

> *What: eating protein derived from insects instead of animal meat.*
> *Why: sustainable, cheap and environmentally friendly as well as delivering more protein and less fat.*

For this behaviour, as with all the others, we wanted to know whether respondents had heard of it, whether they felt it unacceptably strange – or thought that others might – and, most importantly, whether they would like to learn more about it or even try it. What was surprising, given the contentious nature of some of the other behaviours explored, is how low on the list insect protein came for willingness to try – one of the least likely to make it into that category.

This was replicated in the qualitative work, where we had more time to explore the reasons why some people choose to eat insects (including grubs and mealworms) and gauge the reactions of people who do not. Our stimulus captured a wide range of the arguments made by proponents of this nutritional life choice, which include the fact that insect farming produces significantly lower greenhouse gases than traditional livestock farming, that it requires less land and water, that we need alternative protein sources if a world of nine billion people is not to starve, and that insects are 60 per cent protein by body mass and healthily low in fat.

In a sense, given this weight of argument, the wisdom of eating insect protein is a no-brainer. But respondents were in any case in no hurry to respond with their brains, or at least not the rational side of them, since their reactions were located somewhere more visceral, below. They were disgusted at the thought, deemed insects dirty, and found it almost impossible to get beyond that emotional pinch-point. Here are some of the verbatims from the groups:

> 'It makes me feel sick, to be honest, looking at this.'
> 'Insects are dirty, I don't see them as food.'
> 'It's dirty, unhygienic and will taste awful.'
> 'I'll eat anything. But, like, there's no way I'm buying an insect flour burger or Grub bars that have insects in them, I just don't want to do that.'
> 'I don't know, I get a bit of the shivers, it's just, like, they're creepy-crawlies.'
> 'It's dirty, it's for the poor and starving.'

So extreme and universal was this dirty/disgust reaction that you would think it might have already seeped out and reached the awareness of groups and individuals who advocate for this diet choice. If it has, it isn't being heard. Advocates are more apt to double down on the ecological and sustainability arguments, celebrating insect protein as a 'future food', with positive implications for humankind and the environment.

Paraphrased and condensed, the dialogue between margin and mainstream goes something like this:

> 'We can save the planet if we all sometimes eat insects to get our protein.'
> 'Yuck!'
> 'But don't you care about the planet?'

This is exactly the kind of misalignment entry point that marketers could step into – showing first that they understand the visceral reaction, echoing it back, and offering reassurance on hygiene and taste, before seeking to be understood on the higher-order 'planet' points. If you look at the efforts of those businesses so far that trade in insect protein products, that marketing nuance appears not to be there. Most simply expound the sustainability arguments, while a few try to defuse the natural squeamishness around insects by showing them in cartoon form. It is unlikely to be enough.

Since a little reframing would not go amiss here, we will pick up the insect protein case again a bit later, in the section devoted to the 'reframing' beacon. First, though, a look into group dynamics to help understand why a group can be a far more extreme amplifier of a singular point of view than loosely connected individuals.

The inner world of groups

Not all marginal behaviours attract advocates that coalesce into groups. Of those we have already looked at, uniform wardrobe, polyphasic sleeping and home burial are as likely to be practised by scattered individuals who see little need to coordinate and club together on what is usually a quiet, personal choice.

But many marginals do very much have a group attraction – committed veganism, extreme carnivorism, naturism, modern-day witchcraft and neo-Luddism are all examples where advocates come together to form some sense of 'us'.

Where there is an 'us' there will also be a 'them' – in this case, the wider, fuzzy entity of the mainstream, which is not really a coherent group at all, but more a population of disconnected souls who are giving scant thought to the subject in question until confronted with it.

There is an asymmetry, then, between the tight, impassioned group with a single theme or cause at its core and the unfocused, half-attentive, big, blurry populous on the outside. Misalignment occurs because the tight group's own feedback mechanisms create an ever-more inflexible narrative that ignores the wider mainstream's vaguely articulated 'ifs' and 'buts'.

GROUPTHINK AND RAISING THE STAKES

Why are tight groups so inflexible and impervious to ideas, objections and critiques from outside? An important theory was suggested in 1952 by the renowned US social scientist William H. Whyte. In an interview with

Fortune magazine, he first introduced the concept of 'groupthink', and gave reasons why groups cleave increasingly inwards in their desire for harmony, and how that can result in a sacrifice of diverse cognition along the way. Whyte pointed to what he saw as 'a rationalized conformity – an open, articulate philosophy which holds that group values are not only expedient but right and good as well'.[8]

The problem of groupthink has been extensively explored since, most forensically by the US research psychologist Irving Janus, who in 1982 set out a list of 'symptomatic elements' that tended to characterize the trait.[9] These include illusions of invulnerability; belief in inherent morality; stereotyping those outside the group, to the extent of sometimes dehumanizing them; self-censorship – where the group eliminates ideas that deviate from the consensus; and illusions of unanimity – where silence is interpreted as consent.

More recently, the US behavioural economist Cass Sunstein has shown that tight groups fall prey to a kind of intensity inflation when they come together either physically or remotely to round on a subject. In his 2009 book, *Going to Extremes*, Sunstein showed that a group will tend to exaggerate any slight bias that was there at the outset. So pernicious is this that, by the end of the session, the overall group bias will be more extreme than that of the single most biased member beforehand.[10]

In the process of encouraging a marginal behaviour, then, groups tend to demonstrate two opposing influences. At the outset, as we saw in Chapter 3, the group dynamic can help get a marginal behaviour off the ground. The possibility of getting together with like-minded others, especially in a digitally connected world, brings cohesion and heft to what otherwise would be just scattered and individualized eccentricity. But once the group is well established, with its own codes and practices, its inwardly turned narrative, its tendency to raise the stakes, it can become a barrier to open discourse with those less committed on the outside.

The empathetic go-between has a fine line to tread. The danger is to be deafened by the forcefully argued group narrative and not hear the less articulate but no less felt concerns of the neutrals. The group may have all the passion, but the mainstream has the numbers. If the behaviour, cause, idea or way of life is to gain traction, those misaligned mainstream objections need to be addressed – but without losing all the positive themes that got the thing going in the first place. It is not the work of a moment – but is greatly helped where some inside the tight group begin to recognize the problem of misalignment and try to solve it from within.

A marketing take on misalignment

You will not find many marketers claiming to underinvest resources in understanding their consumers. It is an established tenet of modern marketing that business should work back from customer needs, and that all avenues must be explored in the duty of discovering what they are. Marketers really do seek to understand before seeking to be understood.

But understand whom? Most marketers, when seeking fresh insights into consumers, turn first to their heavy users, on the premise that those who most love the brand are the ones most likely to reveal its innermost satisfactions. Sometimes marketers might add in light users for balance or will turn to lapsed users to see what might bring them back.

But it is rare for marketers to canvass people who never buy the brand or even the category. Yet there, in that usually large population, resides considerable opportunity for growth. If marketers reached out that far in their quest to understand, they would likely walk into the issue of misalignment: despite all the brand's or category's benefits, something unrelated is erecting a barrier.

To resolve that misalignment and unlock opportunity, marketers will need to defuse objections, either substantively or perceptually or both, and still communicate positive reasons and benefits to get consumers beyond just neutral. It is a harder – and always a dual – task than just responding to the latest round of loyal consumer research.

Marketers who go further and seek to find growth at the behavioural margins will for sure need techniques to understand misalignment and to get inside it and find ways to resolve it. To achieve that, they will need a bigger toolkit than the one they typically carry now. And one of the tools inside it will be reframing, coming up next.

Understanding reframing: refocusing the eye of the beholder

There was a time when a person, if they were so minded, would go out and buy a used car. To do so they would venture to a used auto mart and seek to navigate the astute bargaining tactics of the used car dealer. On their way back home, at the wheel of their shiny acquisition, they would sense the bittersweet emotions of driving something that was thrillingly new to them but still, well, *used.*

What a smart bit of reframing it was when 'used' morphed into the more neutral, less dispiriting 'preowned'. And what genius it was to go way beyond that and coin the epithet 'preloved'. As long as the car in question could credibly match that description – there are limits – the new framing would help the buyer see their acquisition in a wholly positive light.

In the UK the term more normally employed was 'second-hand', rather than 'used', but the principle still applies, and not just to cars. Your child shows an interest in music. Would you rather buy a second-hand piano or a preloved piano? If two were locally on sale and otherwise similarly priced and described, which would you orient to? It's hard to imagine the more sweetly framed 'preloved' as not feeling more emotionally right.

The reframing also lends more positive associations to the place you buy from, not just the item itself. A second-hand clothes shop suggests one thing, a purveyor of preloved clothes quite another. A used car dealer – with all the unfortunate and often undeserved associations that accompany that term – becomes a specialist in preloved autos.

In the buyer's eye, it is the reframing that has made the difference. Nothing substantively has changed. And yet what was seen negatively is now brightly positive. That is a remarkable kind of power, if you think about it.

The roots of reframing

Marketers didn't invent reframing. It is a concept that has been borrowed from psychology, with its roots in the subdiscipline of cognitive therapy, first explored by the US psychotherapist Aaron T. Beck in the mid-1960s. What Beck had found, when working with clients who were depressed or given to panic disorders, is that the accepted Freudian techniques of the day had serious limitations. So, he began to experiment with a series of behavioural therapy techniques that helped patients see their own interpretations of their situation in a more positive light. The new suite of techniques, which rapidly became accepted practice, was bundled under the term 'cognitive restructuring', of which 'cognitive reframing' is a focal part.

The theory behind it is that in any new situation an individual rapidly decides what meaning it holds for them personally. This is the 'frame' through which they see it, and that frame is likely to persist unless actively modified. But perspective is, to an extent, a choice. If the frame is negative, it can be reassessed and changed. So, Beck and his followers would work with patients to 'change the conceptual viewpoint', by 'placing the situation in a different frame that fits the facts just as well but changes its entire meaning'.[11]

Note the absence of smoke and mirrors from this therapeutic technique. There is a straightforwardness to Beck's approach, evident in interviews with him right through to the years before his death, at 100, in 2021. It is open and obvious and achieved with the co-operation of the patient.

Similarly, in the marketing sphere, it is not necessary to see reframing as some sort of marketing 'dark art' sneaking in a clever switch while consumers are not looking. It is out in the open, and can be achieved with consumer input, with recipients very much party to the reasons for the linguistic change. Or, of course, consumers might make the reframing adjustment themselves, without any external marketing influence at all.

Reframing marginal behaviours

In the sphere of marginal behaviours, reframing is often welcomed by sympathizers in the mainstream mass who might consider adopting the behaviour but are put off by current unwanted associations. They would actively *prefer* to see it reframed. We saw this with our original research when exploring the relatively recent mainstream drift towards veganism.

Alongside the qualitative groups we conducted with longstanding vegans (as touched on under 'intensity' in Chapter 4), we also ran sessions among people only recently experimenting with the diet, to assess what had got them to modify their nutritional habits. Their reasons were of course substantive – usually a combination of health and ethics – but there is no doubt that a change in terminology helped. And that change, as already noted, was the easing from 'vegan' to 'plant based'.

How big a part did that loosening of the semantic reins play in their propensity to switch to the principles of a meat-and-dairy free diet? Here are some verbatims from our qualitative work:

> *'Plant based is better, vegan has a stigma, you think of tree huggers.'*
> *'People are more open to hearing about 'plant based' than they are about vegans. If you're a vegan it's all or nothing, isn't it?'*
> *'I've got a few friends who are more extreme vegan. It's a bit too much for me...it's not that deep to me.'*
> *'It's (plant based) less preachy and more factual.'*

Clearly, where the reframing has helped in this example is to soften the intensity surrounding veganism and give people a way to buy in without having to commit wholesale and embrace all the fierceness and dogma that came with it.

A deeper takeout from that is the importance of understanding just what it is that makes people hesitant about the behaviour in question, since it won't be the same for each one. With other marginal behaviours, as we have seen, resistance could present in many forms, some strongly felt, ranging from fearful disgust to doubts about practicality.

When unveiling our eight selected marginal behaviours in the qualitative groups, we ensured that there was always a gradual exposure of more factual detail about each one. We wanted to know what kinds of new information might prompt a little reconsideration after the first outpouring of negativity. This was not, of course, an attempt at reframing on the hoof, but the exercise did, nonetheless, work to identify broad thematic territories where reframing could potentially focus.

It should be noted that in some cases there was to be no softening; respondents would hang on to their initial doubts and be unpersuaded by new information. Where they did relent and reconsider, though, we could usually identify one of three thematic motifs at work:

1 **Antiquity:** it evolved with us or was a part of normal life at a different time. For example, when we showed that our ancestors often used to bury people close to where they lived, people felt the concept of home burial to be more normal and accessible.

2 **Cultural diversity:** it is a norm elsewhere. We showed (and sometimes respondents volunteered) that in Thailand, insects are routinely eaten deep-fried at street-food stalls. This wasn't enough, alone, to command active reconsideration, but did at least prompt pause for thought and more open discussion.

3 **Benefit:** focus on the personal gain. Microdosing is framed by what advocates *do* – and was generally judged to be illegal and misguided. But when shown examples of otherwise ordinary people whose reason for doing it is to focus better, respondents themselves began to reframe it, along the lines of this verbatim: 'It's not really about drug taking, it's about enhancing *you* every day'.

Sympathizers in the mainstream, adherents in the marginal group, entrepreneurs and marketers with a commercial interest in turning things round – all will confront very different perceptual framing challenges related to gaining widespread acceptance for a given marginal behaviour. And all will be enjoined to consider very different kinds of reframing approaches. Although the three pointers above will help, there is no magic formula for reframing, because, as we'll remind ourselves next, every challenge is unique and brings its own particular set of hurdles to surmount.

Insect protein revisited: a tough reframing challenge

You'll recall that the 'frame' through which respondents saw this behaviour choice was one of squeamishness about insects in general, disgust at the thought of consuming them, and a conviction that they are dirty. Since this was the overriding perceptual frame, it was hard to get respondents to embrace the positive, environmental arguments. They might well agree intellectually, but their 'conceptual viewpoint' was already strongly negative.

This is not an easy reframing challenge, but that is not to say that alternatives could not be tried. Since the very concept of 'insects' is a trigger, it might be worth considering the avoidance of striding in with that word at the first, general level. But what could be used instead?

A clue might be found in the first of our three reframing motifs above: the antiquity of our species' co-evolution. Insects predate birds and mammals by about 53 million years and were flourishing before almost all other land-based creatures. They became a protein resource, an early link on the food chain, on which later evolutions – including humankind – would feed. That could give us:

Original protein.

At some point in the communications hierarchy, of course, it would need to be spelt out what this means, but the avoidance of the term 'insect' at this first level could help. This is not without precedent. There was a time when the concept of eating raw fish would have seemed unthinkable in Western cultures but was softened by reference to 'sushi' and 'sashimi' at that first-order level rather than the frank, and unappealing, 'raw fish'.

Original protein goes in the opposite direction to 'future food' and is probably the better for that. Rather than evoking an unknown and uncertain tomorrow, it reassures through reference to our long, shared past. The reframing may also have practical advantages, since avoidance of the term 'insect' brings a certain elasticity that might permit the broadening out later to other ancient proteins – for example, those that derive from the sea.

Other reframing options are of course possible. One way through the 'dirty' perceptions might be to attach a little 'science' to the revised term, using the taxonomic 'ento' prefix rather than the word 'insect' itself (as some brands are already trying) and to signal a refinement process, rather than fix minds on the whole, creepy-crawly thing. For example:

Purified entoprotein and
Refined entoprotein.

Alternatively, it is not necessarily too crude to simply reframe by taking the negative perception head on and reversing it:

Clean insect protein.

A final point here is that the power of branding, itself, as an element of reframing should not be underestimated. It is one thing to offer up insect protein as a challenging nutritional choice – and another to offer it up under the reassuring logo of a known, trusted brand. Any food brand famous for its high standards in sourcing and hygiene would be bringing its own hint of reframing to – literally – the table.

A marketing take on reframing

Reframing is by no means unfamiliar in marketing but is nevertheless under-used. Most marketers have their heads down in their own brands, whereas reframing is often more applicable – as we explored with insect protein – at the category or subcategory level. Much has been written about that subcategory reframing opportunity, notably by the US marketing academic David Aaker,[12] but it is still a tactic rarely deployed.

Another area where the power of reframing is ignored is that large part of marketing known as internal brand engagement. Often, considerable resources are expended with the objective of galvanizing people who have direct contact with consumers, to get them to better embody the spirit of the brand.

But they still get called 'service teams' or 'cleaning crew' or 'contact centre employees'. In a famous example from the 1980s, Ritz-Carlton showed the deep effect of a beautiful linguistic switch. When launching an internal brand programme aimed at the people who worked in its premium hotels – chambermaids, cleaners, porters – it was careful not to use the term 'service staff' or anything like it. Instead, it reframed their role with this overarching 'motto': 'We are ladies and gentlemen serving ladies and gentlemen'.

Yes, the gender-specific language will now seem dated, but imagine the effect in self-esteem and comportment that was achieved at the time. The Ritz-Carlton case – which included a well-conceived incentives programme – has since become celebrated in the sphere of best-practice internal brand engagement, with that judicious reframing at its heart.

Given the insight that functions, not just products or categories, can be reframed, might it be too much to suggest that marketers turn the tactic on themselves? Are marketers simply the people who are there to grow the corporation's brands? Or are they the *entrepreneurs inside the organiza-tion*? How might that 'reflexive reframing' alter the way marketers see themselves and, every bit as important, the way they are viewed by others in the boardroom?

Entrepreneurs eschew process and seize opportunity. They are alive to change and the new chances for growth that it brings. As we will see next in Chapter 6, when it comes to exploring marginal behaviours, the opportunities that cascade from chance and change are there to be seized.

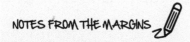 NOTES FROM THE MARGINS

Polyphasic sleeping

Should you be sleeping like a genius? Leonardo da Vinci eschewed the notion of lying in bed all night and instead took 20-minute naps every four hours, around the clock. Inventor Nikola Tesla famously did the same; both seemed able to get stuff done. This became known as polyphasic – many phases – sleep.

There's also biphasic – two phases – sleep, with a long night-time block and another in the heat of the afternoon, depending on your location. Churchill had his own take on it too, with a traditional long sleep at night and a two hour nap from 5pm daily (kicked off with a large whisky and soda).

Of course most humans take monophasic sleep, but start off polyphasically (as babies and infants), until their circadian rhythms develop, taking an environmental cue from darkness to trigger the single block of sleep we need to repair and recharge our brain function. Scientists and doctors agree this is vital. Without one long period of time spent asleep, we're denied the cycles of light, deep and REM sleep which each work in different ways to restore the brain and body and set us up for the day to come.

But there's no doubt that for some, and not just the odd few, polyphasic sleeping works. US student Marie Staver's insomnia was so bad that she decided to deal with it head on, rather than trying to sleep when her body wasn't letting it happen. Instead, she completely redesigned each 24-hour period and settled into taking just one 30-minute nap in every four hours, throughout the day and night.[13] Inspired by their studies into Nietzsche and his scholarly treatise *Ubermensch*, Staver and a fellow student who joined her in the experiment named the process Uberman, a nod to the philosopher they were studying and to the heightened creativity and alertness they were enjoying. They were losing sleep, but in a good way.

As Staver moved from student life to employment it became more difficult, in a practical sense, to continue with Uberman. She adjusted the schedule to fit around her working life and called it Everyman – in her case a three-hour block of sleep at night and three 20-minute naps during the day. Admittedly this was only possible as she had the kind of job which comes with an office, a desk to snooze under when required, and a broad-minded and understanding boss.

Along with her other preparations, British sailor Ellen MacArthur trained with a specialist to sleep polyphasically for 2001's Vendee Globe race – on this solo round-the-world adventure, she slept efficiently and restoratively in 10 short sleeps in each 24 hours in order to keep herself healthy and her boat on track. During the 94-day circumnavigation, MacArthur took 891 naps.

It mightn't suit all of us, or our lifestyles – da Vinci wasn't operating heavy machinery after all – but these extreme sleep patterns clearly work for some.

After all, monophasic sleepers (most of us) spend an average third of our time asleep; that's 26 years in bed out of the average life expectancy of 78 years old in the United States. If you were to adopt a polyphasic sleep pattern you'd claw back around 21 years … and just think what you could do with that.

06

Shakers of place and pace: the opportunity beacons

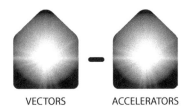

VECTORS   ACCELERATORS

Standing slightly apart from one another along the M2M pathway are two beacons that in different ways reflect the concept of movement. Vectors – Beacon 4 – are a conduit for the transference of a marginal behaviour from one subgroup to another, or from subgroup straight into the mainstream. They are about *place* – a shift from one orbit of society to a different one. Accelerators – Beacon 7 – are about *pace*. Here, we are talking about factors in the wider context that put rocket fuel into the take-up of a marginal behaviour. What was moving at one speed now ratchets up to surge at another.

Where there is movement there is opportunity, and entrepreneurial marketers will want to be aware of the forces and factors that underlie these dynamic waystations on the pathway. Sometimes, these will be obvious and linear. At other times, though, it will be anything but obvious and will require some joining up of the dots. As we shall see, there are both temporal and cultural nuances to these beacons, with the result that similar background influences can have very different results by timeframe or geography. This subtlety, paradoxically, adds to the opportunity; if everything were so obvious that everyone could see it, everyone would react at once. So, these beacons are especially pivotal for those with the commitment to combine observation with insight and draw meaningful conclusions ahead of the crowd.

VECTORS AND BLOCKERS

At the base level, the concept of vectors is simple enough. In any sizeable subculture (like bikers) or counterculture (like punks) or tightly defined group (like the military) there will normally be a bundle of behaviours that help to separate the group from outsiders. These behaviours might not be immediately obvious in their relationship with the overarching reason-for-being of the group entity. Some appear to incidentally come along with it – as we saw with punks and veganism, for example.

The point is that those who join the subculture, counterculture or group, through a need to demonstrate belonging, adopt these incidental behaviours. But they don't live their entire lives inside the group entity. When they interact with others on the outside, they can become a vector – a human conduit carrying the behaviours into the mainstream.

Where vectors get complicated is when time and place come into play. At a point in time or in a part of the world where the subculture, counterculture or group is vilified or demeaned by outsiders, the very association of the behaviour with that entity might be counterproductive. In this case, the potential vector acts more like a blocker, deterring the uptake of the behaviour. But when it is more neutral than that, or when the subculture, counterculture or group is deemed by some in the mainstream to be cool or in some other way worthy of respect, so our human vectors seed the behaviour with greater ease.

As a kind of generalized example here, imagine a behaviour that is a routine part of life within a society's underclass. For most of history that underclass association would have acted as a blocker on the behaviour's uptake, since the flow of emulation typically goes in the other vertical direction, down the class structure, from the top. But if a rapport develops between members of that underclass and, say, an edgy music culture, then behaviours will get transferred in a vector effect. And from there, via the music culture's 'cool' associations, onwards towards the mainstream. (We'll see a practical example of this in the case that follows a little later.)

ACCELERATORS AND OPENINGS

Accelerators are developments or events in the wider geopolitical, societal, economic and environmental background that exert a force on all human endeavours, and which can propel a hitherto slowly developing behaviour forward with surprising force. Relatively recent accelerator events would include the economic crash of 2008 and the 2021 commitment to net zero carbon. Accelerators can be global but are not necessarily so; some will apply to just one region of the world. Recall how the 2011 Fukushima nuclear disaster gave veganism a push in East Asia, as fear of contamination prompted people to seek alternative protein sources from those that derived from the sea.

There is no doubt, though, that the most dramatic accelerator of recent years has been both global and all-encompassing: the Covid pandemic. Some of its effects on behavioural changes that will endure are obvious and have been much discussed. Dispersed productivity – working from home or, increasingly, from anywhere that takes your fancy – is one shift. This work-place alternative was growing steadily before the pandemic but has gained a significant boost since, with hybrid work arrangements – part office, part home – fast becoming a norm.

But accelerators can exert their force in subtler ways, for those prepared to look. So, let's do that now. Of the marginal behaviours we have encoun-tered so far in this book, which might be given a thrust by the new, post-Covid reality? Polyphasic sleeping might be one – as a corollary to the move to dispersed productivity described above. Working from home didn't just change *where* people worked, but *when*. Barring scheduled meetings, and with the proviso that deadlines were met, people became free to create their own work schedules, and new possibilities opened up from that.

As we saw from our original research, many people are attracted to the notion of multiple naps through the day, rather than one long nocturnal stretch of sleep, but were daunted by the practicalities involved. Working from home reduces these frictions, since the practical and interpersonal difficulties disappear. Related commercial opportunities might range from daytime sleep-wear, to pre- and post-nap teas, through to more exciting ideas, such as windows that shade automatically, like those on the Boeing Dreamliner 787.

But our analysis need not stop there. What happens when our newly-polyphasic sleepers start to go back to the office, at least for part of their working week? One possibility is that they will be reluctant to forego the wellbeing benefits that they have now become used to with their more personally attuned sleep patterns. Smart employers might seek to keep their best talent with flexible working hours and 'rest booths' for daytime napping. (And smart entrepreneurs have already picked up on that with the invention of portable 'sleep pods' – on which, more in Chapter 8.)

So, for marketers, the concept of accelerators can repay a kind of wargam-ing approach. Ask which kinds of global or local events are conceivable in the near future, and then work backwards to imagine what it could mean for your category – or for the invention of new ones. And in doing so, allow for the fact that the same accelerator might have different effects in different cultures, since the underlying societal and economic structures will not be the same.

Later down the chapter we'll look more closely at the beacons of vectors and accelerators when we explore them in greater depth, one by one. But for now, we'll turn to a case-length example that includes all the dynamism – and all the subtlety – of both.

Tattoos: how a fringe behaviour made its mark (and didn't)

If you were to find yourself on a public beach, or alongside a public swimming pool, anywhere in North America, South America or Europe, you would notice that a great many of the people around you had at least one tattoo somewhere on their body. Or perhaps you wouldn't actively notice, since tattoos are so ubiquitous as to be accepted without a second thought and remarked upon only if the design, scale or location happens to be unusual. Tattoos are everywhere. Estimates of the number of adults with at least one tattoo in 2018 were 40 per cent in the UK, 42 per cent in Spain, 43 per cent in Argentina, 46 per cent in the United States, and very nearly half in Australia, Italy and Sweden.[1]

It wasn't always so. Step back in time to that same beach or pool, say, 35 or 40 years ago and a tattooed torso or forearm might leap out at you as something unusual. Tattoos would be noticeable because of their rarity. Few men, and virtually no women, displayed them. And assumptions might be made about those who did – that they were ex-servicemen, bikers or perhaps gang members or people with connections to the underworld. Something happened in that intervening period to thrust tattoos into the mainstream.

But not everywhere. Put yourself on a beach in Japan and, even today, you are unlikely to see more than the occasional discreet tattoo on the flesh of your fellow bathers. If you were to be sitting naked in an onsen – a Japanese, communal, hot-spring spa – the absence of tattooed skin anywhere on the body or face would probably have been a condition of entry. They are almost always forbidden. The irony here is that the art form of Japanese tattoos is more sophisticated than anywhere else in the world, with designs of astonishing intricacy that can take a year to complete. They are beautiful, but they are rare.

The reasons for this disparity in uptake are many and involve an array of historical and cultural factors. But among them are the divergent roles played by vectors, blockers and accelerators in different parts of the world. And those nuances were in evidence from the outset.

WESTERN ORIGINS: FROM OCEAN ISLANDS TO ROYAL COURTS

The original vectors for the transmission of body art into Western cultures were Captain James Cook's sailors in the Pacific voyage of 1769. Tattoos had been known before in Europe – some evidence of them dates to 3250 BCE – but, through a combination of natural atrophy and papal edict, the practice had long since died out.[2]

So, Cook's men were stunned by the expansive body and face ornamentations of the native islanders they encountered in Tahiti and other Pacific landing points. When the company brought the art and its associated crafts back to England, Cook used the term 'tattau' – Polynesian for 'mark' – to delineate them. The leap to 'tattoo' was easily made.

The leap in practice went upwards, from sailors to aristocrats, who began to adorn their skin with tattoos as a novelty. The future King George V opted for a dragon on the forearm in 1881 and somewhat later the mother of Winston Churchill was said to have gone for a winding snake around the wrist. But the sailors never abandoned them – though the designs were cruder – and the practice spread to other members of the armed forces on both sides of the Atlantic. That association with what were perceived as the coarser elements of society, combined with the fickleness of fashion, led to them falling out of favour within the elite.

Wars were always an accelerator. As conflict loomed, military ranks would horde to practitioners to get designs that displayed patriotism to country or allegiance to cause. In 1846, Martin Hilderbrandt, the first known US tattoo artist, claimed to have tattooed soldiers on both sides of the Civil War.[3] By the time of the world wars of the 20th century, as many as 90 per cent of military personnel had at least one tattoo. It became a mark of military service.[4]

But not yet a vector into the mainstream, as obvious associations with the armed forces waned in appeal in the years of relative peace – or cold war – that followed. Neither employment nor romantic prospects were improved by a flag on the shoulder or a bomber on the chest. And nor did it help that the other main constituency for tattooed skin came with associations that were not, at the time, either decorous or glamorous: prisons and crime.

PERMANENCE AND PAIN: THE PRISON TATTOO

Prisoners have always been massively over-represented in the universe of people with tattoos. To start with, this was not a matter of choice. In Russia, France and other European states from about 1800 onwards, tattoos were forced on convicts, as enduring stigmata of criminality.[5] When that imposition came to be revoked a century or so later, an interesting thing happened. Prisoners protested and then began to break the rules by getting tattoos themselves, while incarcerated, in spite of the sanctions involved.

Different methods were invented to accomplish this, including the use of sharpened guitar strings and biro ink, which gave prison designs a distinctive, 'fine-line' look – one that came to be emulated in the backstreet parlours on the outside.

And different reasons have been proffered by psychologists and social scientists for the persistence of the inmate tattoo. They are emblems of endurance, since they both take time and inflict pain; they are symbols of defiance that cannot simply be erased away in conditions where few such expressions are available; and they are markers of individuality to resist the crushing and deliberate uniformity of prison life. More bluntly, tattoos could also be calibrators of crime, with different designs associated with particular offences, or with particular gangs, to the extent that those in the know could assess at a glance the level of malice they were dealing with.[6]

AN UNLIKELY VECTOR

Behaviours strongly associated with a criminal class would not normally be expected to gain easy transference to the mainstream, and for decades tattoos did not. There were subcultures that adopted them – bikers, and to an extent, hippies – but emulation was not remotely automatic in societies that still tended to aspire upwards, to elites, not downwards, to the underworld.

But societies, or strata within them, can reach levels of comfortable prosperity that see large groups of essentially middle-class youth looking for symbols that communicate edginess and rejection of bourgeois norms. The vernacular of prison life became one. 'Lowriding', for example – wearing pants without a belt, low on the body – was a reflection of the norm in US prisons where belts were not permitted and slacks were badly, and loosely, made. Streetwear emulated inmate wear – and when Barack Obama intervened to discourage the trend in 2008, it would have only added to the appeal.[7]

A similar vector effect was in evidence with tattoos, with the borrowing of prison tattoo iconography being picked up in rap and hip-hop culture and that, in turn, becoming emulated by middle-class youth as a bit of instant cred. Celebrities and elite sports people were to follow in short order. In later years, that celebrity appropriation would become more blatant and direct, with uncontentious music acts and artists such as Adam Levine of Maroon 5 choosing to display tattoo designs from the super-hardcore domain of Russian prisons.

In her 2000 book, *Bodies of Inscription*, the US anthropologist Margo DeMello dubbed the mid-20th-century tattoo 'the mark of marginality'.[8] But marginality can, in its own right, have an appeal to those seeking expression of the individualized self and outward symbolism of nonconformity. Ironically, that behavioural borrowing can end up going mainstream, and losing some of its desired edge. And equally ironically, in the case of tattoos, forces within the legislative and regulatory structures of the state were to be part of that thrust.

ACCELERATORS: DIVERSITY, EQUALITY AND LEGISLATION

In already heterogenous cultures, calls for the recognition and celebration of diversity act at first as a mirror. They reflect the differences that are there – ethnicity, gender, age, sexuality, health and mobility status – and put everyone inside the frame. That cultural introspection does not at a stroke eliminate prejudice. But it makes it harder. Why should one quality be less equal than another? Why should there be discrimination against any cohort?

Legislation may precede or follow that recognition of diversity to add steel to the rejection of any systemic unfairness. In the United States, the Civil Rights Act dates back to 1964 and there has been time for its effects to infuse the consciousness of a continent. In the UK, multiple laws have been put in place to counter discrimination, including the Race Relations Act of 1976, the Disability Discrimination Act of 1995 and the Equality Act of 2010. Similar legislation is in place in the European Union.

Stereotypical biases will still exist, and the law will not protect all acts of voluntary difference – blue hair, piercings, tattoos – but the mood music is playing an unmistakable theme. Employers might not be compelled by law to accept people with tattoos into the workforce, but rejection of candidates on that basis alone would seem to fly in the face of the values of the times. If footballers are free to ply their craft while displaying multiple tattoos all over their bodies, why should the right to a visible design be denied to those who work in other fields?

And indeed, organizations in both the public and private sectors have voluntarily modified their employment policies. The British Army changed its rules to allow visible tattoos in 2014.[9] London's Metropolitan Police made a similar move in 2018.[10] Air New Zealand ended its staff tattoo ban in 2019, in a move to allow expression of 'individuality or cultural heritage'. Lush, Ikea and Google are among global businesses never to have had an anti-tattoo policy.[11]

Diversity movements and equal rights legalization therefore acted as accelerators for tattoos not so much by encouraging them as by persuading society to get out of the way. They removed social and practical frictions, and uptake of this previously marginal behaviour became non-contentious as a result.

What has been eroded is the usefulness of the tattoo as a mark of rebellion – a loss that some, including DeMello, regret. Perhaps most emblematic of that is the feminization of what was once an all-male domain. In 1970 Janis Joplin was able to flaunt her tattoos as an act of uncompromising feminism. Today, twice as many millennial women are seeking tattoos as men.[12] In the West, at least, across the gender and social spectrum, the mark has become unremarkable.

Tattoos in Japan: still marginal, still taboo

The story of tattoos in Japan is both similar to, and different from, the Western narrative. As in the West, they became associated with gangs and crime. But there was never a vector effect, since that association remained an implacable blocker to their acceptance within any respectable sector of the mainstream. And in a highly homogenous society, the accelerator effects of diversity and equality movements seen in Western cultures have been less influential in changing societal and workplace norms.

As in Europe, there is evidence of tattoos in Japan dating back to antiquity, with figurines from around 5000 BCE depicting complex body art. There is also some evidence of tattoos being used to punish convicts from as early as 720 CE.[13] Better documented is the Edo period (1616–1868) when prisoners were marked on the arm or face to indicate their guilt of petty crimes.[14] Body art was also associated with licensed 'pleasure quarters' in prosperous cities, where courtesans would tattoo the names of their preferred clients on their upper arms.

But by the late 19th century, during the Meiji era, tattoos had become illegal, a prohibition that would remain until reversed in 1948 by occupying forces.[15] The outlawed form went underground, to become adopted by, and thereafter associated with, the yakuza – gangs involved with organized crime.

For a recent recruit into a yakuza syndicate, the rite-of-passage tattoo was not the work of a moment. The first hurdle to overcome would be to prove worthiness to the tattoo master, an artist who would have studied in an apprenticeship lasting at least a decade.[16]

The tattoo itself would be an elaborate depiction of scenes of personal significance to the yakuza member's life, symbolizing the attributes they were known for. It would cover large expanses of the body – the arms and shoulders, the back down to the buttocks, the thighs and sometimes the calves and shins too. It would take time to complete, using non-electric methods in weekly sessions that would continue for up to a year. And it would cost – the equivalent of £10,000 would not be unusual – resulting in a personal debt that would be gradually paid back by the member through services to the gang.[17]

BLOCKERS BUT NO ACCELERATORS

So vivid are the associations of the yakuza with violence and seedy crime – prostitution, drugs, racketeering – and so sensitized to shame is Japanese society that the emblematic symbolism of tattoos of any kind became a powerful blocker. They are routinely banned not only in public spas but in gyms, swimming pools and ryokan – traditional Japanese inns.

This is despite the level of artistry involved – with the intricacy of the irezumi traditional method celebrated on a global scale. Japan may be home to some of the world's most admired artists, but in their own culture, their work is circumscribed. It is not so much a case of mild disapproval as active avoidance. The notion of a vector effect emanating from the criminal strata of society may have once seemed unlikely in Baltimore or Chicago, but in Yokohama or Osaka it is close to inconceivable.

Nor is the concept of diversity one that carries across to East Asian cultures with ease. Japanese society is far more ethnically homogenous than those of Europe and especially the United States, and harmony, cohesion and conformity are more seminal values than self-expression, difference and individuality. The mood music is therefore of a very different kind to that playing in the West. In the workplace, although gender diversity is valued, the presence of visible signs of self-expression, such as tattoos, still strongly inhibits employment prospects.

There are pockets of pushback. In 2015 a former master who had been banned under controversial local laws that allow only qualified doctors to practice, set up an NGO called 'Save tattooing in Japan'. Now with over 200 affiliates, the group campaigns for freedom of choice in body art. And a 2017 survey indicated that 60 per cent of Japanese people in their 20s or younger believe that rules regarding tattoos should be relaxed.[18] Nevertheless, the mass uptake of tattoos in Japan, if it is to ever happen, looks to be some way off yet.

We now turn our attention to the factors and forces that underlie these opportunity beacons of vectors and accelerators by looking at them in more depth, one by one.

Understanding vectors: human agents of behaviour change

Let's start at the extremes here. At one end, you have the individual – an autonomous, sentient human being with a life to lead, an income to earn, a future to build. At the other, at a vastly greater scale, you have the milieu in which that individual swims – society and its culture. In the boundless abstraction of that wider entity there will exist – even if not always consciously perceived at the personal level – a bed of values, norms, beliefs, and accepted behaviours.

A great deal has been written about the relationship between the individual and societal culture, much of it centred on the tensions between the desire to express personal uniqueness and the obligation to meld in with others for some notion of the greater good.

But one of the most important academic contributions – certainly from the point of view of the arguments in this book – is the suite of work devoted to the concept of 'belonging', ably synthesized in 1995 by the US psychologists Roy Baumeister and Mark Leary.[19] Individuals feel a powerful need to belong to something bigger than themselves – bigger, in the main, than their immediate circle of family and friends.

For some, society is that thing, felt and expressed through notions of patriotism or pride in national icons and institutions, such as royalty or sports teams. For many others, though, society is just too damn big. It's way too diffuse, abstract and 'ungrabbable'. The distance between those extremes – the individual at one end and societal culture at the other – is too chasmic and airy to impart the sense of belonging required. And there will also inevitably be those for whom the values encoded in societal culture run counter to their own, leading to an unwillingness to commit to a bond of belonging due to ideological incompatibility.

Getting inside subcultures

Filling a void, then, in this human need to belong, are smaller, though still sizeable, cultural entities. They will be subcultures or – if the need is strongly felt to actively subvert the wider societal matrix – countercultures. Pause for a second to reflect on those you might have come across so far in your lifetime: mods, hippies, punks, bikers, goths, hipsters and, more recently, the tribal groupings of steampunk, dark academia or kawaii – Japanese 'cute culture'. Many more people attach themselves to one or more of these alternative cultural entities than you might think. According to a UK study by the London-based research group, The Nursery, some 56 per cent of adults claim to be part of some kind of subculture[20]. It is not a niche activity.

What is the amalgam that binds any one of these subcultures (or countercultures) together? Well, the clue is in the term that carries across all of them: 'culture'. They are, at a smaller scale, the collection of qualities that societal culture exhibits: values, norms, beliefs and behaviours – often encoded by distinctive symbols, icons and cues (as depicted in the top portion of Figure 6.1).

When an individual becomes part of a subculture (read 'counterculture' too from here on in) they may not at first perceive all the nuances and implicit demands of those values and beliefs. But, assuming they feel an initial 'fit', they are cognitively and emotionally motivated to do as much as possible to increase – to 'earn' – that powerful sense of belonging. As Baumeister and Leary observe, 'As a fundamental motivation, the need to belong should stimulate goal-directed behaviour... Patterns of self-presentation, interpersonal redress, and group conformity may all be seen in the context of enhancing one's chances of inclusion in groups and relationships'.[21]

When it comes to behaviours within the subculture group, the recent recruit may meet some they did not expect to find. Subcultures often exhibit a *behavioural bundle* that comes along for the ride, with some seemingly incidental to the overarching purpose of the group. Veganism came along with hippies and punks; wicca with goths; furniture upcycling with hipsters; hand-written letter writing (black ink) with dark academia. Particularly rich in behavioural byways is the uniquely British steampunk subculture – a subgenre of science fiction – where enthusiasts practise elaborate tea and gin

FIGURE 6.1 The vector effect

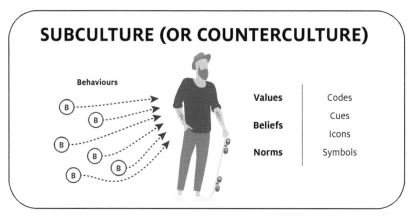

A person becomes attracted to, and becomes part of, a subculture or counterculture – a sizeable group entity with perceived (if not actually codified) values, beliefs and norms, expressed through distinctive symbols, icons, codes, cues and behaviours. As a member of the subculture, through a need to express belonging, the person adopts some or all of its associated behaviours.

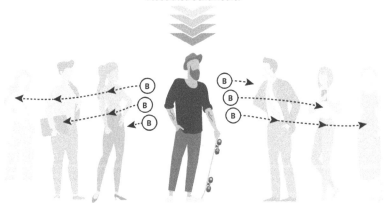

WIDER SOCIETAL CULTURE

When engaging with people outside the subculture entity, the person continues to practise these behaviours and can either passively or overtly influence others to experiment with them and perhaps adopt them.

rituals, invent eccentric subversions of Victorian dress and display an adherence to respect and politeness that can seem at odds with their arresting aesthetic.

Whatever the subculture in question, its behaviours will be experimented with, adopted and indulged by those who become part of it. And the reasoning that comes along with them will likewise be imbibed. Before long, the adopted behaviour will be second nature to the subculture devotee. It will be a part of them, and a crucial element in their sense of belonging.

So, we have zoomed in – to the individual embedded inside the subculture group. But we must now zoom out again to locate that same individual within the wider societal culture. Because they will inhabit both worlds. They need to earn, to live alongside neighbours, to study, to hit the gym, to see the doctor – or be the doctor. The subculture is part, not all, of their tilt at life. Goth by nature, accountant by trade; punk at heart, chef at the local pizza place. So, the behaviours adopted will not be confined to the inner world of the subculture group. They will be expressed, displayed, explained perhaps, extolled quite probably, in the world outside – in the lunch break with colleagues, at home with family, over a drink with friends, across social media platforms.

The conditions are therefore set for transference of what might well be a very marginal behaviour towards other members of the mainstream (as depicted in the lower portion of Figure 6.1). There are two basic modes of propulsion: simple imitation or active influence. In the former, people take note of the behaviour in question and, out of curiosity, admiration, or possibly even boredom, try it out for themselves. In the latter, they might engage the person who has introduced the behaviour into their orbit, probing them on why they do it, challenging them, perhaps – since resistance is still part of the matrix at this stage. The behaviour can then be defended or bolstered with whatever combination of reason, charm or passion that the devotee wishes to bring to bear.

Either way, it helps if the person expressing the behaviour has a little charisma or otherwise-sourced credibility. And of course, the whole engagement could be in person or mediated through communications channels. Vectors are influencers who, themselves, have been influenced – by the powerful sense of belonging felt in their subculture interactions.

YOUTH VECTORS: THE DYNAMICS OF INFLUENCING UP

There have always been alternative cultures, and behaviours and ideas from inside them have always had means to escape the subcultural membrane and leak into the wider societal majority. But there are reasons why that vector effect is likely to be more pronounced now – ones that touch on some of the themes of Chapter 3. Subcultures tend towards the young. Not all of them – bikers will have a relatively high median age – but many are typically phenomena associated with the younger, rite-of-passage years.

In contemporary society (it was not always so) what springs up from the young is more likely to achieve emulation than what trickles down from the middle-aged or old. And the channels through which our youth vectors can broadcast their new behavioural enthusiasms are today more liquid, far-reaching and potent than at any time in the past.

There is also evidence from our original research that Gen Z is showing a different pattern in the adoption of subculture connections – with more tendency to experience 'belonging' in more than one at a time. This fluidity implies a likelihood to experiment with, and eventually adopt, a wider range of marginal behaviours which, combined with extended connectivity, offers ever greater scope for a vector effect.

Affinity groups: subculture 'lite'

Coming down a couple of levels from subcultures and countercultures, we alight on sizeable groups joined by affinity, with perhaps norms, icons, codes and cues but not such a rich seam of values and beliefs. (Inevitably, though, since we're talking about human groupings in a fluid world, there is an element of overlap and imprecision here.) Examples of affinity groups might include surfers, skaters, lifters and e-sporters.

As with subcultures, certain behaviours might get attached to these groups in ways that might not always make sense or seem inevitable from an outsider's point of view. So, a vector effect is again possible. An interesting example of unexpected overlap can be seen in the intense world of committed cryptocurrency enthusiasts.

'Cryptomaximalists', as they often call themselves, are frequently also extreme carnivores – a dietary life-choice that we touched on in Chapter 4, where advocates avoid carbohydrates and plant-based foods or beverages almost entirely. The crossover is high – to the extent that Neeraj Agrawal, communications director for a cryptocurrency policy think tank, thought it necessary to tip off prospective newcomers. In a tweet in 2017 he wrote: 'Thinking about getting into cryptocurrency? Be warned: it comes with a lot of social pressure to only eat meat for some reason.'[22]

Cryptocarnivores were not slow to come up with their 'reasons'. In their social media posts they will often extol the virtues of the all-meat diet – increased strength, enhanced sharpness of thought – and make the link to crypto by noting that both are a natural result of people with the mental freedom to counterthink accepted, societally mandated and, in their view, evolutionarily artificial norms.

The vector effect, as carnivory is picked up in the cryptocommunity and taken into the wider society, is hard to assess. It may be small initially, as resistance is likely to be high, owing to concerns about health and environmental impact. Society currently seems to be moving in the other direction. But as we saw with veganism, things can change fast. The presence of a committed and articulate margin at the other end of the dietary spectrum is not to be ignored.

Finally, a note to observe that groups can be glued together not just by affinity but by circumstance. As we saw with prisoners and tattoos, vectors can emerge from the latter every bit as readily as the former.

A marketing take on vectors

Marketers are often fascinated by subcultures and typically look to view them from an immediate consumption lens: what are the clothes worn, the goods used, the music listened to, the channels preferred? Can we dive in and be first to exploit those more widely?

A less superficial exploration could be more beneficial. What is inside that behavioural bundle? How youthful and connected are the members of the subculture group? What might explode out from that in a vector effect – to ignite opportunity in less expected and linear ways? Vectors are exciting. They are not an abstraction. They are people, at the end of the day. And in a connected world they can lead you to the heady, crazy beginnings of behaviour change at scale.

Now to the potent forces of accelerators, which can achieve a similarly opportunistic scale of change, from a very different starting point.

Understanding accelerators: the great behavioural gear change

One of the 21 marginal behaviours we explored in our original quantitative research was a package known as 'the quantified self' – also sometimes called 'lifelogging'. Proponents use a combination of personal tracking technology and daily journal entries to keep track of, and respond to, a wide range of datapoints about their physical, mental and emotional condition – monitoring sleep patterns, blood pressure, heart rate, oxygenation of blood, exercise taken, food and drink consumed, mental sharpness, mood and score on the 'narcissistic personality index'. The idea is that an individual can use this numerical data to enrich their understanding of themselves and to improve the way they live their lives.

In a 2010 TED talk, science journalist Gary Wolf, who had popularized the term 'quantified self' in a 2009 Wired magazine article, spoke of the self as 'our operations centre, our moral compass', and extolled the possibilities of personalized data to help individuals 'act more effectively in the world'.

In our quantitative survey, though, this richness of background was not able to be captured, since the merciless format of the online questionnaire demands brevity and cutting to the essentials. The 'what/why' description read like this:

> *What: daily measuring and recording of personal metrics.*
> *Why: self-improvement by intense focus on oneself; by visualizing their lifestyle in numbers and graphs, users highlight problems and can be encouraged by small improvements.*

You'll recall that our quantitative format probed awareness of any given behaviour, willingness to learn more and preparedness to try. As it turns out, prior awareness of the quantified self was very modest – fewer than 15 per cent had heard of it before. As a general rule in the quant, awareness and preparedness to try were strongly positively correlated: the more people knew about a behaviour beforehand, the more likely they were to consider trial.

So, it was interesting to observe a break in that pattern here. The quantified self found itself in the cluster of top performers for willingness to try both in the UK and the United States. What we might have thought a definite niche candidate, appealing principally to the self-described geeks out there, proved surprisingly appealing across the board.

What could be behind this willingness to try? One possible clue lay in the timing of the research: October 2021 (UK) and January 2022 (United States). This was deep into the Covid pandemic and by this time, people had been exposed to its ups, downs, deprivations and torments for almost two years. The notion of measurement of self, of testing, of understanding what's going on within the body – and reacting to that, one way or another – had become familiar. It was obvious that self-assessed data – at least in the medical sphere – could sometimes be life critical. So, was the pandemic context working as a kind of mainstream trial prompt here?

Given the bluntness of quantitative research methodology, where nuanced questions get little sway, there was no direct way to check. But the beauty of pairing up methodologies – qualitative as well as quantitative – is that you have another diagnostic tool with which to probe. While quant gives you big samples and broad themes, qual can get into the detail with a little more fluency.

The quantified self happened not to be one of the eight selected behaviours we expanded upon and focused in on during the qualitative groups.

But it came up spontaneously anyway during the opening discussions about burgeoning behavioural trends. There would be one or two people in the groups who knew about it and who offered it up as an example of a behaviour likely to become increasingly taken up. The rest of the group would then concur. Why? Again, timing was key: the qualitative fieldwork took place in June and July 2021. Covid had changed everything. As one Gen Z respondent explained:

> *'Our generation is more health conscious anyway, and with Covid, we will check our health more – more testing and more apps to keep a check ourselves – that's something people are doing…'*

What you have here is the blueprint for an accelerator effect. First, a behaviour practised by only a few, but gaining a little traction nonetheless. Second, a major external event – in this case the pandemic – that makes others take note of it and evaluate it in a fresh light.

There is a third element in the blueprint, though, and that is the commercial response itself, since even a behaviour given a new push of growth by a major event may benefit from a little innovation to help people overcome any impracticalities involved. The principle is:

MARKETING INNOVATION CAN ACCELERATE AN ACCELERATOR

With the quantified self, much of this impetus is of course emerging from the tech sector, with exciting new sensors and personal logging tools such as the first wearable monitor to pick up irregular heart rhythms and tech-enabled smartbeds to optimize sleep. But brands in more humdrum sectors – consumer healthcare is the obvious example – could find imaginative new ways to help their customers understand more about their biorhythms, bodies, minds and moods. 'Know thyself' is a dictum that dates back to Socrates. It is interesting to see something as primal and elemental as plague working as an accelerator to give it a modern thrust.

CONSUMERS AND ACCELERATORS

There will be many marketers out there who have sought to assess what behavioural trends in their own categories will have been affected by the Covid pandemic. Conferences have been attended, articles devoured, expertise sought, to help understand the implications of two years of social, cultural and economic upheaval.

But marketers are generally less diligent at imagining forthcoming events or scoping out the landscape of the relationship between external factors and the development of behavioural trends.

They should change that mindset, because consumers are ahead of them. What was clear from our qualitative fieldwork is that people think about accelerators – even if they don't use that word – and are aware of the possibilities for mass behaviour change prompted by external events.

In both the United States and the UK, during our opening discussions with respondents – and without specific prompting – three themes emerged:

1 *People acknowledge that accelerators can have an effect.* The suddenness and shock of the external event are seen as crucial factors in the 'thrust' for change that may be long overdue.

2 *One accelerator can affect multiple behaviours.* People offered up a range of marginal behaviours that could boom as a consequence of the Covid pandemic: working from home, polyphasic sleeping, homeschooling, freebirthing, quantified self.

3 *People can 'use' an accelerator event to legitimize something they wanted to do anyway.* Many in the groups favoured working from home and taking multiple naps during the day and saw that new workplace practices prompted by the pandemic gave them licence to now do that.

Respondents also articulated an interesting nuance in the accelerator concept. There are truly sudden, major and unpredictable events that seem to come out of the blue – like Covid. And there are pivot points, or crystallization moments, within longstanding issues and themes, that can abruptly come to the fore. So, climate change is a theme that has been part of the collective consciousness for decades, but respondents sensed there would be a defined moment of change, where meaningful behaviour adaptation suddenly takes off at scale.

For marketers seeking to assess the potential of future accelerators, it might be easier to imagine – and even actively prompt – the latter than the former. Either way, though, in the task of mapping out the relationship between behaviours and potential events, it may help to break things down into smaller units – since thinking about anything on a meta, global scale can be daunting.

Figure 6.2 shows one way to approach this. The meta categories in which accelerator events occur are broken down into smaller units; for each unit there is an example of a historical accelerator event and its type ('out of the blue' (OOB), 'crystallization moment' (CM)), followed by the marginal behaviours that are likely to have been given a renewed thrust.

It is one thing to look backwards, of course, another to stare into the future. But a little structure does help. Marketing teams could devise a similar schematic with blanks, to help them imagine and plot potential accelerator events, marginal behaviours affected, and the entrepreneurial opportunities that could subsequently be unleashed.

FIGURE 6.2 Historical accelerators and candidate behaviours affected

Main topic	Event/development	Type	Accelerator for...
Geopolitical	2022 Ukraine invasion	OOB	Prepping[1]
Economic	2008 subprime loans crash (US)	OOB	Extreme frugalism, new nomads
Environmental	2021 Cop26 'consume less' messaging	CM	Zero wasters[2], living without possessions, uniform wardrobe, insect protein, climatarianism[3]
Demographic	2016 WEF presentation on 'The 100-Year Life'	CM	Lifelogging, super-agers[4]
Technological	2004 Graphene discovered	CM	Biohacking
Societal/cultural	2017 #MeToo	CM	Raising gender-neutral kids
Medical	2020 Covid pandemic	OOB	WFH, polyphasic sleeping, homeschooling[5], freebirthing, lifelogging
Legislative	2010 First US state decriminalization of psilocybin	CM	Microdosing

Key: OOB = Out of the blue; CM = Crystallization moment

(1) **Prepping** or survivalism involves anticipating and proactively preparing, at a personal level, to survive global catastrophes and natural disasters. (2) **Zero wasters** aim to eliminate as much waste as possible from their lives, not simply by recycling but by limiting consumption in the first place (3) **Climatarians** adjust their diets to minimize their personal carbon footprints, selecting foods that have made the least environmental impact during their production. (4) **Super-agers** are people in their 70s and 80s who adopt lifestyles and habits that help them maintain the cognitive and physical abilities of people three decades younger (5) **Homeschooling** is when parents elect to educate their children at home, free from a standardized and formal curriculum.

A marketing take on accelerators

It isn't easy to predict consumer behaviour change, but marketers valiantly try, nonetheless. Frequently this will involve the attendance of trends presentations – agreeable sessions in the company of fascinating futurologists in what is normally a one-way, low-demand exchange. Images are shown, music played, and catchy names given to sartorial, social, cultural and consumption trends that are just about to emerge.

In trends presentations, PowerPoint charts and associated commentary often start with the words 'Consumers will...', followed by a description of the new behaviour that is soon to become commonplace. *Consumers will.* But will they? And if so, in what numbers, with what start point and with what likelihood of meaningful continuation?

These are the details the futurologists omit, which is why marketers may leave these sessions feeling upbeat and inspired, but in no great hurry to implement anything relating to what they have just heard. Without answers to those downstream questions, marketers sense they could be exposed to risk.

In truth, consumer behaviour doesn't change that readily. Trends may come and go but profound human behaviour change is rare. The reality with most marginal behaviours is that they usually remain on the fringes for some considerable time before breaking through – if they ever do. So, marketers looking to take action need some way of judging when that moment might be.

The secret – as it so often is in marketing – is to look beyond the consumer. In this case, it is to assess the prospects for change through consideration of bigger, more portentous phenomena. Probing for the possibility of accelerators is one way to do that. Accelerators are one of the factors that explain the two-speed movement characteristic of marginal behaviour uptake: slow, then sudden. And it is this suddenness – this gear change in something that was previously moving only slowly – that can make for consumer-driven disruption, and all the opportunity that comes along with it.

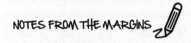

NOTES FROM THE MARGINS

Microdosing

Microdosing is already mainstream, in some ways. Most of us like the pep that a morning coffee gives us, but wouldn't drink 10 double espressos in one go; instead we take a microdose of caffeine. A relaxing pint at the pub is essentially a microdose of alcohol.

But there's a small and growing cohort, often middle-aged and middle class, who are taking microdosing to the next level, self-administering tiny amounts of psilocybin (magic mushrooms) or LSD to sharpen their minds, boost their output at work and even improve their parenting.

Alex is a successful 50-something television executive, recreational drug user and microdosing enthusiast. Though preferring to be pseudonymous here, Alex is effusive about their regular single drop of psilocybin, a tenth of a full dose, which they say helps them benefit from boosted creative and mindfulness effects without any hallucination or trippiness – when a full dose would put them out of commission for a day or more.

Alex is an Oxford-educated Londoner with a successful career, a long-term marriage and teenage kids, and a dealer who responds to queries on WhatsApp with emoji-strewn menus of available drugs and special offers. Making an order couldn't be easier and the goods arrive promptly via a pushbike that looks to the casual observer to be delivering pizza.

Dealers – and they are dealers, it's not (yet) legal in the UK or US at least – have cleverly realized that positioning is all important and psilocybin is often sold in elegant pipette bottles which share more in common with a Lancome cosmetics box than with a baggie full of weed. In liquid form, psilocybin can be taken in single drops, each costing around £1 ($1.40). Clean, odourless and in tiny amounts, no-one else need ever know why you're so upbeat.

Just like the first time round, the microdosing craze started in San Francisco, with evangelists like James Fadiman specifying the correct amounts and citing first-hand evidence of massively-improved productivity.[23] The epicentre at the start of the 21st-century movement was Silicon Valley, where it quickly gained traction within the tech industry. As a clean, non-addictive lifestyle choice to go along with exercise and mindfulness, it served to amplify whatever was happening in their brains. As Diane (another first-name-only contributor) puts it: 'we are all productivity-obsessed, so that's our usage of it. I don't do coffee; I do acid'.[24]

Some users liken the effects of microdosing to having just one great cocktail; enough to lift your spirits and boost your productivity, to make everything seem sharper, brighter and more fun. Keeping it to a minimum is key because in the same way, like having two strong cocktails, or three or more, the effects get stronger, more impactful and less controllable the more you take …

07

An irresistible momentum: the growth beacons

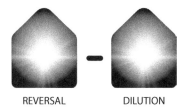

REVERSAL   DILUTION

A reminder: the eight M2M beacons illuminate the pathway from marginal behaviour to mainstream acceptance and practice. The closer to the end of that pathway the beacon is situated and seen, the more certain we can be that the progress to mainstream uptake has become irresistible. So, the presence of reversal – Beacon 6 – and especially dilution – Beacon 8 – are significant. Growth is in the offing and marketers need to be alert.

Reversal won't always be a feature on the M2M journey, but when it is, you can expect progress to be sudden, because it means that resistance to the behaviour has not merely subsided but flipped: the very same force that once acted as a deterrent to uptake switches sides to become a driver. What once pushed back now propels forwards. That's a major turnaround.

The best way to get a feel for the switchback potential of reversal is through the metaphor of gravity. Imagine that you are cycling along a long straight road to reach a point far away in the distance. Let that road stand for the journey from the point where a behaviour is marginal to the point where it is finally embraced by the mass. You are riding that road – with the literal ups and downs ahead of you.

To start with, and for what feels like forever, the road goes sharply uphill. Progress is achingly, grindingly slow. Even after you have been riding for what seems an eternity, you are way closer to the beginning than even the middle, let alone the end. Gravity provides relentless resistance, and there is nothing you can do to pick up speed.

Then – at last – the road flattens out. With the resistance of gravity now neutralized, you can make progress at a respectable pace. You won't reach the end anytime soon at this normal cycling speed, but you are not bogged down either.

Suddenly, though, the road starts to run sharply downhill. From this point on you don't even have to try anymore – gravity has switched from enemy to friend and propels you down the road to the endpoint of your journey with dizzying speed.

That is reversal.

So far in this book we have seen two examples of reversal and witnessed the suddenness of its effects. The first was when the health perceptions of veganism flipped from strongly negative to strongly positive – from concerns about malnutrition to a conviction that the diet was healthier than the meat-and-dairy norm. The second was in the freebirthing narrative, when perceptions of hospitals as the safe option suddenly reversed owing to fears about hospital-acquired Covid infection. Safety concerns – which had long provided resistance to non-hospital birth – became the principal reason to consider it.

That freebirthing example is also a good insight into how the later pathway beacons can work together to promote momentum. Covid was an *accelerator* – one of the beacons we looked at in Chapter 6 – which, in this case, led to *reversal*, which in turn resulted in *dilution*: the uptake of a modified version of the marginal behaviour. New parents didn't suddenly start to adopt the full freebirthing experience, but interest in homebirth, with minimal medical intervention, soared.

Dilution, then, marks the point where the mainstream has got involved, but does things its own way. From the point of view of the adherents who have been practising the behaviour for years, that can sometimes feel like a diminution of the 'purity' of their chosen way of life. But once any concept gets into the hands of the great mass of humanity, a little interpretation is inevitable.

People may mix things up, as they did with blending vegan and non-vegan eating. They might adopt a 'lite' version of the behaviour, like taking two or three naps during the day, but not going for the full-on polyphasic sleeping pattern of 20 minutes every four hours around the clock. Or they might do the thing wholesale but just less often.

An important aspect of the dilution phase is the dialling down of intensity. Mainstream consumers may finally be ready to give things a go and experiment with the behaviour, but they tend not to want to have to engage in all the passion and ferocity that comes with it. Theirs will be a more casual interaction, something to which they would rather not have to give too much thought.

A corollary of that absence of intensity is that frictions are not tolerated. While those impassioned early adherents may have willingly borne the increased costs, inconveniences and discomforts – with their intensity of conviction as a kind of fuel – the mass wants an easy life. It doesn't have that kind of will and it won't make those kinds of sacrifices.

Entrepreneurs and marketers are therefore a pivotal force within this low-intensity phase. They can find ways to remove practical difficulties, increase easy availability of goods and services that could accompany the behaviour, establish price points that reflect 'mass' rather than 'niche' or 'specialist' and communicate with charm, confidence and reassurance to help foster the sense of a new normality.

In the end, though, the underlying reason why dilution inexorably leads to growth lies in the trade-off between full-on commitment (of the marginal few) and sheer numbers (of the mainstream many). A behaviour practised by fewer than 3 per cent will remain small notwithstanding the zeal with which it is embraced. A version of that same behaviour engaged in now and then by upwards of 50 per cent will have a far greater bearing on commercial opportunity. Dilution may sound anaemic, but it is not. It is where growth lies.

Later down the chapter we will come back to each of these growth beacons when we delve into them more deeply, one by one. First, though, let's look at a somewhat counterintuitive example that illuminates the irresistible momentum of both.

Exercise: marginal for millennia, mainstream now

In 1968, a US senator out jogging near his home in Greenville, South Carolina, was stopped by a police officer.[1] In those days jogging was not entirely new – it had been introduced into the US in 1963 by an Oregon athletics coach following a fact-finding trip to New Zealand[2] – but it was unusual enough to prompt suspicion. A man running down the street, in an era when most did not, could be mistaken for a felon.

In a New York Times article that year, on the rise of the new 'fad' of jogging, interviewees explained that they would tend to go out only in daylight hours, since running after dark was apt to promote discomfort, at the least, among neighbours and authorities. One unlucky jogger from Hartford, Connecticut, had been arrested and taken to court for 'illegal use of a highway by a pedestrian'.[3]

It may feel like taking to the streets for exercise has been a norm forever, but it hasn't. In the mid 1960s, running was an activity engaged in by athletes in clubs, or maybe boxers doing their 'road work', not an everyday pursuit of millions. The 1965 Boston Marathon welcomed just 447 runners, and all would have been elite or approaching that status – club or college runners, competing in what was officially designated a road race. All were men.[4] The Amateur Athletic Union (AAU) had banned women from competing in US road races in 1961, citing 'health and safety concerns' – an edict not lifted until 1972.[5]

Similarly, there were gyms back then, but those who used them were a specialist minority – boxers or bodybuilders engaged in serious training, pushing their limits in uncompromising spaces like Gold's Gym in Venice, California, frequented by the young Arnold Schwarzenegger. We were a long way from the notion of moms, students and office workers popping into a climate-controlled studio to do an hour of spinning or Pilates.

Given what we know about the necessity of exercise and its benefits for both physical and mental wellbeing, why, even as relatively recently as the 1960s, was it not a mass preoccupation?

This is one of those questions that is best approached the other way around, to ensure that we retain a sense of temporal perspective. Why, after millennia in which ordinary, everyday people hardly ever engaged in non-productive exercise, did the mass movement (literally and figuratively) suddenly spring up from about the 1970s onward?

A NATURAL AVERSION

Exercise for its own sake, among non-athletes, is by no means a universal human norm. Far from it, as the US evolutionary biologist Daniel Lieberman argues in his 2020 book, *Exercised: the science of physical activity, rest and health*. As part of his research for the book, Lieberman spent time living among the Hadza, a hunter-gatherer tribe occupying a dry, hot, woodland region in a remote part of Tanzania.

What struck him was the contrast between high fitness levels – even grandmothers could walk six or seven miles a day and dig for hours to forage – and the natural tendency of all members of the tribe to take it easy whenever they got the chance. Much of their day was spent 'sitting on the ground ... apparently doing *nothing*'.[6] While the hunting males might sometimes stalk their prey for up to 20 miles, once the pursuit was over, whether successful or otherwise, further discretionary exertion was never countenanced.

When probed on whether there was ever any kind of non-essential physical activity – exercise, training – the response of the tribespeople was similar to what Lieberman had observed in other non-industrial societies: incredulity. Why would anyone expend energy when not required?

The longstanding objection to exercise – the resistance point – can therefore be simply stated: *it consumes energy resources.*

For virtually all of mankind's tenure on the planet, these resources would be deployed elsewhere, in the daily business of staying alive. Nobody got to the end of a long day hoeing the earth with a hand-tool to then declare, 'What I need now is a five-mile run'. No-one emerged from a 10-hour shift in a quarry or a mine to conclude that it was time for a little weight training.

Even into the 20th century, and even in advanced economies, there was an unmistakable physicality to everyday life. In 1910, almost 70 per cent of the US workforce was employed in some form of manual labour[7] – on farms, in factories, on building sites, in steel mills, at shipyards, in the docks, down mines. Much of the lifting, loading, cutting and drilling would be done without the aid of mechanization; the 'machine' involved was the human body and its applied muscularity.

In the home, domestic duties, almost always accomplished by women, were a never-ending round of daunting, energy-intensive chores. Washing consisted in lifting heavy loads into tubs, fetching water, rubbing and rinsing by hand on a washboard, then hauling the wet loads into the wringer, turning the handle to pull them through, before hoisting them up onto clothes lines. Cleaning floors and other surfaces meant first sweeping and dispensing of dirt, then scrubbing with a brush on hands and knees, then rinsing and polishing by hand. Life was a workout called work.

There were of course those who would play sports or ride a bike into the countryside for recreation, and there were social elites who had access to sporting clubs, with their racquets courts, steam rooms and heated pools. But for the everyday working person (the vast majority) the idea of non-essential exercise was both the last thing on their minds and the last thing needed by their exhausted, aching bodies. It made no sense and never had.

As Lieberman concludes, 'Apart from youthful tendencies to play, and other social reasons, the instinct to avoid non-essential physical activity has long been a pragmatic adaptation for millions of generations.'[8]

AN UNNATURAL SLOTH

Let's hold onto that final Lieberman fragment for a moment – *millions of generations* – and keep it in our minds as we move on to what happened next. Because what happened next might have seemed only too gradual from the point of view of people who yearned for the dawning of an easier era – but from a human evolutionary perspective, it was the blink of an eye.

In a period of just 40 years – from around 1930 to 1970 – the daily physical demands on working people in industrialized societies did not merely diminish but plummet. Life became easier, to an extent that we can talk about, first, the rise of the sedentary classes and, by extension, the increasing sedentariness of mainstream society.

This easing up was evident both in the home and at work. In the workplace, there were two kinds of changes: the decreasing proportion of physical jobs, and the increased mechanization for those who still did them.[9] By 1970 the percentage of the US workforce employed in manual labour had reduced to 38 per cent, and was to decline sharply further after that.[10] The era of the dominance of the desk job had arrived. Meanwhile, developments such as machine-cutting tools, powered forklift trucks and craned container systems meant that those manual roles became less arduous – sometimes requiring no more effort than sitting down and pressing controls.

In the home, women became liberated from exhausting chores by a litany of labour-saving inventions: the washing machine, electric wringer, steam iron, vacuum cleaner, dishwasher. These were not all assimilated immediately, by any means, but by the dawn of the 1970s it was a rare US household that did not have some or most. The average number of hours doing housework per week tumbled from 50 in 1910 to 18 in 1970.[11]

All round, people were required to do less – and they willingly accepted the offer. Escalators, not stairs. Power mowing, not pushing. And of course, the car, replacing journeys that would once have been accomplished by walking, bicycling or running for the bus. Even within that automobile domain, though, manual effort was further removed: windows that would once be wound up and down by hand became electric; steering that once required a bit of muscle became powered.

If the big labour-saving inventions were obvious and welcome, this automated takeover of even microexertions was more insidious. When the TV remote control came along in 1950 it meant that people didn't even have to get up from the sofa to switch channels.[12] If you wanted to sharpen your pencils at the office and couldn't be bothered with all that wrist-turning, there was the electric sharpener to help: pop it in, lightly hold, take it out, done.

The outcome – looking backwards – was inevitable. Modern societies – and especially the United States – got fatter, less fit and prey to pathologies that had previously been rare. The big concern was heart disease, which had exploded to 'epidemic proportions' following the end of World War Two. Soon, medics began to conclude that the sedentary habits of its citizens were partly to blame for the soaring death rate from heart attacks in the United States. The concept of hypokinetic disease – sickness caused by lack of movement – was born.

To counteract this dangerous inertia, this unwillingness to expend calorific intake in some form of activity, exercise for its own right was increasingly explored. The reason was simple: *it consumes energy resources*. It gets the heart rate up. It gets the blood coursing. It gets people hot and sweaty. What once acted as a deterrent now switched to a driver. Reversal, right there.

JOGGING AND THE FITNESS REVOLUTION

By the early 1960s a number of professionals were looking at ways to encourage sedentary, middle-aged citizens into some kind of physical exertion in a way that they could maintain on a daily basis. One of them was William J. Bowerman, the Oregon athletics coach who had visited New Zealand in 1963 and come back full of enthusiasm for a new kind of training. Bowerman had been invited by a local, self-taught coach to a meeting of the Auckland Joggers Club – a non-competitive, semi-structured, regular run across undulating terrain. What impressed him was the easygoing enthusiasm of the runners and the fact that Bowerman struggled to keep up with a 74-year-old jogger with no athletic history who had previously recovered from two heart attacks.[13]

Back in the United States, Bowerman teamed up with a cardiologist based at the University of Oregon to devise a programme that could scientifically measure the benefits of regular jogging for sedentary, middle-aged individuals. The pattern they devised was to start slowly, alternate jogging days with rest or walking days, stretch after exertion and gradually add distance. To their initial astonishment the programme was quickly oversubscribed, and – an early example of dilution – people began to just copy the idea of jogging and do it in their own way, in their own time, not necessarily following the rules of the regime.

The thing about jogging is that to do it is also to communicate it. Here was a form of exercise that was public – not confined to gyms or sports tracks but out there, in parks, on sidewalks, along beaches: the social media of its day. People could see that those doing it were not always of athletic build, were not always fast, and often had bodies a bit like their own. They could, without embarrassment, opt in.

And they did. By 1971, jogging had swept the United States and ordinary people were doing it in sufficient numbers that the authorities no longer batted an eye. From there the craze would gradually become prevalent across Europe and other parts of the world.

Bowerman – a pragmatist at heart – was content to see his methods adopted and adapted in haphazard fashion. He turned his attention to working on ways to make running shoes lighter and more efficient for athletes and amateurs alike – which would include borrowing his wife's Belgian waffle iron in his den to burn a pattern into soles to give them more grip.[14]

FIVE DECADES OF DILUTION

The most symbolic expression of dilution in the domain of exercise is the popular marathon. The 2019 Boston Marathon welcomed not 447 participants but 30,234.[15] The elite runners were still there, taking off first and very much still competing in a road race. Behind them were the runners who could clock respectable times, seeking to improve, competing against themselves.

But the vast mass of runners was not there to compete but to take part. These were not athletes, but a pretty faithful cross-section of society. Just under half were women. 2,456 were more than 60 years old. 60 made the 26.2-mile journey in wheelchairs.[16] One runner wore clown's shoes. They ran, walked, hobbled to the finish – did it in whatever way they could. The slowest finishers took the maximum allotted six hours, with some literally crawling over the finish line.[17]

Here, then, is the power of dilution. The hardcore doesn't disappear – it is still there, doing things 'properly', perhaps with a little disdain for those who do not. But these purists are the minority. The vast mass doesn't have a fixed idea of what doing it properly means and are content – to parody one of the most famous slogans of all time – to be just doing it at all.

FIGURE 7.1 Popular fitness timeline

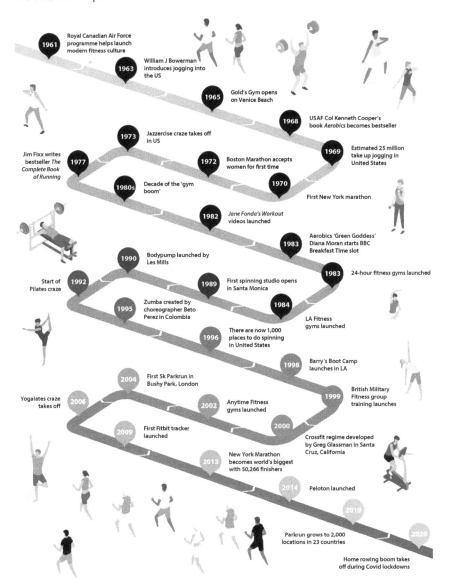

1961 Royal Canadian Air Force programme helps launch modern fitness culture

1963 William J Bowerman introduces jogging into the US

1965 Gold's Gym opens on Venice Beach

1968 USAF Col Kenneth Cooper's book *Aerobics* becomes bestseller

1973 Jazzercise craze takes off in US

1977 Jim Fixx writes bestseller *The Complete Book of Running*

1972 Boston Marathon accepts women for first time

1969 Estimated 25 million take up jogging in United States

1980s Decade of the 'gym boom'

1970 First New York marathon

1982 *Jane Fonda's Workout* videos launched

1983 Aerobics 'Green Goddess' Diana Moran starts BBC Breakfast Time slot

1990 Bodypump launched by Les Mills

1983 24-hour fitness gyms launched

1992 Start of Pilates craze

1989 First spinning studio opens in Santa Monica

1995 Zumba created by choreographer Beto Perez in Colombia

1984 LA Fitness gyms launched

1996 There are now 1,000 places to do spinning in United States

2004 First 5k Parkrun in Bushy Park, London

1998 Barry's Boot Camp launches in LA

2006 Yogalates craze takes off

2002 Anytime Fitness gyms launched

1999 British Military Fitness group training launches

2009 First Fitbit tracker launched

2000 Crossfit regime developed by Greg Glassman in Santa Cruz, California

2013 New York Marathon becomes world's biggest with 50,266 finishers

2014 Peloton launched

2019 Parkrun grows to 2,000 locations in 23 countries

2020 Home rowing boom takes off during Covid lockdowns

The combination of mainstream experimentation, commercial input and public health communications has, over the 50 years since popular exercise got going, spawned a spectacular, splintering array of fitness variations and techniques – from the Jane Fonda programmes of the 1980s, to the hybrid fads of yogalates and high-intensity interval training in the early 2000s, through to the tech-enabled systems like Peloton and Strava today (as depicted in the exercise timeline in Figure 7.1).

Think about the famous brands in diverse commercial sectors that this mainstream uptake has propelled. In fitness footwear and apparel: Nike, Reebok, Adidas, Puma, Sweaty Betty, Lululemon, Asics, Gymshark, 2XYou, Under Armour and countless smaller brands; in gyms and gym equipment: Virgin Active, LA Fitness, Equinox, Jordan, Technogym, Pure Gym – and Gold's, which today has nearly 700 franchised centres worldwide,[18] welcoming dedicated bodybuilders and casual users alike; in IP-protected fitness programmes: Les Mills, Soul Cycle, Barry's; in tech-mediated fitness systems and personal tracking: Peloton, Fitbit, Garmin, Strava, Wahoo. And that is not to mention branded fitness drinks and supplements, nor the network of dedicated personal trainers around the world. All for a behavioural life choice that nobody much was engaging in before about 1968.

For those who see the explosion early and are ready to find ways to serve the mass of people now taking up a given behaviour – interpreting it, broadening it, doing it 'wrong' perhaps – the opportunities for rapid commercial growth are considerable.

As a poignant example of that, let's revisit the image of the late William Bowerman, one-time US Olympics track coach, in his den, with his wife's waffle iron, striving to improve the performance of running shoes for the everyday jogger.

In 1964 he entered into an agreement with a former miler who had trained under him – Phil Knight – to start an athletic footwear distribution company called Blue Ribbon Sports. In 1971, with the pair each owning a near-50 per cent stake, the company began the process of changing its name. To Nike.[19]

We now turn to the growth beacons of reversal and dilution one by one, to explore their powerful dynamics in more detail.

Understanding reversal: the challenge of the 180° change

As we have seen, reversal occurs when a force or factor that served to resist uptake of a marginal behaviour flips sides to become a driver. What once pushed back now propels forward. But it doesn't do that without a reason.

It's not that the resistance side suddenly declares, 'Oh, I'm bored with all this resisting, I'm going to go round the other side and see what it feels like to give things a shove. Gotta be easier – and way more fun!'

For resistance to not merely fade away but actively switch sides there has to be some kind of *spark of ignition*, sufficient to energize the 180° change. Typically, this spark will be either new understanding – in the form of new scientific research, perhaps – or a new context, that suddenly changes everything (as depicted in Figure 7.2).

FIGURE 7.2 The concept of reversal

The intensity of adherents is a force that acts to drive uptake of a marginal behaviour forward into the mainstream – but is countered by the resistance supplied by Factor X which exerts force in the opposite direction. If this resistance were to subside, uptake of the behaviour could advance at a reasonable rate.

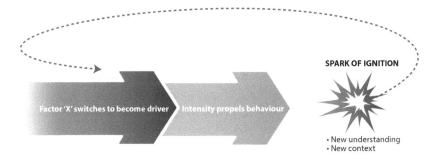

Reversal occurs when a spark of ignition – usually new understanding or a new context – energizes a complete 180° change in the direction of the hitherto resistance force. Factor X now switches sides to become a driver, helping propel the behaviour forward. Uptake is usually remarkably swift from this point.

In the vegan narrative it was new understanding that provided the spark. A range of scientific studies published over a matter of a few years turned the health story on its head: the vegan diet, long assumed to be insufficient in vital nutrients, was now shown to result in lower morbidity than the meat-and-dairy norm. In the freebirthing example, it was a new context – Covid – which convinced people that avoiding hospital birth might now be the safer thing to do. With the mass uptake of exercise, it was a combination of the two: the new context of societal sedentariness met the new understanding of the dangers of hypokinetic disease, and humankind's long-held resistance to discretionary physical activity was reversed.

Clearly, marketers would do well to look out for these sparks of ignition, these potential developments that could energize the reversal of resistance to otherwise promising marginal behaviours. That starts with being better versed in the emerging science of the sector or subject, and gaining deeper intelligence on tectonic cultural shifts – practical topics we'll investigate more fully in Chapter 9. A question that arises here, though, is whether marketers, themselves, could sometimes be the providers of that initial spark – going further than mere observation to embrace active encouragement, where they sense it would be commercially advantageous to do so. An interesting example of that is a brand that succeeded in reversing deeply held perceptions to instigate what is now a global, $33 billion market.[20]

Yakult: when bad became good

Once something has become normal it's difficult to remember the time when it wasn't. Who knows, that might happen with insect protein one day. It might, through some combination of circumstances and communication, become a norm. And we might then all forget how disgusting, dirty and revolting it seems today (as so vividly expounded in our original qualitative research and highlighted in Chapter 5).

Well, if eating insects feels dirty to people right now, imagine how eating *germs* must have felt to people in the 1990s. Back then, there was no background talk of 'good bacteria', no mainstream media coverage of the importance of the 'microbiome', no influencer 'gut-health gurus' on social media and no everyday, mass-market category called 'probiotics'.

Given that backdrop, let's postulate a new-product focus group in, say, 1993, where people are invited to sample an off-white viscous liquid which they are told contains 20 billion live *Lactobacillus paracasei*.

Bacteria! Yuck!

Bacteria were out-and-out baddies. In TV ads they were portrayed as things that 'lurked' in unseen corners – or on surfaces on which a baby might be crawling – always a threat to life and health. They were germs, in the end – the things people bought products to kill 'all known types' or '99 per cent' of, all the while fretting over the outrageous fecundity of the remaining unknown or undead. Just as people don't want to eat crickets and mealworms just yet, who wanted to a gulp down a swig of bacteria and bombard their innards with these unspeakable lifeforms back then?

So, if you were seeking in the 1990s to market a drink containing bacteria, the locus of resistance was clear: it was a drink containing bacteria.

Yakult was not new to the need to encourage people to think about its unusual product more carefully and to reverse prior opinions. Though it delayed launch of its characteristic mini-bottles into English-speaking cultures until 1994 – when it first came to Australia, and then the UK and the United States[21] – it had been patiently marketing the formula in Asia for decades. Since its health message was complex and counterintuitive, one charming way it did this was to employ 'Yakult ladies', going door-to-door on bicycles in Japan, Taiwan and Hong Kong to educate and explain.[22]

The origins of the brand go back to its founder, Minoru Shirota, a Japanese microbiologist who, in 1935, sought to isolate a bacterial strain that could survive all the way into the gut and combat toxic strains in compromised individuals.[23] But the science behind the concept predates even that. In 1907 Elie Metchnikoff, a Russian future Nobel laureate, had discovered while working in Bulgaria that people in remote rural communities who habitually drank a form of fermented milk lived much longer than other citizens. He ascribed this longevity to the benefits of gastrointestinal protection gained from the *lactobacilli* bacteria in the milk.[24]

Building on this theoretical foundation, Shirota eventually isolated a suitable strain that became named after him, and devised the single-dose formula for people suffering from debilitating digestive health issues. Only somewhat later did Yakult broaden its ambitions to become a mainstream, daily health brand.

DRIVE AND RIDE

Since going door to door is hardly a route to reaching critical mass fast in big Western economies, Yakult needed to find a way to crystallize its unique health message without putting people off. It achieved this by introducing the notion of 'friendly bacteria' in its TV commercials, print ads and leaflets.

To contemporary ears that will not sound so remarkable. But the key point is that Yakult faced into the big, alarming issue – bacteria – and called it out. Instead of going for euphemisms of 'healthfulness' or 'vitality' – as branded yogurts had already done – it bravely opened up a new and contentious subject.

That didn't just make it distinctive and newsworthy – useful virtues though these were on a small budget – it gave it the opportunity to ride any new popular scientific understanding that might come along. In this sense, the approach has some parallels with the Oatly US approach that we looked at in Chapter 3 – 'drive and ride'. You use your own communications to get things going – facing candidly into all the polarities of the subject – and ride the wave of new understanding or new behaviour that may follow.

'Friendly bacteria' did not change mindsets overnight. But it began to give people a more nuanced idea of what goes on in their insides and prepared them to be more receptive to the burgeoning science of the microbiome as that became more picked up in mass media from the early 2000s onwards.

The upshot was the establishment of not just a new mass brand, but a new mass category: probiotics – the things people drink *because they contain bacteria.*

On balance, the fairest evaluation is that reversal of a deep-seated resistance factor is not something that can be easily sparked by marketing endeavour alone. When it does come good, there tends also to be some element of serendipity involved – so that marketing's brave thrust both contributes to, and converges with, an upsurge of commentary, interest or new scientific understanding. Luck is part of the matrix. But look at it this way: in marketing, as in so many human endeavours, fortune favours the brave.

A marketing take on reversal

The problem with most marketers is that they know too much – at least, about the relationship between their own brands and the consumers who buy them. The reason they know what they know is because constant research feedback tells them so. Findings from iterative rounds of research get parlayed into 'learnings' which then become ossified as dictums: 'We know from research that...'

Sometimes, this 'knowledge' concerns an uncomfortable consumer opinion about something that would otherwise be dear to the brand. Something it is good at, cares about, yearns to share honestly: a mode of action, perhaps; a story; a process, an ingredient, a 'way'.

But no. 'Consumers don't care about X.' 'Consumers are confused about Y.' 'Consumers are turned off by Z.' They are said to resist, in other words.

Few marketers have the courage – as Yakult did – to lean into this awkward difference and seek ways to turn consumer opinion around. But perhaps more should. Sometimes, consumers are not quite so intransigent as we imagine – even if researchers are. Sometimes, they are up for reversal. Sometimes, the most promising principle might be:

THINK OF THE LEAST CONSUMER FRIENDLY THING YOU ARE GOOD
AT AND EVANGELIZE FOR IT

If you are indeed good at it, you have a head start. And if it is not *obviously* consumer friendly, at least your competitors won't be crawling all over it.

It's a hard call, to be fair. But for marketers with ambition for growth – perhaps daring to seek it at the margins – it is one that, sooner or later, they are likely to have to make.

Understanding dilution: less is so much more

The prevailing motif at this stage of the M2M journey is *scale*. What once was an esoteric pursuit of a few becomes a routine habit of the many. What once was contentious and contained becomes normalized and diffuse. What once was marginal goes mainstream.

The change can have crept up gradually, aided perhaps by the resolution of misalignment, the seeding of vectors, or the softening effects of reframing. It could have happened abruptly, powered by the more violent forces of accelerators and reversal. Or both – to give the pattern so often seen in the uptake of marginal behaviour: slow then sudden.

However it comes about, the change is often apt to take marketers by surprise. If gradual, they might not notice the increments building – marketing's equivalent of the boiling frog. If sudden, they may be blindsided, realizing only too late the explosion of something in a theatre of human interaction they had not been closely monitoring.

Also disguising the change is the shapeshifting tendency displayed by marginal behaviours as they become more accepted by the mass. One minute, there is an 'it' – a behaviour or way of life with a name and a relatively circumscribed understanding among adherents of what it entails. Now there is a 'them', where the behaviour splinters and becomes adapted in new ways in new hands. If, in 2016, the numbers of people becoming self-declared vegans, perhaps joining the Vegan Society, had suddenly grown tenfold, it would have been easy to spot. But the diffuse uptake by the mass of something that wasn't strictly 'veganism', but dilute versions of it, practised here and there, was more easily missed. Many did miss the change. And many were left playing catch-up.

Since marketing is about growth, and since it is axiomatic that growth and scale are linked, it pays to be alert to the nuances at this destination point of the M2M journey. The most straightforward way to do that, and to get more granular on the concept of dilution, is to break it down into its three constituent phases:

1 Dilution of resistance. 'I can see that this behaviour is perfectly acceptable for others – and maybe even for me.'

2 Dilution of intensity. 'I could fancy giving it a go if it just felt a bit more normal – and if I could do it my own way.'

3 Dilution of difficulty. 'As long as it's easy for me to get into, without too much extra hassle or cost, I am happy to try it.'

There is potential overlap between these phases of course, and they aren't necessarily sequential. It's also clear that they can work off one another, to be reciprocally reinforcing. But looking at them one by one gives us a chance to get under the hood and see what's going on at this vital, and final, point in the pathway.

DILUTION OF RESISTANCE

An important sign at the early stages of the beacon of dilution is the simple fact of acceptance. You'll recall from our analysis of resistance in Chapter 4 that people would often feel a behaviour to be 'wrong' not just for themselves but for those currently practising it. 'Immoral, dangerous, illegal' were the kinds of words that cropped up in our original qualitative research. In the spectrum of resistance unveiled in that chapter, behaviours that elicited this kind of disapproving reaction were at the far left – the least likely to prompt curiosity and gain consideration.

So the preliminary step of acceptance – however it comes about – is a force that moves people down to the right of that spectrum, and down the gradient of resistance. Once a behaviour is deemed fine for others, it opens up the conduits of curiosity, even if it is not yet determined fine for self.

The journey from curiosity to trial is by no means mandated and will vary considerably according to personal taste and circumstance. It is one thing to learn more about, say, polyamory, climatarianism, naturism, washing without soap or modern witchcraft – quite another to go out and do it. But working for the propensity to try here is a specific human drive unveiled by some relatively recent theory from the discipline of neuroscience: the 'seeking brain'.

Developed by the late Jakk Panksepp, an Estonian American affective neuroscientist, the theory holds that one of the primary seven human emotions is the 'seeking disposition' which 'drives explorative and approach behaviours and sustains goal-directed activity'.[25] At its crux is the notion that significant emotional reward is gained from daring to find and try new experiences.

Being human, though, our new triallists, in the experimental phase of engaging with a behaviour, are apt to interpret it and add their own touches. And the more they do, the more the stewardship of the concept of the behaviour slips from the hands of the purists and into those of the less committed mass. We are into the next phase of dilution.

DILUTION OF INTENSITY

In our original qualitative research, we would often see a tension between two antagonistic feelings. Paraphrased, it would go something like this: 'I'd like to try that – but I wouldn't want to be one of *them*'.

'That' was the behaviour under review – perhaps polyphasic sleeping, living without money or the quantified self. 'Them' would be the current impassioned enthusiasts who practised it, evangelized for it, directed the discourse relating to it, and, usually, took an all-or-nothing approach to doing it.

Even if people admired the intensity of the committed it was clear that they did not wish to be personally burdened with it. Sometimes it would take respondents a while before realizing that they were free to try the behaviour without needing to enter the circle of zeal. And it sometimes took a little prompting to suggest ways that they could do a scaled-back version of the behaviour. Once they got there though, and the mental shackles were released, their imaginations took off: they could see ways in which some version of the behaviour might pleasingly intersect with their life.

An important motif here is 'behaviour lite' – engaging in a given behaviour in an easier form. Frequency was probably the most obvious way to lighten the commitment. With neo-Luddism, for example (which came up spontaneously in some groups) respondents could imagine going through weekends without tech – taking 'tech breaks' or 'tech holidays' without any access to personal devices – even though they were not prepared to contemplate living entirely without it. Another 'lite' strategy would be to engage in a lower-stakes version of the behaviour – such as using mood-enhancing CBD oils but not risking the illegalities of microdosing LSD.

A clue that this phase has been reached is that the discourse is no longer owned by the dedicated. Tight devotee forums of the few will separate from more casual online engagement by the many. Feelings of intimidation are also softened – the kind of thing that happened when backstreet tattoo parlours gave way to better located outlets something akin to spas, to the mutterings of the hardcore but to the approval of a new kind of consumer.

It may feel counterintuitive that the dialling down of intensity should correspond with a surge in uptake – because we tend to over-interpret 'heat' to mean 'popularity'. But the duller vocabulary of 'normal' and 'everyday' is what characterizes this phase of the M2M journey. The behaviour, or some form of it, becomes an agreeable and accepted part of life. With one caveat: that there are no practical difficulties left to surmount.

DILUTION OF DIFFICULTY

Frictions are an interesting phenomenon. You almost get the sense that diehard enthusiasts for a given behaviour or life choice welcome them, as a kind of badge of honour. They become part of the symbolism of the marginal group, totemic proofs of commitment to the cause.

But the mainstream sees no cause and has no interest in surmounting any frictions. It is willing to have a go – if there is not too much extra effort, social awkwardness or cost involved.

At this late stage of the journey, then, things are not entirely in the hands of any single constituency. Instead, it is a kind of dance between three inter-related groupings. The original marginals, with their impassioned intensity, have got things going and continue to make it newsworthy. The mass is poised to try it in its own time and its own way. The third element is the market context – the part that marketers and entrepreneurs can, and sometimes successfully do, influence.

It is not easy to recognize when this phase has been reached because, inevitably, there is a chicken-and-egg paradox to it. If sufficient numbers are interested in trying a new behaviour then, obviously, the market will respond – making it easier and cheaper for them to do so. But those consumer numbers might not be there in the first place without that market adaptation. Which comes first?

In the end, the entrepreneurial marketer – seeing clues ahead of rivals – makes a bet here. That bet is to invest in the ease, ready availability and reduced cost of any consumption elements of a given behaviour. Or to innovate entirely new ones.

Investment implies risk and it is only right that you look deeply into the dynamics of the behaviour in question before making that bet. Is this the next veganism, the next mindfulness, the next tattooing, the next fitness revolution? It is easy, of course, to look backwards and sense the seeming inevitability of the soaraway growth of these once marginal movements. It is a far tougher call when you're staring at the future and assessing the inchoate opportunities of behaviours that haven't yet made that transformative leap.

But if you have been carefully monitoring a marginal behaviour and your analysis tells you that it now stands at the threshold of this final phase of this final beacon, then you are as close as you will get to certainty that consumer-driven disruption – with all the crazy challenge and opportunity that implies – is about to be unleashed.

A beacon complete

You will recall from Chapter 1 that a beacon consists of some combination of up to four elements: signs, clues, principles and motifs. Any given beacon will embrace one or more of these. (See Figure 7.3 for a reminder.)

FIGURE 7.3   A reminder of the four constituent elements of a beacon

Since the beacon of dilution features all four of these elements, and since this is the last of the eight beacons on the M2M pathway, it seems apt to capture it in totality (Figure 7.4), as a complete, fully developed whole.

FIGURE 7.4   The beacon of dilution in full

A marketing take on dilution

If we're honest, it is virtually impossible to consider dilution without there being some kind of marketing 'take', because marketers will become involved at this stage whether they like it or not. They can become involved as pioneers, forging ways to bring their brands and their markets in line with the burgeoning behaviour as it crashes through into the mainstream. Or they can end up involved as laggards, doing what they can to catch up with the new paradigm and struggling to ride the waves of consumer-driven disruption that will inevitably accompany it.

Marketers will tend to fall into one of these two camps. The more you are part of the former, the more Part 3 of this book is for you.

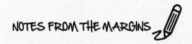

NOTES FROM THE MARGINS

Lifelogging

Fictional singleton Bridget Jones famously kept a daily diary noting personal metrics that mattered to her: weight, number of cigarettes smoked, units of alcohol drunk and amount of calories consumed.

Her mood was lifted when any of these were lower than they had been the day before... a simple example of the benefits of keeping a daily diary, or journalling, which mental health professionals often 'prescribe' as a de-stressor. The focus on detail seems to help, giving a hyper-awareness and visualization of the different elements in one's life.

Advocates of lifelogging take this self-knowledge through numbers to the extreme, often but not only related to their health. The behaviour has been dubbed the Quantified Self, and advocates measure all kinds of personal data in the aim of using the numbers to understand how to live a better life, which is the underlying goal. As the QS saying goes, you can't hack what you don't track.

Benjamin Franklin is an early low-tech example. His 18th-century journals show a hand-drawn grid, listing 13 virtues he aspired to, from industry and cleanliness to justice and sincerity. Each day he'd mark with a dot whichever he'd achieved, and the visual record could help him adjust his behaviour accordingly. He described it as a 'bold and arduous project of arriving at moral perfection'.

300 years later, the 21st-century entry-level lifelogger might use a Fitbit to keep track of step count, heart rate or stairs climbed. The visualization of positive messages on achieving targets helps with motivation, delivering a hyper-awareness and focus on health and body. (Canadian blogger and YouTuber Lillian Karabaic recommends the llamalife.co task management app, which showers the screen with confetti – and the user with a flush of wellbeing – when a goal is ticked off). In London, The Times journalist Robert Crampton shares with his readers an annual New Year update gleaned from his measurements: 'miles (and steps) walked, floors climbed, miles cycled, alcoholic units consumed, food eaten, hours slept, flights and trains taken, nights spent away from home and... er... other activities I'm too much of a gentleman to reveal. But not too much of a gentleman not to write them down in my diary next to a big hand-drawn smiley emoji'.[26]

So-called Quantified Self advocates take it further still, and extend their record-taking from one-dimensional tech, linking that data with mood trackers and journals to build a picture of their lives. With the phrase coined by Gary Wolf in The New York Times and expanded on in his 2010 TED talk, Wolf also drives the online site and forum where advocates share their experiences and ideas.[27]

For example, adopting QS behaviour could help someone struggling with poor sleep hygiene, beginning by simply data-capturing their night-time routine. Taking measurements on the time the pre-bed bath was taken, its temperature and its duration and comparing it to the quality of their sleep – which itself is captured on paper each morning on waking up – over a number of weeks, they'd be able to see which combination of heat and timing works best.

One QS self-tracker wanted to optimize their work days, feeling that it wasn't just drinking too much that made the morning-after-the-night-before unproductive. They started to track all the foods they were eating and, correlating their nutritional intake with the quality of their work on the following day, a pattern began to emerge.

Another user flagged that their heart rate was always noticeably raised two days before the onset of flu symptoms, and many others reported the same as the thread grew. This personal insight could have something in it; a Stanford paper based on 250,000 daily measurements from 43 people found that tracking heart rate, among other physiological signals, can give warning of an impending sickness.[28]

So while these self-recorded biometrics are being used creatively to improve the user's own personal situation, perhaps there's a broader public health value too. Meticulously kept patient-generated data could be ultimately time-saving for doctors, short-cutting the usually inaccurate or anecdotal taking of medical history and feeding scientists with the numbers they need for research and development of medicines and vaccines.

In the time of Covid, like never before, mathematician Clive Humby's saying is true: data is the new oil.

PART THREE

A strategy for growth

Research overview for Part 3

The following chapters outline how entrepreneurs and established businesses can apply the opportunities presented by the margins as fuel for growth.

In Chapter 9 you will find a list of marginal behaviours for the UK and the United States ranked according to their likelihood to go mainstream. This ranking was created by The Nursery statistics team using the findings from the quantitative surveys.

Below is the scale methodology that was used to create the rankings.

Methodology to create behaviour ranking

Data from the quantitative surveys was tabled and charted to help visualize any clear relationships between these measures and openness to trying a behaviour.

From this, and our qualitative research, we found clear patterns that helped us to create four hypotheses:

1 For a behaviour to move into the mainstream in the near future, it relies on enough people having knowledge of it to allow more people the opportunity to try the behaviour. This alone, however, isn't enough for it to become mainstream.

2 Behaviours that elicit strong negative emotions, such as disgust, are less likely to be something people are willing to try, and so create a strong barrier to becoming mainstream.

3 Behaviours that are impractical are also less likely to be ones that people are willing to try – but to a lesser extent than the above. In other words, behaviours that are impractical, but that create fewer strongly negative emotions, have a weaker barrier to becoming mainstream.

4 Risk takers influence the risk averse. When a higher proportion of 'risk takers' are willing to try a behaviour, the behaviour can be tipped into the mainstream and the risk averse will follow.

Based on these hypotheses, a composite score was created by summing together top three scores (on 11-point scales from strongly disagree to strongly agree) for each behaviour on each of these measures:

From a practical perspective, I could easily do this if I wanted to

This would easily fit into my day-to-day routine

I would like to try this out (including have tried already)

Bottom three scores (same scale as above) across these measures:

I feel disgusted by this behaviour

Other people find / would find this behaviour offensive

Plus, the percentage who had:

Some or good knowledge of the behaviour

Are risk takers and have already tried the behaviour

This produced a single percentage for each behaviour, to suggest how likely it is to become mainstream. Each behaviour was then ranked based on these composite scores and put into a scale, with those most likely to move into the mainstream with higher scores at the top, and those least likely to do so with lower scores at the bottom.

08

Entrepreneurs get it – they are marginals too

Are entrepreneurs born or made? Academia pulls in two directions on this one. On the one hand, there is a rich seam of academic research into 'the entrepreneurial mindset' – a cognitive hard wiring that predisposes entrepreneurs to think, act and even feel differently from the rest of us. On the other hand, business schools and schools of management are bursting with regular courses, electives and summer programmes devoted to 'entrepreneurship'. Clearly, for all that the mindset might appear to be innate, academia believes it is transferable.

Students, for their part, attend these sessions in droves, drawn from a range of disciplines, or none, to learn the secrets of building new ventures and breaking new ground. Though for those coming from the established corporate world, it might be more a case of 'unlearning' first; the two modes of approaching business often pull in diametrically opposite directions.

There is a kind of echo between thinking differently, as entrepreneurs do, and behaving differently, as those on the extremes of any life-choice continuum do. So, it is only to be expected that entrepreneurs are already exploring opportunities on the societal and commercial fringes. Of course they are – and we'll be looking more deeply into that as we progress through the chapter. For now, though, let's do that academic theory justice, and get a better feel for just what makes entrepreneurs so different, and why these brilliant, brave – and sometimes flawed – individuals are the very heartbeat of innovation.

The entrepreneurial mindset: a brief guided tour

In June 2020, three professors from the Kelley School of Business at the University of Indiana published a meta-analysis entitled *Unraveling the*

Entrepreneurial Mindset.[1] They had examined over 80 separate papers spanning nine decades to reach their conclusions, performing that most useful of scholarly tasks – synthesizing and making sense of disparate, overlapping and occasionally contradictory original research material.

After duly noting the relationship between entrepreneurialism and innovation, the authors propose that 'three distinct aspects of the entrepreneurial mindset exist' – cognitive, behavioural and emotional. The diagram in Figure 8.1, depicting this, is taken from the published paper. So, it makes sense to conduct our tour by visiting each of these focal points of importance in turn, perhaps peeling off now and then down the odd anecdotal alleyway where an interesting curiosity is to be found.

FIGURE 8.1 The triad of the entrepreneurial mindset

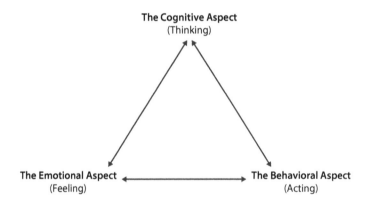

SOURCE *Unraveling the Entrepreneurial Mindset* (2020) Kuratko, Fischer, Audretsch.

THE COGNITIVE ASPECT: 'DON'T EXPECT ME TO THINK LIKE YOU'

Entrepreneurs aren't linear, and they tend not to fixate on objectives – remaining flexible for far longer than would seem feasible to those more used to the cognitive rhythms of corporate life.

In her seminal 2001 study, *What Makes Entrepreneurs Entrepreneurial?*, Saras D. Sarasvathy, of the University of Virginia, drew a distinction between the 'causal' thinking patterns typical of managers and the 'effectual' reasoning of entrepreneurs.[2] Good managers select the best of the available routes to a desired, agreed goal – or, if they are imaginative, invent new ones. Entrepreneurs, with their effectual rationality, don't bother with an objective at all, but start with a set of circumstances and imagine a range of potential end points from there. You won't know which one they'll run with because they won't know either, at first.

This *cognitive adaptability* is a theme endorsed by the work of a suite of academics quoted in the meta-analysis paper, defined by the authors as 'the ability to be dynamic, flexible and self-regulating in one's cognitions, given uncertain task environments'.

There is more to it than flexibility, though, since it also involves arcs of connection that require a creative leap. Mitchell et al (2002) argued that entrepreneurs 'use simplifying models to piece together previously unconnected information that helps them invent new products or services'.[3] Clearly, when looking to the margins, especially when behaviours are not well documented or researched, this ability to join 'previously unconnected information' could be key to breakthrough understanding.

Entrepreneurs think differently, and it is tempting to speculate whether they somehow 'see' the world differently from others, as an innate trait. Literally, that appears to be so. An interesting anecdotal finding was related by Malcolm Gladwell in his 2013 book, *David and Goliath*.[4] Quoting the work of Julie Logan, of City University London, he reported that a remarkably high percentage of successful entrepreneurs – around a third – are dyslexic. Could that reflect a 'big picture' bias, as a concomitant of the inability to discern or get tied up in fine detail? Or is it not about cognition at all, and reflects the resourcefulness of having overcome adversity? Either way, it is further fuel to the notion that entrepreneurs are, themselves, at the marginal end of things.

THE BEHAVIOURAL ASPECT: 'READY, FIRE, AIM'

It will not come as any surprise that entrepreneurs are driven to act – that they abjure theory, deliberation and procrastination to favour getting out and making things happen. It might surprise some more accustomed to the cadences of the corporate world just how abrupt – premature, it can seem – this leap from considering to doing can be.

As Sarasvathy shows, many entrepreneurs embrace the 'zero cost to market' approach. It's not just that they will minimize or even eliminate market research, it's that they will get out selling before the new product or service has been built. As one of her respondents told it, 'I'd just go try to sell it. Even before I have the machine. Even before I started production. So, your market research would be hands-on selling'. Another – a serial entrepreneur – summed up the approach more pithily: 'Ready, fire, aim'.

The relationship between the entrepreneur's natural assumption of action and the very existence of an opportunity can be glimpsed by looking at questions entrepreneurs tend *not* to ask. They don't ask, 'Does this opportunity exist?', in the sense that it is there as an independent phenomenon, irrespective of their actions. For the entrepreneur, it exists *as a consequence* of what they go out and do. Alvarez and Barney (2007) call this the 'creation theory', where opportunity is contingent on action, as distinct from the 'discovery theory', where opportunity is viewed like fruit hanging on a branch, ready for whoever happens to be passing.[5]

Similarly, entrepreneurs tend not to speculate long on what the future holds in any given domain because they believe their actions will shape it. It is the reverse of the marketing approach. Marketers come at innovation by first staring into their consumer-research crystal balls and asking, 'What's next?'. If it is a question that entrepreneurs don't much bother with, it is because they are too busy building the answer.

Clearly, where entrepreneurs can most effectively intersect with the margins, it is around the beacon of dilution, where the mainstream is ready to try the behaviour just as long as steps have been taken to make things simple, intuitive and inexpensive. The *opportunity is contingent on action*, in other words. That action will likely be taken by entrepreneurs – or, conceivably, by marketers taking a leaf out of their book.

THE EMOTIONAL ASPECT: 'HOPE TRUMPS FEAR'

When asked in a 2019 interview why she had chosen to focus on emotions in a newly published paper on entrepreneurship, Wharton Professor of Management Sigal Barsade responded, 'Entrepreneurship is incredibly emotional; there's so much uncertainty.'[6]

The emotional side of entrepreneurship has until relatively recently been downplayed compared with the cognitive and behavioural aspects. Barsade's co-authored 2019 paper – examining the roles of hope and fear when crises hit start-ups – had rounded on uncertainty as the aquifer from which these fulsome emotions spring.[7] It offers an explanation for the dramatic, and occasionally treacherous, emotional contours of the natural entrepreneur, and why, for the uninitiated, these driven individuals can sometimes seem so difficult to work with.

Uncertainty will breed emotions that can be both uplifting and challenging – reflecting, respectively, Barsade's 'hope, fear' duality. On the uplifting side is the entrepreneur's bundle of energy, passion and sheer enthusiasm for the cause. This is needed to carry others with them. Kuratko (2020) talked about the 'vison to recognize opportunity where others see chaos, contradiction and confusion'. But those conditions are rarely just the *perceptions* of others; they actually exist as challenges, as contributors to uncertainty, and a huge force of optimistic zeal is necessary to confront them.[8]

A less appealing outcome of the challenge of uncertainty – leaning into the 'fear' dimension – is the desire for control. Defiance and will are strands of emotional content necessary to overcome what others might see as unsurmountable obstacles but, as Beaver and Jennings observe (2005), this *control combination* can become 'a destructive force that could lead to negative consequences'.[9]

As an aside here, it is interesting to note the personal quality most sought by venture capitalists when deciding whether or not to back a start-up. According to a 2021 Harvard Business Review article, although experience, passion and leadership are important, the virtue at the top of the list is *resilience*.[10] The implication is clear: stuff will go wrong, failures both great and small will happen. It's inevitable. What counts are the reserves of tenacity and resourcefulness the team can dig down into and mine when confronting them.

Professor Barsade died of a brain tumour in early 2022 at the age of 56, so it is fitting that the concluding words in this section should be hers. In the co-authored 2019 study, the team had focused on those moments in a start-up's life when failure does indeed loom and asked whether group hope or group fear was more likely to achieve an 'escalation of commitment' to the troubled venture. In that 2019 interview, Barsade summed up the findings in three words. 'Hope trumps fear.'

From theory to practice

We've looked at what academia has to say about entrepreneurship. Now it is time to view entrepreneurship in action, with examples of where entrepreneurs, and entrepreneurial managers, have explored, created and scaled up opportunities rooted in marginal behaviours and ways of life.

So – brief signpost – here's how the chapter will work from here.

We'll start by delving into two business cases that come at the subject from very different directions. The first – the tech-enabled mental-wellbeing start-up Spill – tells the story of a classic entrepreneurial partnership, starting something completely from scratch, developing a new kind of offering in a space where it was by no means obvious that growth would be found. The second – Oatly US – takes a different tack, looking at how a remarkably entrepreneurial management team faced into unexpected headwinds when bringing an established European brand to a much tougher US consumer.

After the two cases, we'll look at a range of the marginal behaviours we've explored so far in this book – microdosing, polyphasic sleeping, insect protein and more – and give brief snapshots of some of the entrepreneurial start-ups already exploring them. Throughout this remaining section on entrepreneurs, where relevant, we'll touch on the M2M beacons – but we don't propose to get slavish about it.

Spill: taking therapy into the mainstream

If corporate success stories tend to be crisp, linear and heroic – especially when related by the leaders who drove them – the equivalents in entrepreneurial start-ups tend to be a mess. Pivots, failures, near bankruptcies, restarts, switches in everything from pricing models to customer targets – and partner fallout – are reliably part of the narrative. Gains are hard won, the struggle never simple.

Spill, founded by two partners in 2018, fits that mould. And the founders themselves – who met at school – pretty well fit the mould of the natural entrepreneur. Gavin Dhesi was the kid in the playground who sold sweets that a family member would bring home as part of the perks of working in a chocolate factory. Calvin Benton was the teenager who dreamed of owning a bakery, and spent a year learning to code, where others might be off travelling for a gap year. Neither considered getting jobs after university. Both tried other ventures – a cake delivery service in Canada, a chain of fish and chip shops in the north of England – before moving to London to 'start something awesome'.

In typical entrepreneur mode, they did not immediately settle on the 'what' of that 'awesome something' but had a clear view on the 'how'. They believed in the power of technology to make good things more accessible for more people and wanted to unleash it.

The initial venture – in education – failed. Called the Infinity School, it had been conceived as a way to make early access to education easier – but ran into the brick wall, as Benton relates it, of 'too many gatekeepers and stakeholders'.

The move to applying the same 'accessibility' principle to mental health wasn't entirely out of the blue. Benton's parents were both professionals in the field – his father as a clinical psychologist, his mother as a counsellor. He grew up, he claims, seeing first-hand the power of therapy to change lives for the better.

MAKING THE MARKET

At this point, it is instructive to stand back and take a wider view, because it is one thing to have personal reasons to consider a given field, quite another to establish that a market is there. In objective terms, in the UK, as things stood, it wasn't.

Think about who voluntarily pays to go to therapy for a moment. In the United States, as depicted – more or less parodied – in Woody Allen films, it was a trope of a certain class of person to spend money and time with their 'shrink'. It was, for the upscale urban elite, an accepted part of self-understanding and improvement. But even in the United States, outside New York and Los Angeles, the number of people routinely engaging in the behaviour was small.

In the UK it barely existed. Those who were clinically mentally ill could – though not always easily – access the state-provided support they needed. But beyond that, the notion of exploring therapy for more general self-improvement, or for lower-stakes issues such as vague anxiety, was rarely a consideration. Therapy was a marginal choice, a privilege of the rich. This is despite the fact that the UK charity Mental Health Foundation reported in 2018 that 87 per cent of people said their mental health was less than good.

Benton and Dhesi determined to change that. Observing that the mental health system was 'broken', and sensing that many would take advantage of the benefits of some form of therapy or counselling if it were more of a norm to do so, they set to identifying the resistance points that got in the way. There were two.

First, there was cost. Privately paid-for therapy was beyond the reach of the average citizen because the hourly face-to-face rates were high and there would normally be a requirement to commit to a minimum number of sessions. And second – but every bit as problematic – there was the stigma. Going to see a therapist was tantamount to admitting to some kind of mental or emotional frailty. It wasn't – then – something you did as a routine step to healthier mental wellbeing, the equivalent of going to the gym to enhance physical fitness.

With the help of the democratizing influence of technology, and a more positive reframing of the concept of therapy, the founding duo believed they could dismantle both of these barriers and open up a new market, to the benefit of all.

FAILURE, PIVOT, PROGRESS

It is a myth that entrepreneurs embrace failure like a dear friend. Who wouldn't want their venture to be a massive success fast and early, opening up paths to even greater things? Who, genuinely, yearns to fail? Where entrepreneurs are different, though, is in their capacity not to be bowled over by failure, but to put it to one side, reflect, and try again.

Benton and Dhesi were to have several attempts in the mental wellbeing space before getting it right. At first, branded as Sphere, they tried a business-to-consumer (B2C), peer-to-peer model, where people could connect with likeminded others who had been through similar experiences. But it quickly became apparent that the user base was too variable to make for a consistent, quality-controlled offer.

Sticking with a B2C model – this time branded Spill – they built an offer around online therapy, delivered by professionals, via text and app. This didn't fail completely but neither was it a conspicuous success, partly because the default price setting in people's minds for apps was anchored too low to offer the service profitably.

The breakthrough came in 2020 with the decision to pivot to B2B. The switch didn't alter the ultimate recipient of the service – the individual who, for whatever reason, feels they might benefit from therapy – but it changed the buyer. In this new Spill iteration, businesses – employers – would pay a flat monthly subscription for all of their employees to use the service whenever they felt the need, as a part of their employment package.

From the employee's perspective, it was an additional bonus, something they could take advantage of – for personal growth, to resolve issues, as a sounding board – without personal cost. The mechanics were simple and clean. Accessed via Slack or Microsoft Teams, users could spend an hour over video call talking with a qualified therapist or counsellor about whatever was on their mind. The service was completely discreet, and although employers would know the total numbers using Spill, they would have no more information than that.

From the employer's perspective, it was a way of showing commitment and care to employees without huge cost implications. And in the struggle to attract and keep talent – which became more marked after the pandemic – it was a small added benefit that could, at the margins, make a difference.

From Spill's perspective, it made selling much more streamlined. They could target the HR function in firms of the optimum size – 50 employees or more – rather than having to convince endless individual users to pay. Spill was good use of the HR Health and Wellness budget – just so long as employees made good use of the service. If nobody took it up, HR managers would notice and not repeat-purchase.

So, the reframing element was still key to success, even though businesses, not individuals, were now the paying customer. It was vital to 'de-medicalize' mental health, and frame it as a positive, active consideration. Here, Benton's passion for the benefits of therapy and counselling really kicked in. The guiding principle was that the Spill app was not merely something you were not embarrassed to have on your phone, but something you were proud to display – a sign that you invested in yourself, and that you cared about mental and emotional wellbeing in the same way that a fitness app might show you cared about your physical shape.

In this attitudinal shift also lay the secret of *scale*. In an interview for this chapter, Spill's marketing director, Will Allen-Mersh, summed it up like this:

> If you just try to go into the big addressable pie of people who sometimes don't feel great and you talk about not feeling great, or feeling a bit anxious, or feeling like you're not sure how your relationships are going, or feeling stressed at work, you're then a) in a space where there's less ambiguity around the words, people know what that stuff means. And b) it's just a much bigger pie.

ACCELERATORS, AMBITIONS, MIGRATIONS

In an earlier chapter we observed that fortune favours the brave. Spill got its share of fortune in the shape of accelerators that hoisted the subject of mental health high on the cultural agenda. In the UK, the Royal Family vivified the dialogue with Prince William's TV-interview confessions of 'dark clouds of depression'. The anxieties of the Covid pandemic, and the rigours and constraints of lockdown, further raised sensitivity and awareness. The 'great resignation' that ensued as the pandemic retreated was an accelerator of a different kind, as companies discovered they had to dig deeper and offer more to keep talent on board.

Spill lost a strand of its own talent in 2020 when founding partner Dhesi moved on to pursue ventures in food, which was his abiding passion. Benton's ambitions remain undiminished: one million active users and a launch into the much larger US market.

Spill is a young business and there will undoubtedly be twists, turns and untidiness in its narrative yet, contingent as it is on rounds of funding and the forbearance of investors to trade profit for growth. As a start-up case, though, it is a wonderfully illuminating window not just into the entrepreneurial mindset (cognitive flexibility, the prioritization of action, tenacity under pressure) and the M2M beacons (resistance, reframing, accelerators, and aspects of dilution too) but an inspiring evocation of the courage to try something in a space that is eerily unexplored and yet matters to people's lives. Hand-to-mouth start-ups can have their shades of heroism, too.

Now to our next case – Oatly US: the headwinds it faced, the creativity it showed, and the backstory that brought the brand there in the first place.

Oatly US: overcoming the obstacles in entrepreneurial style

In 2017, Oatly US introduced not just a new brand but a new subcategory – oat milk – to the North American consumer. Both had existed in Europe, though, for some time.

The concept of using oats to make an alternative to dairy milk had been explored during the early 1990s by a team led by Rickard Öste, a professor of applied nutrition at Lund University, Sweden. Since the country's soil and wet climate favoured the growing of oats – and little else – it made sense to seek additional uses for the superabundance of the crop. In 1997, Öste partnered with his serial-entrepreneur brother, Björn, who felt there was a market that could be exploited for the unusual product. At first, they tried a B2B route, selling the formula as an ingredient for lactose-free yoghurts and ice creams. Sales were disappointing, so the brothers opted to create a B2C brand and, in 2001, Oatly was born.[11]

The brand went nowhere much for about the next decade. It certainly didn't look the way it does now. Packs were bland and predictable, the logo recessive and the usual visual tropes employed – pouring shots and idealized usage options, with the product splashing onto cereal or fruit. The appeal was limited to a narrow group of consumers with allergies and a few with animal welfare concerns.

Things started to get interesting in 2012, when, after making product formula improvements, the team declared ambitions to drive Oatly beyond its narrow, niche status. In search of growth – with alternative milks by then gaining traction in Europe – the business recruited a previously successful manager and former pop singer, Toni Petersson, to run the show. He, in turn, sought out a celebrated creative director, John Schoolcraft, who had been working in a Copenhagen ad agency, to join him in the challenge of broadening the brand's appeal. The pair turned out to be the dream team who would utterly transform the fortunes of the brand.

In classic creative style, Schoolcraft took out six months to ruminate on the new direction for the brand's iconography. The resulting solution – with its artisan, almost homemade, vernacular – was testament to that combination of time and talent, since it is one of the hardest things in branding to get right. Underdo it and it comes across as risible amateurishness. Overdo it and it's ersatz, the corporate version of dad dancing. Hit the sweet spot, though, and you lay claim to not just distinctiveness but a kind of easygoing authenticity and bags of charm.

If you look hard at those packs, and compare with those of other alternative milks, and indeed packs in supermarket food aisles more generally, the creative leaps are remarkable. Schoolcraft sliced an already short brand name into two, splitting it vertically with a playful and eye-catching hyphen. The logo could now be huge on the packs, even though they were tall and narrow. Clichéd pouring and usage shots were gone, leaving the communication of the brand's virtues to a disarming combination of verbal wit, wiggly type and 'naïve' icons and drawings. At Schoolcraft's insistence, the brand tonality was taken beyond design to embrace an attitudinal palette, set down in a wood-covered brand strategy guidelines book.

That gave way to ads that were similarly disarming, with one poster heralding the product as 'like milk, but made for humans' – a reframing of 'alternative' that made it seem a far more natural thing for people than something that was forced from the udder of a cow. Although other non-dairy milks had long existed, none had put it quite like that. In Europe, Oatly took off, growing to €103 million revenue by 2018.[12]

US HEADWINDS

The US team, then, did not start from scratch. Headed up by General Manager Mike Messersmith and an in-house creative director, the operation had distinctive packs, iconography and attitude already going for it. Also working in its favour was the fact that alternative milks were becoming more established in the United States, with recent growth led by almond milk, reflecting the huge importance of almonds as a US crop.

But there were headwinds as well as tailwinds and the most serious of these was the issue of taste. In trials, over and again, people would baulk at the taste of Oatly. US consumers were used to the sweeter notes of almond and many could not get past the blandness of oats. Worse, even those who did not get to taste showed no hurry to do so. The very idea of oats seemed strange for a milk – incongruous and odd – even though not just almonds but also rice and soy were already accepted in the US market as credible bases for non-dairy milks. Taste – actual and perceived – was a worrying fulcrum of resistance for the new brand.

This is the point at which misalignment could have kicked in. What many brands do when confronted with a barrier to purchase is to double down on the communication of their core benefits – in Oatly's case, as a non-dairy milk, contributions to nutritional health. At the same time, they might give a cursory nod to the taste issue in the time-honoured fashion, with 'product enjoyment' shots and hopeful copy about the brand's 'great flavour'.

The Oatly team's response was both more original and more courageous. They took the entire side of the pack to address the taste issue – not by outright denial but by leaning into the problem. At the top of the side panel, in big, bold type was a short but extraordinary statement: 'This tastes like sh*t! Blah!'

The copy underneath it explained that this was 'a real comment from a real person who tried one of our oat drinks for the first time'. Leavened with touches of wit, the copy then went on to observe that 'taste is personal' and that Oatly's taste may not be for everyone – before noting that there is, nonetheless, 'a growing number who find oat drinks delicious and can taste the fine balance of protein, fiber, unsaturated fats and carbs and know that it makes them feel good'.

If you think about it, this is a bit like the reflective listening technique we looked at in Chapter 5. The brand shows it is listening by repeating back, verbatim, what it is hearing from consumers – before sensitively addressing the point and going on to make its own points, in return.

Playing into a problem is a way of taking some of the heat out of it – and of communicating a deep confidence rare in branding. It also arouses curiosity – and Messersmith knew the importance of consumers who might be curious to give the brand a try if the circumstances proved right. Get them on side and they could form a bridgehead to the mainstream. Yet Oatly did not target them, nor any consumers, directly, just yet.

LOWERING THE STAKES

Clearly, for any new brand competing in an everyday grocery market the overriding objective is penetration – which can only be gained via trial. You need to quickly get numbers on board. Yet for the first six months of its US journey, the Oatly team confined the brand's targeting to an audience that represented, perhaps, 0.1 per cent of the US population. With verve, wit and dedication it focused its efforts on baristas working in upscale or fashionable coffee shops. It strove to get them on board first. Why?

As Messersmith explained in his 2019 ANA Masters of Marketing talk, it was all about consumer risk, and in doing so, he introduced a central concept in the marketing of a contentious new product, where curiosity is just about the only thing going for you: *lowering the stakes*.

The point is that curiosity is a weak force – a long way short of visceral desire. It amounts to a kind of momentary, 'Shall I or shan't I?' decision that can be easily swayed one way or the other. There is, as Messersmith observed, a sizeable element of risk when you fork out $5 for a half gallon pack and take it home for family or housemates to try, with the possibility that it doesn't go down well. But to try it solus in a $2 latte, with a bit of professional barista endorsement to help, is to de-risk that choice; it becomes the kind of fleeting, low-stakes decision that curiosity is sufficient to prompt.

There was another reason to court baristas. Oat milk just happens to blend particularly well in coffee – so it worked for them, and in turn helped ensure their customers' first experiences of oat milk were positive. And they were. Before long, regulars at the nation's coffee places were requesting their cappuccinos, flat whites and lattes to be made with oat milk, and from there began seeking out the Oatly packs in supermarkets. This counterintuitive, indirect, approach to penetration had got the new brand up and running.

NORMALIZING THE WEIRD

There were still those who found the concept of oats as a basis for a milk a bit weird. So, communications would be an important plank in the task of normalizing the brand and its key ingredient. In any consumer-facing business, but in a small one particularly, marketing resources are finite, and you have to make choices where you will focus that communications effort. Oatly made the brave call not to invest in social media – to more or less ignore it – in favour of gaining an unmissable presence in a medium it called 'surfaces'.

These were not just print media like magazines but outdoor spaces like posters, walls, benches – anywhere in the neighbourhood where it could put up or paint on one of its insouciant, laid-back messages, offering its product as something you might want to consider, but no worries if not.

The point about this choice of neighbourhood presence is that everyone knows that everyone else is seeing it. It's public, open, out there – part of the local street culture. And that makes for a far more normalizing out-take than sniping at individuals on their devices.

Over the years, as the brand has grown, Oatly has gained a strong presence in social media too – but it still claims to be a 'print brand' at heart, and its confident use of outdoor is still a feature of its culture-based communications style.

FIVE INCREDIBLE YEARS

If you think about it, Oatly US is a kind of brand-specific M2M-style story. The brand began as a super-marginal choice (oat milk) in a minority category ('alt milks') which, in 2016, accounted for about 7 per cent of total US milk consumption.[13] By 2021, alt milks had grown to be present in 12 per cent of US households[14], and Oatly had both ridden and driven that surge to become one of its most dominant players. Across five incredible years, through to the global IPO in 2021, Oatly US grew from zero to revenues of over $130 million.[15]

The team that got it there were not entrepreneurs – they were managers, with a little less skin in the game. But they displayed those characteristic entrepreneurial traits of iconoclasm, cognitive adaptability and sheer guts in the way they broke free from the accepted way of doing things, to back both their carefully weighed judgements and their offbeat intuitions. Marketers everywhere could take note.

Twenty entrepreneurial ventures based on marginal behaviours

This is the section where we return to some of the marginal behaviours we've encountered so far in the book and showcase the entrepreneurs who have also taken a good look at them and decided to plant a start-up flag squarely in one of them. Never mind that the behaviours are seemingly confined to the fringes; these founders believe there is scope for mainstream expansion and see growth where others see only issues, confusion or nothing much at all.

A few caveats, though before we launch into the list. This is entrepreneurial start-ups we are talking about, and that is always a fast-moving subset. Facts that were correct as this copy went to press might have changed by the time you read it. Some businesses will have moved on, some pivoted, some joined with competitors, some sold, others run out of cash, or luck or time. And who knows, one might have punched that vaunted hole in the universe. There's no way of knowing which is which at the outset. That is just how it is.

For the remainder of this section the format will be consistent. We'll headline the marginal behaviour in question, make a few brief observations, and cameo two or more of the entrepreneurial ventures that are commercializing it and going all out for growth.

Marginal behaviour: polyphasic sleeping

As noted in Chapter 6, the Covid pandemic – with many more people working from home – gave the notion of adapting work and life schedules around personal sleep patterns a boost.

Some interesting businesses were already seeking to help make that happen.

MetroNaps was founded in 2003 based on the then 'crazy idea', as co-founder Christopher Lindholst puts it, of 'encouraging employees to sleep at work'. The need was clearly there. In their initial empirical research, the founders noted that people would nod off at the office anyway, or on the train home, but did not want to be caught 'sleeping on the job'. Some admitted that they would sneak off to the toilet, a parked car, or an unused conference room for an afternoon nap. The remainder simply 'caffeinated their circadian rhythm in an attempt to keep their focus'.

The business believes that helping people adapt to their natural sleep rhythms at work makes them both happier and more productive. Its lead product is the EnergyPod, an ergonomically designed recliner with a low-slung privacy hood, purpose built for sleeping at work, and costing upwards of $15,000. Customers today include Google, HuffPost, Virgin, Accenture and the NHS.

Apps are another obvious play in this space. One of the most downloaded is **Polyphasic Sleep by Alexey Kuzokov**, which offers seven different sleep schedules ranging from biphasic (5–7 hours at night and 20 minutes during the day) through to what it calls 'Uberman', which is the full-on polyphasic schedule of 20 minutes every four hours, round the clock.

Marginal behaviour: Microdosing

Legality is the thorny issue here. Psychedelics (principally psilocybin, or 'magic mushrooms') are banned in most jurisdictions. But they are legal in in the Netherlands, and in the US state of Oregon[16], while other parts of the United States and Canada have voted to decriminalize them in medical therapeutic settings. Entrepreneurs have come at the opportunity and the challenges in different ways on both sides of the Atlantic.

At the top of its homepage, Amsterdam-based **Blissed** declares: 'The psychedelic renaissance is underway!' To help it along, the venture specializes in packing dried and magic ground truffles into a capsule format. Even a tiny amount, according to the site, can 'trigger the body's serotonin receptors, releasing hormones essential for health, wellbeing and happiness'.

Mojo skirts round the legal issues by producing soft chews laced with a blend of 'carefully selected bioactives', which it claims will mimic the effects of a psilocybin microdose. Founder Peter Reitano, a serial entrepreneur, calls the product 'the world's first productivity gummy'.[17]

Other businesses are finding ways to blend product and service offers in interesting combinations. The Canada-based **Field Trip Health** aims to provide a 'safe space' to engage in 'psychedelic assisted therapy'. The business, co-founded in 2019 by a group of five partners comprising bio-scientists, 'visionaries' and entrepreneurs, went public in a 2020, listing on the Canadian Stock Exchange with a market capitalization of 102 million Canadian dollars.[18]

In Jamaica, where psilocybin is legal, **MycoMedications** and **Silo Wellness** offer psychedelic retreats in beautiful island locations. In Holland, **Synthesis** aims to live up to its name by fusing experimentation with truffle mushrooms in both high and moderate doses with the relaxation of a three-day retreat.

Marginal behaviour: eating insect protein

As we saw in Chapter 5, many in the mainstream are viscerally repulsed by the idea of eating insects and mealworms. That hasn't deterred entrepreneurs from seeking to explore ventures rooted in the burgeoning science of insect protein. Here are three that have come at it in very different ways.

It's not hard to see how the idea for **Bug Farm Foods** came about. The UK-based venture is the brainchild of entomologist Dr Sarah Benyon and her husband and chef Andy Holcroft. Established in 2017, the business sells its cricket cookies and yellow mealworm powders for protein shakes both online and through stockists.

Pet industry veteran and sustainability enthusiast Tom Neish has solved the problem of human squeamishness around insects by circumventing it. His **Yora Pet Food** venture, based in the UK, offers a complete range of dog and cat food entirely based on insect protein. By his calculations, cats and dogs consume about 23 billion tons of meat a year, with serious implications for the environment. So, he worked with experts in animal nutrition and entomophagy to arrive at *Hermetia Illucens* larvae as the optimum ingredient for both pet and planet.

In the United States, **Chapul Farms** is an insect agriculture company – a B2B play. That's a pivot from where it started back in 2014, when founder Pat Crowley won investment in his idea for a cricket protein bar on *Shark Tank*, a TV show where hopeful entrepreneurs attempt to persuade seasoned investors to back their projects. In 2018, the business embarked on a more ambitious vision to transform food systems with insect biology. Its focus is industrial farming units using black-soldier fly larvae to eliminate food waste and turn it into animal feed and biofertilizer products. In 2022 the venture raised $2.5 million[19] to continue the farms project and claims to have seven more insect-based initiatives in development.

Marginal behaviour: home burial (and other forms of alternative deathcare)

This one sets up the concept of direct or indirect commercialization. Direct focuses in on the marginal behaviour itself. Indirect is when the behaviour inspires ideas in adjacent space.

That's what's happened with home burial. Practicalities and legal constraints make it difficult to directly commercialize, although some conventional undertakers offer it as an option. But the recognition that people are seeking non-standard, more personal, ways of disposing of the remains of their loved ones has inspired some fascinating business concepts.

Based in Austin, Texas, **Eterneva** makes diamonds out of human ashes. The concept came about in 2015 when Adelle Archer was made guardian of the ashes of a good friend who had recently died. Finding the existing options underwhelming, she chose to have them turned into a black diamond.

Co-founded by Archer and Garrett Ozar, the venture uses machines to replicate natural diamond formation and so grow a real diamond from the carbon of human ashes. They claim to have honoured thousands of lives and the website showcases rave reviews. Investors are seeing the potential, committing more than $10 million to date.[20]

Recompose comes at a similar need in a different way. Founded by Katrina Spade in 2017, the Seattle-based enterprise specializes in human composting, in a process known as natural organic reduction. The deceased is laid in a vessel surrounded by wood chips, alfalfa and straw. The body and the plant material take about 30 days to form nutrient-dense soil, which is then cured and can be used to enrich the land. This is deathcare as part of the sustainability effort, with the claim that for every person choosing it over conventional burial or cremation, one metric tonne of CO_2 is prevented from entering the atmosphere.

Marginal behaviour: New nomads

Motorhome living has enjoyed more prominence following the release of the films *Nomadland* and *Into the Wild*. It's beginning to feel more like a viable life choice for the adventurous, and businesses are popping up to support those wanting to take the plunge.

One of them is **NomadCreations**, founded in the UK by entrepreneurs who self-identify as 'nomads at heart'. The venture offers both pre-built campervans and a van conversion service that creates tailormade, bespoke campervans 'to get as many people as possible out on the open road'.[21]

Going at it more indirectly is the remote job platform **Wanderbrief**, founded in 2015 by the Dutch 'Backpacker Intern' Mark Van Der Heijden. The business offers a virtual home to remote professionals or, as Van Der Heijden prefers to call them, digital nomads.[22]

Marginal behaviour: biohacking and the quantified self

There is overlap between these two lifestyle choices. Both incorporate the full embrace of technology to measure, assess or more directly enhance mental, physical and emotional responses.

The emergence of Elon Musk into this space is not insignificant. His 2016 co-founded **Neurolink** venture helps people with brain or spinal issues gain direct control of their personal computers or mobile devices through micron-scale threads that are inserted into the brain. The aim is to eventually broaden out to life-enhancing biohacking technologies for the wider population.

At the more accessible end of the market is Swedish start-up **Mendi**. Founded in 2017 by three entrepreneurs with backgrounds in technology and neuroscience, the business seeks to 'improve the brain health of millions of people'. Its launch product is a headband that monitors brain activity. It costs $350 and works by sensors that measure the oxygenated blood and neural activity of the brain. Customers wear the headband and then use the Mendi training game to help strengthen neural pathways.

Marginal behaviour: living off the sea

What is the next 'veganism'? That is a question asked by entrepreneurs and established food manufacturers alike.

Living off the sea is a plausible candidate. This isn't about plundering our already overfished oceans, but harvesting or farming kelp and other edible sea plants, which grow naturally at a phenomenal rate, are a good source of protein and are rich in iodine, calcium and vitamin C. Here are three pioneer ventures already exploring the commercial opportunities.

New York-based **AKUA** claims to be the maker of the world's first kelp burger. The business was created in 2019 by entrepreneur Courtney Boyd Myers, who learned about regenerative ocean farming through her connections with charity Green Wave. She was inspired by the nutritional benefits and wanted to find a way to get more people eating sustainable sea greens. Customers buy directly from the website, choosing from products such as kelp 'ground meat' and kelp jerky – voted one of Time Magazine's 'best inventions of 2019'.[23]

The founders of **Atlantic Sea Farms** created the first commercially viable seaweed farm in the United States. But this was a pivot from their prior focus as a traditional fishing business based in Maine, reliant on lobster and shrimp – both of which were increasingly under threat from climate change. Products include jarred Sea-Beet Kraut, Sea-Chi (a kimchi garnish), and frozen kelp cubes for smoothies.

The UK-based **Notpla** does something even more original. It makes edible and biodegradable packaging for drinks and sauces out of a seaweed and plant-based material. Its lead product, named Ooho, biodegrades in a matter of weeks... or can just be eaten.

What now for mainstream marketers?

We have spent a chapter in the company of entrepreneurs. We have observed the traits that make them different, the actions they take to overcome challenges and the risks they are willing to bear along the way. We have also noted how they are doughty pioneers, daring to venture to the frontiers of human behaviour in search for growth.

But mainstream marketers may find themselves working in businesses that are not especially entrepreneurial. So how does this balance of risk and reward work then? How does a corporately trained marketer break old habits and embrace new ones? How do you even begin to convince the multidisciplinary, hierarchical management structures that characterize the corporate world that the whole idea of venturing to the margins is worthwhile? These are the questions we'll be answering as we move on to Chapter 9.

And yes, working in new ways with new kinds of potential customers can feel challenging, scary even. The risks are real. But on the upside, this is where meaningful growth is to be found. So, if there is one axiom that we carry across from this chapter to the next one, let it be this: hope trumps fear.

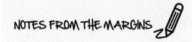

NOTES FROM THE MARGINS

Extreme frugalism

A few radical outliers make an intentional, philosophical choice to live completely without money – to remove themselves from the notion of currency, or even barter and exchange, in an attempt to challenge societal norms and make a difference.

Extreme frugalists sound similar on the surface but have quite a different motivation. This determined group continue earning but opt to minimize spending and maximize saving, often to a fanatical degree. They too are in search of financial freedom – but aren't expecting it to kick in until their middle age.

Advocates take ordinary money-saving habits and make them extraordinary, completely re-shaping how they live. For the frugalists, every little helps. They minimize outgoings by sofa-surfing, house-sitting or living with family, by not having a car, going on holiday or going out to eat or to cultural events. They don't buy new clothes, makeup, or presents for friends, they use washable menstrual and baby products (if they've had children, which many don't) and collect and use every voucher or special offer they can find to buy the basic ingredients they use to make all their own meals from scratch. They maximize income by renting out rooms, driveways or parts of their gardens and working extra hours wherever they can on top of their regular jobs.

After deciding to change their lives, Elizabeth Willard Thames and her husband targeted saving 80 per cent of their earnings and within two years, were able to pack in their 9–5 jobs and move to rural Vermont.[24] They'd always been regular savers so weren't starting from nothing, but the conscious decision to turn up their frugality and step away from the 'arms race of possessions' fast-tracked their move. As well as securing them the freedom they'd hoped for, the couple found unexpected advantages to ultra-frugal living. The environmental benefits were obvious straightaway, from reduced waste to the sustainability tick that comes from not buying anything new.

Beyond that, however, the pure satisfaction of doing practical things themselves – using someone else's unwanted paint to re-do their kitchen for example – surprised them both, and the fact that they were team-mates on a project brought them closer than ever in their marriage. Until then, like so many other busy working couples they simply paid other people to do stuff for them, while they focused on making money which meant working on separate tracks. Their radical shift to 'insourcing' strengthened their intimacy, boosted the respect and gratitude they had for each other and got the couple back 'on the same page'.

Living without money

Imagine no possessions… it's actually not easy, even if you try, but converts have found it liberating to step away from the culture of money and live wholly self-reliant, sustainable lives.

Freeconomics doesn't have to mean living without a roof over your head, good food or holidays. A growing concern for the planet's welfare, a desire to live in tune with nature, a rebuttal to rampant consumerism – whatever the reasons for trying it, living without money IS achievable.

Business graduate Mark Boyle wasn't even that keen on the mindset of exchanging goods and services to get by without money. Inspired by watching the film *Gandhi*, Boyle was struck by his mantra: be the change you want to see in the world. Setting up home in an unused caravan on a remote corner of a Welsh smallholding in 2008, Boyle figured out how to use solar power to run his laptop and lighting, foraged for wood to power a stove for heat and cooking, and basically nailed his attempt to live a rich and fulfilling life without cash.

Boyle quickly relished the feeling of self-reliance, of not being a burden on anyone else – or on the planet. Wanting to share his experience he wrote a book, *The Moneyless Man*, which sold well (and ironically made him some money).[25] Five years on, he adjusted his entirely cash-free life to buy land in Ireland, where he lives not entirely without money, but self-sufficiently. Ambitious and inventive, with a group of friends he even threw a banquet for 1,000 people using only waste food, complete with a bicycle-powered cinema. He is by all accounts still majoring in gift economics...

German psychotherapist Heidemarie Schwermer also wanted to try a different kind of life. She'd grown up extremely wealthy in World War Two, when the family fortune was lost; for some years they struggled with nothing before her father became prosperous again. For the rest of her life, Schwermer hated being defined by money, whether as a rich person or a poor one.

Always fascinated by people's values, and with a hunch that money was the problem, she established Germany's first exchange circle in the mid-1990s. *Gib & Nimm (Give & Take)* connected locals and enabled them to barter goods and services around her home town – and was also her first step towards a whole new kind of life.

Her initial idea sounded good in theory: she would offer free therapy sessions to a landlord in exchange for free room and board. In practice, of course, not many people could bear to have a live-in therapist... The second step was a housesitting offer, which sparked her big idea: to live without cash for 12 months. She sold her apartment and gave away all her possessions apart from one suitcase with a few basics in it, and from then on simply traded odd jobs from cleaning to babysitting for any tangible goods she needed.

The one-year experiment turned into 21, and Schwermer lived happily and successfully money-free until her death in 2016. In her *TedxReset* talk in 2013, Schwermer said her plan had been triggered by her outrage about the situation in the world; she asked herself, what can I as a single individual do to make the world a bit better?[26] At the beginning of her experiment, Schwermer had given away all her belongings apart from the one suitcase, and €200 which she left in a bank account for emergencies. Two decades later, when she died, those €200 remained untouched.

09

Growth from the margins:
a marketer's playbook

This is a practical chapter, a 'how to', a playbook to get you from where you are now as a marketing team to one that is willing and able to hunt for tomorrow's growth in today's marginal backwaters and fringe ways of life. Inevitably, it will be a lot about process – high on detail and diagrammatic flow. That's what you'd expect from a playbook, and that's what you'll get.

But before we immerse ourselves in all that, let's first take a breath, step back, and reflect on how we've come this far on our journey of marginal discovery through the pages of this book, and the milestones to recognize when you begin your journey as a dedicated team. Because, in the fractal nature of things, there is a resonance between the two.

Ahead of everything was *objective*. Growth. We began by observing that the ambition of soaraway growth was unlikely to be met in today's sclerotic commercial world through the typically dour struggle for market share. Meaningful innovation, instead, could come from being first to spot marginal behaviours that break through to the mainstream – the ones that feed consumer-driven disruption.

A book about marginal behaviours needs to exemplify marginal behaviours, but these were not just sitting there out in the open, waiting to be plucked. There first had to be a phase of *exploration*, one that involved a small team of researchers using diverse methods to prise out ways of life in unexpected niches. That research phase included reaching out and talking to adherents of marginal behaviours to get their perspective, understand more about their life choices, and to satisfy ourselves that the behaviours met our marginal definition set out in Chapter 3.

A fair portion of the book has involved *sharing* those marginal behaviours with you – describing them briefly or fully, in the main body of the chapter text, in the 'Notes from the margins' panels, in the overviews of our original qualitative and quantitative research methodologies, and occasionally in the captions to figures, like the one in Chapter 6 on accelerators. Overall, if we include everything through to the end of the book, we will have shared and described 42 marginal behaviours or ways of life in all. Let's briefly remind ourselves of all of them – summarized in Figure 9.1.

FIGURE 9.1   Full list of marginal behaviours (in order of where first described in the book)

Marginal behaviour	Where first described	Comments
Transhumanism	C1	
Freebirthing	C1	More fully described in C3 NFTM
Polyphasic sleeping	C1	More fully described in C5 NFTM
Homesteading	C1	
Survivalism	C1	
Living without possessions	C1	
Urophagia	C1	
Veganism	C1	Now mainstream in dilute form
Biohacking	C1 NFTM	
Insect protein	C2 NFTM	
Uniform wardrobe	C3	
No-soapers	C3	
Polyamory	C3	More fully described in C4 NFTM
Cosplay	C3	
Ice-shower converts	C3	
Neo-Luddites	C3	
Mindfulness	C3	Example of complete marginal-to-mainstream journey
Tattoos	C3	Now mainstream in the West, still marginal in some Asian cultures
Extreme frugalism	C3	More fully described in C8 NFTM
Polygamy	C3	
Off-grid living	C3	
Wicca	C3	
Voluntary celibacy	ROFP2	More fully described in C4 NFTM
Home burial	ROFP2	
Living without money	ROFP2	More fully described in C8 NFTM
Microdosing	ROFP2	More fully described in C6 NFTM
Raising kids gender-neutral	ROFP2	

(continued)

FIGURE 9.1 (Continued)

Quantified self	ROFP2	Also called lifelogging; more fully described in C7 NFTM
Ayahuasca	ROFP2	
New nomads	ROFP2	
Living off the sea	ROFP2	More fully described in C9 NFTM
Neo-tribalism	ROFP2	
Homeopathy	C4	Marginal/minority cusp in some cultures
Naturism	C4	Also called nudism; marginal/minority cusp in some cultures
Extreme carnivores	C4	
Working from home	C6	Marginal/minority cusp pre-Covid pandemic; widespread now
Homeschooling	C6	In caption to accelerators table
Prepping	C6	In caption to accelerators table
Zero wasters	C6	In caption to accelerators table
Climatarians	C6	In caption to accelerators table
Super-agers	C6	In caption to accelerators table
Nudiens	C10	Naturism subset

A description of a marginal behaviour is just that – a static snapshot of the way things are at the fringes right now. But we are interested in the likelihood that some of them might grow in popularity, to cross over to the mainstream. That, after all, is the central theme of the book. So, it is to be expected that many of its pages have been devoted to some form of *evaluation* of the marginal behaviours and ways of life we have discovered, to gain a sense of the prospects for expansion and for the commercial opportunities that come with it.

This evaluation has taken many forms. We have assessed marginal behaviours through the prism of our eight beacons, plotting them on the spectrum of resistance, probing for the possibilities of vectors, reversal and accelerators, judging the potential for reframing and mainstream-friendly elimination of frictions. We have probed some in considerable depth in our original qualitative research, and more through a broader-sample quantitative survey. Some behavioural choices – like homeopathy – have enjoyed more forensic analysis using a range of diagnostic inputs. Others have been evaluated more briefly. But for almost all, we have moved beyond mere description to get a feel for potential momentum.

So significant is this phase of evaluation that we have also developed, as outlined in the research overview to Part 3, a scale to help us prioritize the most promising behaviours of the ones we explored in our quantitative research (see Figure 9.2). The methodology is described in detail in that overview section. Essentially, it upweights prior awareness as a positive indicator, adjusts for different shades and strengths of resistance and recognizes the influencer potential of 'risk takers'.

FIGURE 9.2   Behaviours in scale order of likeliness to go mainstream for the UK and the United States

UK	United States
1. Living off the sea	1= Extreme frugalism
2. Extreme frugalism	1= New nomads
3= New nomads	3. Living off the sea
3= Voluntary celibacy	4. Quantified self
5. Quantified self	5= Polyphasic sleeping
6= Polyphasic sleeping	5= Freebirthing
6= Naturism	7= Living without money
8. Living without money	7= Neo-tribalism
9= Freebirthing	9. Neo-Luddites
9= Neo-Luddites	10. Naturism
11. Neo-tribalism	11= Raising children gender-neutral
12= Insect protein	11= Wicca
12= Home burial	11= Insect protein
14. Wicca	14. Polyamory
15. Raising children gender-neutral	15. Microdosing
16= Polyamory	16. Ayahuasca
16= Microdosing	17. Biohacking
18. Biohacking	18. Urophagia
19. Ayahuasca	
20. Urophagia	

The ranking results from a specially created scale applied to the marginal behaviours explored in the UK and US quantitative studies. The scale methodology is described in detail in the research overview to Part 3. It upweights prior awareness as a positive indicator, adjusts for different shades and strengths of resistance and takes into account the influencer significance of 'risk takers'. NB: two fewer behaviours were explored in the US quantitative study than in the UK.

Finally, in the previous chapter, we moved on to *execution,* to observe how entrepreneurs in different parts of the world are finding exciting ways to create ventures and build opportunities based on some of the marginal behaviours we have explored in the book. Importantly, we noted a fork in the road here – between direct and indirect commercialization, where the former explores possibilities in the marginal behaviour itself, while the latter uses the behaviour as a springboard to imagine possibilities in adjacent space.

So:

Objective

Exploration

Sharing

Evaluation

Execution

That is the journey you've been on as you've worked through the book thus far. That – in essence, in brief – is the spine of the process for discovering new behaviours of your own as a marketing team, and turning them into opportunity for genuine growth.

But why venture down that hard road when we have already uncovered behaviours for you, and done a fair amount of helpful evaluation? Why not simply work with one or more of those, and explore the relevance for your organization? You could. It is a start point. There is plenty there to work with.

But the ambitious marketer will want to go further, be fresher, look deeper into the culture and discover a gem of their own. Because the great thing about the margins is that they are fluid, dynamic, fertile, exciting, fast. Imagine how it will feel to be the very first to spot the entrepreneurial possibilities of a hitherto unconsidered marginal behaviour, to be an early prophet of consumer-driven disruption. If you happen to have that exceptional marketing ambition, take another breath now; then join us as we get stuck into the M2M playbook, coming up next.

The M2M playbook in overview

The process follows the flow depicted in Figure 9.3. Once the decision to embark has been made, it starts with being realistic about the overall *objective* – essentially, long-term growth.

FIGURE 9.3 A schematic view of the M2M playbook process

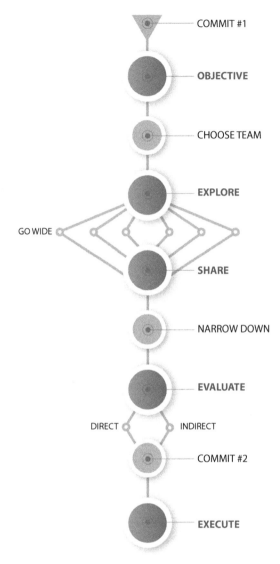

Then it's about choosing the right team – getting the balance right both numerically and functionally – to ensure the optimum mix of skills and temperaments.

That team will first come together to discuss the initiative then break up into smaller units for the *exploration* phase – the seeking out of promising marginal behaviours. This is about going wide, before narrowing down. A range of discovery techniques will be discussed when we get into the detail of the playbook.

The next step is *sharing* – where the group gets back together, and each unit shares the fruits of its exploration with the others. Inevitably, there will be some narrowing down, informally, here, through team reflection and discussion.

Evaluation is a key step in the process – and not a fast one. The aim is to probe the most promising of the behaviours for their potential to go mainstream, and to assess the commercial relevance to the organization. A range of diagnostic techniques – including questions deriving from the beacons – will be employed.

As part of that evaluation, the team will consider the potential of both direct and indirect commercialization.

With the process of evaluation complete, the team agrees on the most promising M2M candidate and develops a plan for *execution*.

That is the process in overview. Here's how it plays out in detail.

The M2M playbook in detail

Obviously, somebody needs to press the 'start' button. Somebody needs to commit. That will typically be a CMO, or a tight leadership group, determined to do things differently to ignite new growth. It is not a slight consideration since, as will now become clear, the process implies considerable investment of talent, budget and time.

Objective

Being both realistic and clear-minded about the overarching objective is crucial. Most marketers are expected to deliver both short-term and long-term brand growth as part of their corporate remit. Often there is tension between these objectives, and it is usually long-term planning that loses out, in the fight for this quarter's numbers.

An M2M strategy is about the longer term. It is about significant, sustainable growth starting 18 months to three years from when you begin the process. It is an answer to the question, 'Where are our future, sustainable returns going to come from?'

Team and time

The ideal to aim for when building the core team is a combination of agility and diversity.

Agility is best served by ensuring the numbers do not become bloated. In today's consensus-driven corporate cultures there is always the temptation to add names to the list, but this should be resisted. Aim to keep numbers to around six to eight. Above that, things start to get cumbersome, even down to basics like diary management.

Within that core group, casting is important, and you'll want to aim for the right kind of experiential, professional, and cognitive mix. Think hard about the kinds of talents you want around the table – and about temperaments, too. Ideally, there should be no obvious hierarchy within the process itself. And it has to be said that this is not an initiative to completely assign to graduates or juniors as a 'development opportunity', tempting though that often is with this kind of 'blue-sky' investigation. One or two bright young thinkers might find themselves on the team, but you'll also want some people who are at the top of their game.

What kind of disciplines do you want to see represented? It is better not to be too parochial and to think beyond your own department to include others from across the organization, or from your agencies. A typical list might look something like this:

- Marketing (brand management, research, customer experience)
- R&D, product development
- Communications (maybe agency)
- Digital (maybe agency)

But the most important element of diversity is diversity of thought. You need some mavericks and right-brain thinkers as part of the mix. Perhaps that means being comfortable with at least one person who makes you uncomfortable. In his 2019 book *Rebel Ideas: the power of diverse thinking*, Matthew Syed stresses the importance of not having too many 'clones' in a team:

> 'The critical point is that solutions to complex problems typically rely on multiple layers of insight and therefore require multiple points of view.'[1]

In terms of time, a little management of expectations will be in order. It is not a one-stop, workshop process. You should reckon on commandeering about 20 per cent of each person's diary, over a period of about three to four months. Within that there will ebbs and flows.

Exploration

Here we are talking about voyages of social discovery, going wide before narrowing down – staying open-minded and resourceful in seeking out unexpected behaviours and ways of life.

With the team thoroughly briefed and hopefully inspired by existing marginal-to-mainstream stories – veganism, mindfulness and the personal fitness revolution are all contenders – the first step is to split the party up into pairs. The idea is that each pair will first focus on a different 'big, fat area' within which they will be charged with discovering and getting to understand promising behaviours out there. The aim is to give each unit something to home in on, and, by splitting and assigning, to avoid too much overlap.

What are these 'big, fat areas'? They need not be obviously connected with your category – not at this early stage – but neither should they be so wildly at the other extreme as to have zero potential for future relevance. It is a judgement call. Here are some that you might want to consider.

Candidate 'big, fat areas'

- Health, wellbeing and looks
- Friends and social life
- Home, children and family
- Food and drink
- Self-improvement
- Work and money
- Morals and beliefs
- Travel, sport and hobbies
- Dating and sex

As well as seeking behaviours in their allotted big fat area, each team pair will also have the option to come back with a 'wild card' – with a behaviour drawn from anywhere within the panoply of human affairs – perhaps borrowing from some of the examples in this book. Either way, there are techniques and tips that will help get pairs beyond the obvious and into the more interesting and less exposed folds of life.

DISCOVERY TECHNIQUES AND TIPS

Obviously, digital search and social platforms will be a natural start point for everyone. One way to approach it is to isolate a subtopic – say, 'sleep' –

and add the term 'extreme' and see what it throws up. On social platforms, look for behaviours or actions in your area of focus that are inducing other commentators to laugh, weep or worry.

But this is a start point, no more. Sitting at a computer is unlikely to get you to places that will be much beyond the obvious. So, a good tip is to get away from the screen and engage in real life, before coming back to it when you have more specific ideas to follow up on.

Friends and contacts survey

Ask a simple question to friends, family and colleagues: 'What is the most unusual behaviour that you've seen in the area of ____?'

Mini focus group

Convene a focus group with the four most iconoclastic thinkers you know. Or choose people who have lived in other countries or cultures. Ask them to come to the group ready to talk about the most unusual behaviours they've seen – or been part of.

Prompts

- What behaviours in this area make you laugh, cry, worry?
- What are people doing now that their grandparents would never do?
- What unusual thing have you seen when travelling that you never see back home?

Get out there and observe

Go to relevant places associated with the big fat area you have been assigned. So, if it's 'health and wellbeing', head for the gym, juice bar or hospital. Observe.

Go to the area of your city that attracts the rebels, performers and mavericks. And hang out: observe.

Serendipity is your friend. Welcome it. That way, there'll be more to play with and develop when you get back to exploring online.

Keep the time tight

This doesn't want to become a long, drawn-out process or it will lose vigour from too much overthinking. Two weeks should be long enough to complete a shortlist of behaviours in your big fat area, or for your wild card, and from that to choose the ones you most look forward to sharing with the wider team.

Sharing

The sharing phase – when the group comes back together again – will inevitably involve some discussion and narrowing down of ideas. That is both natural and desirable, since it would be cumbersome to take everything through to the full evaluation phase.

But sharing, discussion and narrowing should be done in a way that gives each team pair, and each behaviour idea, the best chance of fair and equal consideration. It would be better for the process as a whole if those who happen to be most forceful or persuasive are not allowed to dominate at this early pivotal point. One way to achieve this is with a three-step process of unifying, silent reviewing ('brainwriting') and moderated reducing.

1. UNIFY THE PRESENTATION OF THE IDEAS

Ask the teams to capture the behaviours in a unified way – in writing and with no more than half a page for each to cover these points:

- What it is
- Why people do it
- Why it's on the shortlist

These summaries should be anonymized – so it is not obvious where each has come from.

2. SILENT REVIEWING

Take the first 30 minutes of the sharing session to silently and individually read through the anonymous behaviour ideas. In order to ensure everyone has the time and space to express their views, give everyone a small deck of index cards and ask them to write down a simple one- or two-line thought on each idea – including their own – then toss the cards into the middle of the table so the writer can't be easily identified.

Leigh Thompson, Professor of Management and Organizations at Kellogg School of Management calls this *brainwriting* – a simple way to take hierarchy, dominant personalities and superior persuasive skills out of reviewing ideas. Professor Thompson's research shows that in a typical six-person meeting, two people will do more than 60 per cent of the talking. Brainwriting puts a brake on that potential skew.[2]

3. MODERATED REDUCING

Have each behaviour idea ready on a poster (the moderator could do this in a break or before the session) and pin them up with the relevant review cards around them. Allow everyone time to read and think.

Aim to reduce from the overall number you have on the wall – which could be as many as nine or ten – to get down to something more manageable for the evaluation phase, maybe two or three. You'll find that some will drop out easily, without contention, while others may need more discussion. The moderator would use the individual cards to guide the discussion and reduce.

Once two, three or perhaps even four behaviour ideas are agreed upon as candidates to go forward, the phase of structured evaluation can begin.

Evaluation

There are two parts to this phase of the process, driven by two overarching questions to ask of each of the behaviours under consideration. They are:

1 *How likely is this behaviour to go mainstream?*
   In other words, could this be the next veganism, the next mindfulness, the next fitness revolution? Could we be looking at consumer-driven disruption down the line?

2 *What are the commercial possibilities for us in response to this behaviour?*
   This would involve consideration of somehow interacting with the behaviour itself (direct commercialization) or using the behaviour as a springboard for exploring ideas in adjacent space (indirect commercialization).

The astute reader will note a potential overlap between these two question-based stages of evaluation – since the commercial response itself could be one of the drivers of the movement of the behaviour towards the mainstream. For now, though, as we move onto the tasks the team will need to confront, we'll approach them separately, outlining actions, tools and techniques for each – while staying alert to the possibility for overlap at key points along the way.

Answering Evaluation Question 1:

How likely is this behaviour to go mainstream?

The way to come at this is through a series of sub-questions that derive from the eight M2M beacons, plus the 'meta-beacon' of awareness (see

Figure 9.4). Since the beacons illuminate the pathway that takes a behaviour out of the margins and into the mass, it makes sense to first focus there.

But teams need not be slavish about this. Some beacons, and some questions, will be more significant than others, for any given behaviour. Nor is there any need to proceed in a given order. So, the table of questions is not a straitjacket; it should be viewed as a series of helpful prompts that teams can work around and review, according to instinct or need.

What should emerge at the end is a more granulated understanding of the behaviour in the context of its likelihood to break through to the mainstream.

FIGURE 9.4 Questions deriving from the beacons

Beacon	Questions
Meta (awareness)	How well known is this behaviour or life choice? What kind of general population awareness of it exists right now?
Intensity	Is there a 'purist' version of the behaviour? Do current practitioners form a coherent group?
Resistance	What is the nature and strength of mainstream resistance? Where would this behaviour sit on the spectrum of resistance?
Misalignment	How likely are the arguments of devotees to inspire or persuade people from the mainstream? Do devotees and doubters 'talk past each other'?
Vectors	Are there any countercultures that have embraced the behaviour or are linked to it? Are they likely to help carry it into the mainstream?
Reframing	Is there any language associated with the behaviour that might help 'soften' resistance to it? Is language and mainstream mental framing currently a strong barrier to mass uptake or consideration?
Reversal	Is there any emerging science or new understanding that could provide the spark of ignition for resistance reversal?
Accelerators	Is there anything about this behaviour that links to a move in popular culture, or legal frameworks? Is it possible to imagine external events that might give this behaviour a massive push?
Dilution	Are people beginning to experiment with this behaviour in a 'lite' or diffuse way? Do you sense that the removal of some key frictions could open up the behaviour to a mass population?

We'll now break down the table into its constituent parts, focusing on one beacon at a time, outlining the methodologies, techniques and tips that are most likely to help for each.

Meta (awareness)	*How well known is this behaviour or life choice?* *What kind of general population awareness of it exists right now?*

The point of the questions is to get a baseline feel for how known and mentally salient the behaviour is right now – either globally, or in key countries (according to your geographical footprint). The behaviour might be practised by few but known by many – in which case it stands a better chance of gaining trial by newcomers. If it is relatively obscure, both in practice and awareness, uptake could be much slower.

With that in mind, your goal should be a fast, relatively inexpensive 'read' on awareness.

METHODOLOGY
Online quantitative survey
Online platforms like Google Surveys are a quick, cost-effective starting point for probing simple awareness and salience questions. Name the behaviour and add a brief 'what/why' description to help people get a feel for what it is and why some people engage in it.

You could also consider adding questions on how people feel about the behaviour to give you an understanding of actual or potential resistance (for later in the beacon questions).

TECHNIQUE
Consider some social listening. As a baseline, look at whether, and by how much, search on the subject has increased. Then assess the level and nature of online conversations.

TIP
Do you have any existing research studies that you could hijack? Perhaps by adding a question to your regular panel or including it in a current social listening project?

If you work for a large global company, consider putting a couple of questions on your internal communications platforms.

Intensity	Is there a 'purist' version of the behaviour? Do current practitioners form a coherent group?

Intensity can be a double-edged sword in the spread of a marginal behaviour. On the one hand, it can help keep the behaviour front of mind and give advocates the resolve to overcome frictions. On the other, for the mainstream, it can be off-putting.

One of the things that can put people off is the presence of a dogmatic 'hardcore' who insist on a 'purist' form of the behaviour; all or nothing. So, it is worth checking that out – and whether, around that nucleus, is a fuzzier element who take things less pedantically. For example, the purist ideal for zero wasters is to fit their family's entire weekly recycling into a single jam jar. Mass uptake of the behaviour is likely to be lower if people feel they have to match that ideal – but higher if they can be inspired by the fuzzier element who take recycling and waste more seriously than current norms but without succumbing to dogma.

It's also worth gauging to what extent practitioners form a coherent group, since, if they do, it may be necessary to work with them if you seek to encourage a spread of a version of the behaviour.

To come at both questions, it's worth considering the following:

METHODOLOGY

Ethnography, depth interviews

The aim is to gain some first-hand knowledge of the practitioners. You could consider bringing in a research partner or take a first pass at getting closer to the behaviour yourself. Ethnography is not fast, but it is a good way to achieve the desirable goal of 'rich description'. Essentially it would involve participant or non-participant observation of the behaviour over a period of days to weeks. You could also consider approaching a practitioner and asking for a depth interview.

TECHNIQUE

In the depth interview ask open-ended questions to encourage description of how the behaviour works in practice.

TIP

Find out about any group events and simply go along and chat to people. Ask if you can take some pictures and observe. When The Nursery (a research partner for this book) were seeking to understand more about the steampunk subculture, members of the team went along to, and took part in, steampunk events – informally chatting, observing closely, and listening carefully for language and verbal tropes.

Resistance	What is the nature and strength of mainstream resistance?
	Where would this behaviour sit on the spectrum of resistance?

Resistance is seminally important in the understanding of marginal behaviours, and any sign that it might soon vanish or fade is a signal that the behaviour could advance into the mainstream.

For any given behaviour, both the strength and the nature of the resistance need to be assessed. You'll recall from Chapter 4 that resistance is not a single, even phenomenon; some kinds are more powerful than others. In our *spectrum of resistance* from that chapter, the more viscerally felt, 'danger/disgust' reactions to the left were the ones that were more intractable and harder to shift; whereas the shades of resistance to the right of the spectrum, rooted in practicality, were more amenable to softening, in light of new information. (And the ones in between were, well, in between.)

So, the key task at this point is to plot where the behaviour under review might sit on that spectrum – and, either now or later in the process, to assess whether brand action could help move resistance ever further to the right, and open up potential for spread of the behaviour.

METHODOLOGY
Online quantitative study
This is the way to achieve the most robust data, since sample sizes can be high without addition of too much cost. You could undertake just one survey across all your shortlisted behaviours, and approach it by mirroring the 'what/why' behaviour descriptors, and battery of questions, that we used for our own quantitative surveys in this book (described fully in the research overview to Part 2).

You could give the survey an early dry run to iron out glitches by restricting version 1.0 to a sample of 'friends and family' – aiming for around 10–20 people.

TECHNIQUE
Online 'drag and drop'
In an online questionnaire, show an extended version of the *spectrum of resistance* by including further zones to the right, to embrace non-resisters

(eg those curious, willing to try, or current practitioners), as depicted in Figure 9.5. Online it is possible to give respondents a simple drag and drop device to show where they would 'land' on the spectrum, providing an instant snapshot of how they feel about the behaviour.

TIP

Explore how people feel personally about the behaviour (right/wrong for me) and also how they feel about others doing it (right/wrong for others), since this can give a feel for the strength of any resistance. Gauge resistance across different age groups. When talking informally to people, observe body language as well as verbal response.

FIGURE 9.5 'Drag and drop' spectrum for online research

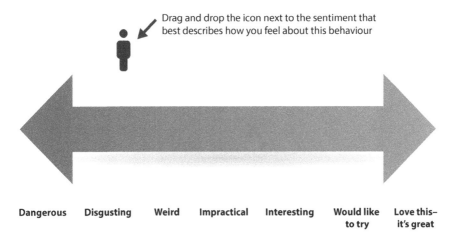

| Dangerous | Disgusting | Weird | Impractical | Interesting | Would like to try | Love this– it's great |

| Misalignment | *How likely are the arguments of devotees to inspire or persuade people from the mainstream? Do devotees and doubters 'talk past each other'?* |

Impassioned advocates of a behaviour are often very poor at communicating its virtues to the wider population – partly because they are so caught up in their own reasons for pursuing it that they fail to appreciate or even hear mainstream concerns, which could be unrelated to the aspects adherents most hold dear. Over time, the two sides can begin to 'talk past each other'.

The aim of the questions is to sense whether this kind of misaligned exchange is a feature of the discourse and whether that might present an opportunity for a third party (which could be your brand) to infiltrate, promote better understanding and thereby grow the behaviour.

METHODOLOGY
Ethnography 'lite'
Observe online communities of the behaviours, note the reasons why people do it and where the passion is. Interviews with participants: when we were researching our 'Notes from the margins' we were able to get depth interviews with devotees and simply ask them to talk about why they engaged in the behaviour and what they got out of it.

You then need to assess those impassioned 'why I do it' reasons against the 'why I don't' reasons for mainstream resistance that you will already have uncovered in your work on that beacon.

TECHNIQUE
Ask a new participant what persuaded them to take part. Ask if there was anything that nearly put them off.

TIP
Develop some hypotheses about what could better engage mainstream audiences and try them out with friends and colleagues.

Vectors	Are there any countercultures that have embraced the behaviour or are linked to it? Are they likely to help carry it into the mainstream?

Subculture and counterculture movements such as punk, hippies, goths, hipsters, steampunk and kawaii have all been significant disseminators of marginal behaviours. Group members pick them up as part of their involvement within the subculture, then help take them out into the mainstream.

The exploration of sub- or countercultures is fascinating in its own right, as they are a dynamic feature of the social landscape of influence and change. Not all marginal behaviours start out in these groupings, but it is worth exploring whether the behaviour you have under consideration is practised within one, and to get a better understanding for the potential of its adherents to become vectors.

METHODOLOGY
Desk research
The aim is to delve into and better understand current subcultures and countercultures.

TECHNIQUE

Interviews with people who practise the behaviour to understand more about the wider context of their lives – and the possibility for overlap with a subculture, counterculture or simply affinity group (like the overlap we saw in Chapter 6 between extreme carnivores and cryptocurrency enthusiasts). Once any consistent overlap is identified, switch focus to learn more about the subculture, counterculture or affinity group, and probe for the strength of any wider vector effect.

TIP

Subculture and counterculture understanding may come from academics in social science. Google Scholar is a good place to start.

Reframing	Is there any language associated with the behaviour that might help 'soften' resistance to it? Is language and mainstream mental framing currently a strong barrier to mass uptake or consideration?

As we saw with veganism, language associated with a behaviour can come with connotations that serve to deter mainstream uptake. What the veganism story also showed is that sometimes, even within the marginal behavioural group, there exists 'softer' language that could be lifted and amplified by brands keen to reframe things in consumers' minds. It was interesting to see how swiftly McDonalds reframed its 'McVegan' burger as the softer, more inclusive 'McPlant'.

Reframing is a major opportunity with contentious marginal behaviours, so it pays to be aware of verbal tropes and associations that could be imaginatively transformed to help people view things through a more positive mental frame.

METHODOLOGY

Co-operative inquiry

This is a form of research that involves breaking down the barrier between researcher and participant. In this case you would be asking practitioners to research themselves and fellow practitioners, with the brief of conducting a language and practice audit. For example, is there a spectrum of language from 'hardcore' to 'softer'? Are there less impassioned participants who talk about the behaviour in a different way?

NB: This methodology could also help with some of the other beacons. It lends itself well to behaviours where there is a grouping – like new nomads, Wicca, or cosplay.

TIP

Simply try and reframe the behaviour or associated concepts yourself – as we did in Chapter 5 when we explored 'original protein' as an alternative way to think about eating insects. Try your ideas out on mainstream colleagues.

Reversal	Is there any emerging science or new understanding that could provide the spark of ignition for resistance reversal?

You'll recall from Chapter 7 that reversal isn't always a feature of an M2M journey – but that when it does occur, progress can get suddenly swift. This is because the force of resistance doesn't merely fade or disappear but switches sides to become a positive driver of the behaviour.

You need to be on the lookout for new science or understanding that could be the *spark of ignition* that propels that sudden switch.

METHODOLOGY

Desk research

The first thing to do is to make sure you know what the primary resistance factor is, so check back on your resistance research. Then look for new scientific, technological or cultural understanding that could provide the spark of ignition for reversal. Again, Google Scholar is a good place to start, exploring new academic research into the subject. Relevant lifestyle or cultural changes might be found in trends research reports.

TECHNIQUE

Ask your own innovation team for latest relevant understanding.

TIP

Come at it the other way. Imagine what the spark of ignition would have to be to propel a full-scale resistance reversal, then look for emerging evidence.

Accelerators	Is there anything about this behaviour that links to a move in popular culture, or legal frameworks? Is it possible to imagine external events that might give this behaviour a massive push?

Accelerators can be hugely important in the abrupt mass uptake of marginal behaviours – yet, by their very nature, they can be hard to predict. Disruptive global events – such as the Covid pandemic – invariably blindside almost everyone, springing up by surprise, even though they may then look more inevitable with hindsight.

That said, a 'what if', 'wargaming' approach is still viable, imagining broad geopolitical or environmental outcomes, probing for their likelihood, and determining what they might mean for uptake of the behaviour. And it is also possible to look for 'crystallization moments', when longstanding cultural, demographic, environmental or legal issues burst through to create some kind of meaningful popular shift. Either way, the framework towards the end of the section on accelerators in Chapter 6 will offer some structured guidance.

METHODOLOGY
Desk research
Monitor commentary on burgeoning cultural, environmental, medical and legal issues.

Check think tanks and policy research for forthcoming legislation.

TECHNIQUE
Try a 'self-brainstorm'. You don't always need a group to come up with good ideas; you can do it yourself with some time and alternative ways of thinking. Ask yourself: What would need to be true for this to massively take off? How likely is that to happen?

TIP
Simply checking macro demographic trends can be an eye-opener.

Dilution	*Are people beginning to experiment with this behaviour in a 'lite' or diffuse way? Do you sense that the removal of some key frictions could open up the behaviour to a mass population?*

If the behaviour has arrived at, or is on the threshold of, the beacon of dilution, then its spread into the mainstream is now more likely than not. At this point, people outside the hardcore are already experimenting with it, adapting it in new ways, and maybe finding 'workarounds' for any frictions they happen to encounter. Resistance hasn't been completely overcome – there will still be those who have their doubts – but the appeal of some form of the behaviour is seeping through to more new recruits.

This is one of those points on the pathway where overlap between organic growth and brand action is definitely a consideration. The thing that might stop it breaking right through could be frictions – cost, inconvenience, social awkwardness – and innovation or brand action could be key in overcoming these. If it is not your brand or business that achieves that, it may end up being one of your competitors. So, the assessment of frictions is key here.

METHODOLOGY

Ethnography, depth interviews

Can you develop a typology of practitioners? Are there already people doing it in a more 'dilute' way – less often, less 'properly', with lower intensity?

Ethnography is going to help again here, as will interviews with a broad cross-section of practitioners.

TECHNIQUE

Can you identify the frictions that might stop people adopting the behaviour and, either now or later in the process, brainstorm ways to overcome them?

TIP

If you see people adapting some kind of 'workaround' to help overcome a friction associated with the behaviour, it is a perfect hint that innovation would be massively welcomed. This is one of the ways entrepreneurs sense that an untapped market is out there.

What the team will have at the end of this process is a more granulated understanding of the behaviour and a better idea of its likelihood to break through into the mainstream and ignite consumer-driven disruption.

Nevertheless, it is still a judgement call. There is no algorithm to tell you with certainty what the future trajectory of the behaviour will be. That said, there are three simple principles to take into account.

1 Higher awareness equals higher likelihood of breakthrough.

2 The position of the behaviour on the spectrum of resistance is a critical diagnostic input; the further to the right, the better.

3 If you have evidence that the behaviour shows signs of arriving at the beacon of dilution, breakthrough is likely, and speed is of the essence.

Answering Evaluation Question 2:

What are the commercial possibilities for us in response to this behaviour?

There are two aspects to this question: direct and indirect commercial potential. We'll take them in that order.

DIRECT POTENTIAL

The beacon questions will have helped the team narrow down from perhaps three or four behaviours to land on the one that looks to have the most promising trajectory for growth. The task now is to probe that behaviour for its relevance to your category and for the prospects for direct commercial involvement – where the business finds ways to engage with the behaviour itself, for the benefit of all.

That starts with bringing the team back together for a deep-dive session to imagine what those possibilities for commercialization might be. At the start of that session, it is vital to give yourself as much flexibility and breathing space as possible through the discipline of 'expansive definition'.

First, define the category the business is in as broadly as possible. So, a financial services brand might define itself as a 'partner working with money to enable life options and possibilities'. This helps prevent ideas for products, services and interaction with the behaviour getting too constrained.

Second, do the same thing with the behaviour itself. Define it generously, giving it as broad a canvas as credibly possible. Veganism, for example, tended to be viewed strictly through the lens of diet, even as the movement took off. But we know that committed vegans shun animal-derived materials in many other aspects of life, from furniture to footwear, so veganism could have inspired – and still could inspire – innovations way outside just those related to food and drink.

Combined, this exercise in expansive definition will offer a greater area of overlap between organizational capability and candidate behaviour for the business to explore.

Once the team has agreed definitions, the next step is to embark on a brainstorming session that seeks to find a sweet spot between what the business could credibly innovate or offer and what the growing band of practitioners of the behaviour might want or need. As with all good marketing, the aim is mutual benefit.

Obviously, the precise way these brainstorms might unfold would vary considerably by broad category: the detail and the challenges would differ between, say, a technology brand and a refreshment brand. They will also differ according to the precise nature of behaviour under review. But at a higher, general, level there are three important prompts that can guide, shape and invigorate the conversation. They are:

1   How can we bring the benefits of this behaviour to more people?
    Those who practise the behaviour may still be relatively few in number, but they clearly get something important out of it. There are many shades to what those benefits might be – emotional, practical, communitarian, symbolic, health-giving, life-affirming, planet-protecting – or simply just fun. The task of the business, then, is to build a bridge to carry one or more of these benefits across to a mainstream population.

2   How can we eliminate or reduce the frictions associated with this behaviour? Can we reduce cost? Can we offer more convenient distribution? Can we innovate products and services that might be less perfectly designed for the hardcore devotees but more suitable for mainstream dabblers? Are there 'workarounds' that people are doing now, that we could neatly resolve? Can our communications serve to 'normalize' the behaviour and help people feel freer and more confident to try it?
    Frictions are often one of the big drawbacks about marginal behaviours and prizes will go to businesses and brands that overcome them. The team will need to be imaginative, though: if these frictions were simple to smooth away, others would have already got there first.

3   How can our capability, expertise and skills best interact with this behaviour?
    If the first prompt was consumer focused, and the second anchored in problems to resolve, this one comes the other way around and starts with the organization itself. It can be approached by first asking, 'What are we really good at?', then moving on to 'How could that special capability interact with this behaviour?' As always, the addendum would be '…to the benefit of all'.

With these three prompts as the heartbeat, it should be a lively session. It can be a thrill to look at the possibilities of a burgeoning behaviour and either slowly or with a sudden burst of brilliance imagine a daring innovation or route to market that is, at once, both outside the normal scope of the business and yet still connected to it. Growth suddenly seems not a grinding slog but a more tangible and proximate possibility.

But the team hasn't finished yet. Such is the plasticity of marginal behaviours and ways of life that there is a second way to gain inspiration from them in marketing's eternal quest for growth: indirect potential, coming up next.

INDIRECT POTENTIAL

This is where the business does not, or cannot, interact with the marginal behaviour itself, but reflects on it as inspiration for activity in adjacent – or even distant – market space. An important nuance is that it can apply even where the behaviour itself is not destined to achieve mass uptake – so opens up possibilities for shortlisted behaviours where the team is less convinced of the likelihood of a full M2M journey.

For the team session, indirect potential is approached by considering a big, open-ended question:

What is this behaviour telling us?

Think back to the example we looked at in Chapter 8, where home burial was simply too impractical for most people to actively embrace. But the fact that some were doing it or contemplating it, despite its unusualness, tells us something important – that people yearn for a more personalized experience than those they currently find within the deathcare category. We saw that entrepreneurs were already stepping into that void offering imaginative new options to help people honour and remember recently deceased loved ones.

In a way, that is a relatively simplistic example, since it takes place within the same broad category. But behavioural inspiration can be more encompassing than that, to cross from one aspect of life, and one commercial category, to another. To discover these possibilities, teams need to be supple in their thinking, and be ready to consider how the behaviour might *intersect* with other elements of the cultural zeitgeist.

As an example here, let's revisit one of the behavioural byways that we have touched on a few times in this book: uniform wardrobe, where people elect to wear the same thing every day. If your sphere of business happens to embrace clothing or fashion retail, that might have an obvious, direct relevance. But what about for businesses in other sectors? What could the behaviour be telling them?

At a base level, it signals that decision fatigue is a genuine phenomenon, such that some will go to the extreme of severely limiting their look. And in fact, the stress of decision making induced by an overabundance of choice in the modern world is well documented in the social and behavioural sciences. That, alone, may be enough to make brands in unrelated sectors think about editing ranges and appealing more by offering less.

But add in an *intersection*, and it gets more interesting. For many people, environmental concerns are becoming an ever more pressing factor in consumption decisions. It's not hard to see that sustainability and choice are related. When manufacturers make fewer versions of things, the result is more efficient production and less waste. So now, at the intersection of 'decision fatigue' and 'environmental concern' you have the potential to pioneer something as brave and trenchant as 'The low-choice economy', which could become a rallying call for brands in multiple sectors (as represented in Figure 9.6).

FIGURE 9.6 The concept of intersection

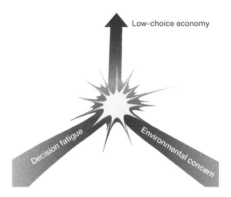

Intersection occurs at the confluence of two motivators that relate to the same marginal behaviour, giving it renewed power to transfer more broadly to other realms of life and other commercial sectors.

In this case, the behaviour of 'uniform wardrobe' is interpreted as indicative of the presence of decision fatigue, where people become overwhelmed by the superabundance of choice in the modern world. On its own, decision fatigue may not prompt significant social change, but it collides with another motivator – concern about the environment – since superabundance of choice is inefficient, overconsumes resources and creates waste. Together, these two motivators combine to propel a social and organizational movement – 'The low-choice economy', which can be relevant to multiple sectors.

'What is this behaviour telling us?' is a penetrating, deeply revealing question, one that marketers should be asking even if a full-scale, long-term M2M initiative is beyond their current resources. If approached with imagination, and combined with the technique of intersection, it can be a deceptively powerful way to open up new paths to growth.

Go or no-go

We have arrived at the point on the roadmap in Figure 9.3 marked 'Commit #2'. The most promising combination of behaviour and idea for commercially engaging with it has emerged and been agreed by the team. It is now a question of 'go' or 'no-go'. If the answer is the latter, effort need not be considered wasted; looking to the margins will undoubtedly have broadened the mindset of the team and will pay dividends in small ways down the line. If the decision is 'go', then the final step on the journey is a credible plan for execution.

Execution

It is abundantly clear that the optimum route to execution will vary considerably according to a whole suite of particulars: category, geography, investment ambition, whether the innovation is a product or service or both, whether it's B2C or B2B or both, and the general appetite of the corporation behind it for risk.

And there will be risk. So, some form of validation of the team's brave new idea will normally be an intermediate step. CEOs may call for their senior managers to be more entrepreneurial, but few would be comfortable with the 'ready, fire, aim' approach of the true entrepreneur.

Validation might involve classic concept testing, experiments, or A/B testing if the product or service idea is digitally led. Once confidence of success is at the required level, there are four broad execution options that the leadership team might go on to consider.

1 Test market
   Launch into a test market or region – where you are most likely to learn how the mass market might evolve. Think about where the regulatory, legal or cultural environment might be easier to work with.

2 Slow burn
   Treat it like a corporate side-hustle: minimal investment but with a constant eye on the opportunity and some low-key experimental launches.

3 All-in
   Go for it like a start-up, maximum investment, full dedicated team.

4 Acquisition
   Look for a company to buy (or partner with) that is already operating in the space.

We have reached the end of the M2M playbook. But of course, for marketers who do get this far and launch something truly innovative into the world, it is more like a beginning – the start of a journey in which the brand, the business and the behaviour all grow together, reciprocally, for the benefit of all. That is the aim. And, for all the detail planning it will have involved, for all the doggedness of spirit it will have taken, it is an exciting one. Let's never lose sight of that.

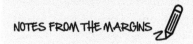

NOTES FROM THE MARGINS

Living off the sea

Vegans must feel pretty good about themselves, doing their bit for the planet by sticking to a plant-based diet. A kelp-preneur, however, would argue that there's still an environmental price to pay for growing the vegetables, pulses, legumes and nuts in their diet, all of which use vast tracts of agricultural land, require fresh water for irrigation, fuel to power harvesting machines and transport crops, and so on.

Kelp is a 'zero input' crop, growing naturally in coastal waters so needing no land clearing, sowing or maintenance. In huge kelp forests, the rootless crop simply attaches itself to rocks on the sea floor. Once it's farmed, it quickly starts to re-grow at a phenomenal rate of around two feet a day and up to a height of around 250ft.

In powder form kelp is already used as a superfood supplement in smoothies, as it's rich in iodine, calcium and vitamin C, and one of its 30 varieties, kombu, is used widely in Japan where it's the key ingredient in dashi broth.

Here comes the science: the high level of antioxidants in kelp, including carotenoids and flavonoids, fight against disease-causing free radicals, and minerals such as manganese and zinc help combat oxidative stress (a plus in the fight against cardiovascular disease and cancer).

What's happening out on the margins is even more interesting though, as leading-edge eco-minded producers are using kelp to create food products rich in nutrients and umami, positioning it as a low environmental impact ingredient which also happens to be incredibly good for you.

Courtney Boyd Myers' Maine-based company AKUA hopes to push 'climate cuisine' into the big time while becoming the key driver in the nascent industry, trusting that 21st-century customers now want to add environmental considerations to their usual food purchasing decisions related to price, taste, nutrition and even advertising.

Sometimes rebranded as sea greens, AKUA is now manufacturing and marketing kelp in snack jerky and as burger patties, and is promoting the new products hard on social media where they hope to find early adopters and influencers.

Testimonials on their website kick off with the disruptor king, Sir Richard Branson, whose message says: 'I was prepared to come up with a nice response after eating this, but actually it's really rather delightful. It's incredibly delicious. Well done.'[3]

The second environmental tick is that kelp farming at scale could shoulder some of the pressure on the fishing industry, who have to balance sustainable fishing while maintaining income. Fishermen could become 'ocean gardeners' and for that the rewards could be good for everyone... the non-profit World Resources Institute claim that every $1 invested in ocean sustainability generates $5 of benefit to the planet.[4]

It tastes good and does no harm. Can a crop that's growing quietly in the ocean really be the win-win it sounds like, and make it from the margins to the middle of the food page?

10

The M2M advantage: seven things every leader should know

1. Your marketers are doing great, but face an uphill battle

Marketers know what is expected of them. It comes down to a single word: growth. At the 2022 Festival of Marketing, held live and online in front of a huge, post-pandemic audience, Diageo CMO Cristina Diezhandino summed it up with a searing blend of precision and passion: 'Growth is at the heart of all we do'.

It is. And to achieve it, marketers continue to hone their skills in product and service improvement, communications, customer acquisition and retention, brand experience, and emotional consumer connection to keep market share buoyant and competitors at bay.

But it can be a war of attrition out there. Incremental gains are often all that is realistically possible, within categories that are, themselves, flat or characterized by anaemic growth. The forces constraining marketing room for manoeuvre are the ones we laid out in Chapter 2: structural factors that promote unhelpful convergence between brands, a pressure to prioritize lateral innovation to hit short-term targets, and a dearth of macro invention on which all business endeavour depends.

The outcome is that big, scalable, sustainable growth is an ideal more often discussed than delivered. The meaningful innovation needed to achieve it seems ever just beyond the grasp, a kind of tantalizing conceptual nirvana.

Where should marketers look for that category-busting innovation? Maybe the place they always have – consumers themselves – but in a way that puts distance between their brands and those of competitors. That new locus is at the margins of human behaviour because there, as we have shown, lies the potential for the kind of explosive, tumultuous growth for those who see it and act on it first.

As Nike founder Phil Knight observed: 'If Nike didn't start the fitness revolution, we were at least right there – and we sure rode it for one hell of a ride'.[1] What had started as a few eccentrics jogging on the sidewalk turned into a worldwide fitness and exercise phenomenon. Growth can be found in seemingly unlikely grooves, and it can be ridden. If your marketers are alive to that possibility, they are indeed doing great.

2. There are many forms of disruption, but consumer-driven is the one to watch out for

In 1995 the late Clayton Christensen introduced the term 'disruptive innovation' in a landmark academic paper, and business leaders have fixated on it since.[2] The term was originally confined to the difference between incremental innovation, which improves products and services along a continued trajectory, and innovation that cuts across and undermines the current paradigm, often doing it in a way that drastically reduces costs, market prices and therefore profitability.

'Disrupt or be disrupted' has since become a management mantra, as businesses seek ways of monitoring the invention horizon for threats and developing bold innovations of their own – though usually without reference to Christensen's concept of price and profit restraint.

Some leaders take their source of inspiration back further, to Joseph Schumpeter, with his term 'creative destruction', coined in 1942 to describe the incessant mechanism of product and process innovation that he considered 'the essential fact about capitalism'.[3]

What these concepts have in common is that they see disruption as a supply-side phenomenon. It is about the swingeing changes that industry can conjure, mediated usually by new technology or process inventions that get leveraged at scale.

But there is another kind, and an equally powerful one, that comes in the other direction, from the demand side of the equation: consumer-driven disruption. This is when markets get overhauled through sudden new forces of collective consumer preference – where waves that started as ripples crash onto commercial shores and carve out a changed landscape of corporate winners and losers.

Those early ripples can be seen in marginal behaviours and ways of life. We saw it with veganism, with mindfulness, with tattoos, with personal fitness. Not all ripples will be destined to swell, but some will, and conditions today are such that what once took decades now happens with violent suddenness. Digital media, especially video, has massively increased awareness of fringe behaviours; social connectivity gives swift cohesion to movements that would once have been atomized; and the biggest generation in history is emerging into adulthood with the greatest ever openness to new ideas.

Prizes will go to those businesses that sense the swell early, that read the currents and the cultural weather that propels them with greater clarity than their rivals. Prediction is always precarious, but we do not have to resort to the mysterious methods of so-called futurologists to attempt it. A structured approach is possible, and the ambition at the core of this book has been to set one out. Consumer-driven disruption need not take us by surprise.

3. The entrepreneurial mindset is alive and well in organizations, but it needs support

Chief executives of large organizations are frequently given to pleading for their senior managers to be 'more entrepreneurial', occasionally going further to enjoin them to 'think like a start-up'. Frustrated by the sclerotic processes that slow down the pursuit of exciting new routes to growth, they seemingly throw caution to the wind in an effort to shake things up through the byzantine layers of the corporate hierarchy.

In reality, the tolerance for risk within a big, publicly quoted corporation is vastly different from that of, say, a founding duo in a start-up venture with nothing much to lose. Do CEOs really wish for their teams to eschew objectives, prioritize action over understanding to the extent of launching ahead of consumer research and embrace the full entrepreneurial mindset and all the chaos that can accompany it?

Perhaps not. But they are right that the teams below them can be faster, more fluid and more imaginative in how they seek growth. And marketers, with their relatively light attachment to corporate fixed assets, and their antennae tuned to the wavelengths of changing societies, are the layer within that organizational structure best able to bring the spirit of entrepreneurship to what they do.

Some have already started. Marc Pritchard, Chief Brand Officer at Procter & Gamble, launched his 'GrowthWorks' programme into the CPG behemoth's culture in 2019, with the objective of getting every P&G brand team to think and act like a start-up. As he told it in a 2021 interview with The

Drum, 'We studied the start-up world and adopted the principle of lean innovation'.[4]

An M2M approach is both dependent on, and an encourager of, this more flexible start-up mentality. Seeking growth from unlikely and even unpromising behavioural niches is, by its very nature, a more entrepreneurial endeavour than the standard marketing practice of carefully working backwards from known consumer needs. It forces teams to step aside from the one-way mirrors of their normal research settings and engage with people – many of them non-customers of the category – in completely new ways and for more ambitious ends.

Riding the elevators of even the most conservative corporations are the kind of open-minded people who can do it, and who would relish the challenge. The best thing the corporation can do is get out of its own way – and theirs – by loosening the reins of alignment, lowering the hurdles of approval for certain exploratory activities and clearing a simpler route through some of the more paranoid routine checks and balances.

The entrepreneurial mindset is alive in the organizational world. It's the leadership mindset that might most need changing.

4. Your diversity and inclusion strategy is doing good things for your organization, but it could do more

In 2018, a Boston Consulting Group study reported that companies with more diverse management teams have 19 per cent higher revenues that can be directly linked to innovation.[5] The combination of different ethnicities, backgrounds and genders reduces the tendency to groupthink and improves the quality of decision making. In the quest for breakthrough innovation, it's not hard to see that homogeneity is an enemy.

That is an internal perspective, but diversity transmits an external narrative, too. In his 2022 book, *Inclusive Marketing*, Jerry Daykin quotes an ANA study showing that 'progressive' ads – those that reflect cultural diversity without falling prey to stereotyping – increase purchase intent by 42 per cent and drive a 56 per cent improvement in brand reputation.[6]

Could your current diversity and inclusion programmes go further? Some organizations are moving beyond the baseline gender, ethnicity and sexual orientation aspects of inclusion to actively embrace hardwired cognitive differences, recruiting people on the autistic spectrum or those with ADHD.

An M2M strategy both thrives upon and reinforces this kind of broad-based organizational diversity. The more varied the internal culture, the more life experiences there will be to draw on – some from unexpected quarters where behavioural norms are way out of kilter with the repertoire found within the mainstream. The more varied, supple and even challenging cognition patterns are, the more your employees will be able to imagine connections between organizational capability and these unorthodox, but possibly burgeoning, fringe ways of life.

Diversity and inclusion are a 'must have' for today's corporations. But taking it further, and intertwining it with internal programmes that look to today's margins for tomorrow's growth, can turn an imperative into an edge.

5. Throughout the M2M journey, the originators deserve respect

When a marginal behaviour captures the popular imagination and bursts through in some form to the mainstream, it can be easy to lose sight of the pioneers who started it all. And those originators – the hardliners perhaps, who have always thought it right to do things a certain way – can come to resent the general uptake of what once was theirs. In part that will be because the mainstream tends to bend the rules somewhat, doing things in a more diffuse and unapproved way.

We saw that brooding resentment as early on as Chapter 1, where committed, long-term vegans would be scornful of those who dipped in and out of only the dietary aspects, and did not see the movement as a way of life embracing many other facets of consumption.

Brand owners that have alighted on the fresh enthusiasm of the mass for a given behaviour tend to focus all efforts and communications on the new crowd. Up to a point this is understandable – because the mainstream is where the numbers are.

But taken too far it is an error. The originators deserve recognition and respect, for two reasons. The first is unrelated to commercial considerations. Of course, it is right to celebrate and salute those who have had the courage, foresight and resolve to get something going that might once have been held up to ridicule, or worse. We are talking here of simple courtesy.

The second reason brings us back to a truth about growth. It cannot always be attained by venturing ever outwards from a core ideal. To simply follow a behavioural or consumption path where consumers lead it is to be prey to the sin of offering the ersatz. Keeping close to the originators, giving them more attention than might be justified by commercial size alone, will help keep the mainstream version of what you are bringing to market more authentic. It is not, to be fair, an easy balance to strike. But start with respect and it gets a little easier to sense when you have strayed too far.

6. Business succeeds when it improves lives. An M2M approach is one way to achieve that

Businesspeople, and marketers especially, are given to talking about 'adding value' through the endeavours of the organization and what it brings to market. It's one of those all-purpose terms that straddles the transactional divide, with applicability to the business itself – adding financial value – and to the recipient – adding some kind of value to a given consumption choice.

But business success, and marketing practice, are best served when the causal arrow runs backwards, with exploration of the value to the consumer coming first, and the potential value to the business coming later. The fundamental question at the heart of business decision making should be: 'What are we doing to bring new and exceptional value to people's lives?'

The new and exceptional value that an M2M approach can bring lies in the opening up of possibilities. The linear lives of yesterday – school, college, military, marriage, career, retirement – have given way to something more fluid, organic and potentially far more satisfying. The opportunities to try new things and new ways of being are greater than ever before. Hiding in the margins of society are fizzy new ideas that could enrich today's lives, if only more people knew about them or could find easier ways to engage with them.

Business can help facilitate that. It can step into a space where people might be glad to try something they are not yet asking for. It can inspire experimentation, make the obscure more accessible, and smooth away tiresome frictions. An M2M approach is about opening up – lives, futures, possibilities. That is something of real value to a broad mass of people, and one way or another, they will reward you for it.

7. The M2M advantage is multifactorial

This book has faced into the challenge of growth and argued that a marginal-to-mainstream strategy can help generate it. Instead of slugging it out in hand-to-hand combat for more share within mature markets, attention is turned to fringe ways of life and unorthodox consumption patterns where the returns may be small right now but are apt to surge later. It is an unconventional route to capitalism's conventional goal.

That goal is growth, and when you deploy the word in a business context the most natural interpretation is the financial one. But there are other kinds that a well-executed M2M approach can foster: a growth in human understanding, a surge in team fulfilment, a boost to innovation prowess. In part that is because there is so much about looking to the margins that runs counter to the usual business norms. It is stimulating and exciting, in a world where much of the business of bringing goods and services to market has become routinized and cautious.

But let us not shirk from that first, most natural, meaning of that pivotal capitalist word. An M2M strategy would not be worth the risk and investment of resources if it were it not for the prospect of straightforward dollar gains – of a maintainable upward curve in the corporation's revenues and the value of its brands.

Given that ambition, a more sobering challenge arises from the school of thought that questions the entire precept of economic growth, arguing that it is incompatible with environmental sustainability. It is an insistent mantra emanating from pressure groups and publicly funded bodies alike. In a 2021 European Environmental Agency report, the authors start by acknowledging that economic growth is 'culturally, politically and institutionally ingrained', only to then refer to these truths as 'challenges' to be overcome in the quest for change.[7] It is sustainability that must win through, at economic growth's expense.

But need these ends be so rigidly juxtaposed? The M2M approach offers glimpses into why the zero-sum argument may be simplistic. An interesting observation about the marginal behaviours considered within this book is how many have an environmental rationale as either a primary or secondary motivator: veganism, climatarianism, eating insects, uniform wardrobe, no-soapers, living off the sea, zero wasters. Clearly, businesses that work with the groupings at these exotic points on the cultural compass will be doing more to grow the behaviours found there and to disseminate the sustainability aspects that are part of them.

Even advocates of behaviours further removed from obvious environmental themes are looking inwards to ruminate on their sustainability impact. In a 2022 Spectator article, the British author Jonathan Miller reports on a naturist subset cult in France called *les nudiens*, which seeks to normalize nudity in all public places, motivated 'not by health or sport but by ecology'.[8]

If the shedding of clothes is seen as a means of reducing the ecological harms of sartorial overconsumption, it is one that will be more practical in Lyon in June than it is in Boston in January. Prospects for emulation are not high, although you never know. But the point is that even where uptake remains modest, marginal groups, and smaller cults embedded within them, are spreading an awareness of sustainable considerations that outpunches their size. Business would do well to stay close and take heed.

That will still leave business looking for an answer to the much cruder 'consume less' dogma that is emerging from environmental congresses such as that of Glasgow's COP26. This blunt, oft repeated two-worder appears to leave little room for negotiation. Taken literally, it implies a wholesale decimation of commercial interaction, with all the consequent economic pain, reduction of the tax base and impact on public service funding.

The answer for business is surely to preach the gospel of 'consume better' – for both sides of the transactional divide to think harder about the broader implications of everyday production, acquisition and disposal. Or for there to be no divide – but instead for a process of co-creation with consumers to be encouraged, with the objective of working through new ideas to achieve both the goods and the good environmental outcomes that everybody craves.

It is axiomatic that these ideas will not be forthcoming through conversations conducted by the usual researchers in the usual focus group settings viewed by the usual corporate attendees. Outreach will have to be more imaginative and more daring than that, seeking out the mavericks and ideas makers who have the suppleness of thought and the strength of character to challenge the current paradigms – and those people are not likely to be found within the current mainstream flow of society.

There are some corporate leaders who get this intuitively, but not many. That is not to boast that the authorial and research teams behind this book got there at the outset, as a matter of judgement or prediction. One of the satisfactions of working with people at the behavioural margins during the writing of these pages has been the serendipity of coming across a rare blend of eloquence, intelligence and defiance within the consumption discourse. From homesteaders to home schoolers, from zero wasters to no-soapers, from polyamorists to polyphasic sleepers, the level of insight has been high and the passion and polemical themes deep.

That is a further reason why marketers should spend a part of their research budgets reaching out to the fringes of society and engaging with the behaviours and beliefs of the people they find there, no matter how removed they might seem from the brand and the category. They will discover, as we did, that the margins are not just fascinating and fertile, not just iconoclastic and original, but are the seedbed of bold ideas that will make for a better kind of growth and a better kind of world.

ENDNOTES

Chapter 1: From 'Does *anyone* do that?'
to 'Doesn't everyone do that?'

[1] Forbes (n.d.) High-end Vegan [Online] Available at: https://www.forbes.com/pictures/ehlk45jhll/high-end-vegan/?sh=4b5f30604df4 (archived at https://perma.cc/8A5X-LL4U) [Accessed 12 September 2022]

[2] Vegan Society. Available at: https://www.vegansociety.com/whats-new/news/find-out-how-many-vegans-there-are-great-britain (archived at https://perma.cc/7CCT-KV5V) [Accessed 3 May 2022]

[3] Hancox, D (2018) The unstoppable rise of veganism: how a fringe movement went mainstream, The Guardian, 1 April. Available at: https://www.theguardian.com/lifeandstyle/2018/apr/01/vegans-are-coming-millennials-health-climate-change-animal-welfare (archived at https://perma.cc/U5YH-QPAY) [Accessed 12 September 2022]

[4] Vegan Society. Available at: https://www.vegansociety.com/about-us/history (archived at https://perma.cc/9CZ4-UMSX) [Accessed 3 May 2022]

[5] Vegan Society (2014) Ripened by human determination [Online] Available at: https://www.vegansociety.com/sites/default/files/uploads/Ripened%20by%20human%20determination.pdf (archived at https://perma.cc/FR3A-2SCP), p 4 [Accessed 12 September 2022]

[6] Vegan Society (2014) Ripened by human determination [online] Available at: https://www.vegansociety.com/sites/default/files/uploads/Ripened%20by%20human%20determination.pdf (archived at https://perma.cc/FR3A-2SCP) [Accessed 12 September 2022]

[7] Vegan Society (2014) Ripened by human determination [online] Available at: https://www.vegansociety.com/sites/default/files/uploads/Ripened%20by%20human%20determination.pdf (archived at https://perma.cc/FR3A-2SCP) [Accessed 12 September 2022]

[8] Information on the US vegan society was found from this source: Vegan Society. (2014) Ripened by human determination [Online] Available at: https://www.vegansociety.com/sites/default/files/uploads/Ripened%20by%20human%20determination.pdf (archived at https://perma.cc/FR3A-2SCP). Information on the German vegan society came from this source: Vegan Society (1953). Deutsche Vegan-Gesellschaft. The Vegan, p 24. Information on the Indian vegan society came from this source: www.vgan.in. (n.d.). Satvik Vegan Society (formerly Indian Vegan Society) - More About Us [Online] Available at: http://www.vgan.in/about_us (archived at https://perma.cc/3XEA-ECMP) [All sources last accessed 12 September 2022]

[9]   Plamil Foods. Available at: https://www.plamilfoods.co.uk/about (archived at https://perma.cc/VP5V-6VDE) [Accessed 3 May 2022]

[10]   Tancock, K (2015) Vegan cuisine moves into the mainstream, Globe & Mail, 13 January. Available at: https://www.theglobeandmail.com/life/food-and-wine/food-trends/vegan-cuisine-moves-into-the-mainstream/article22430440/ (archived at https://perma.cc/LTZ2-T9U2) [Accessed 3 May 2022]

[11]   Russell, P (2020) The seeds of veganism, FT Magazine, 17 January [Accessed 12 September 2022]

[12]   Anarchist Library. Available at: https://theanarchistlibrary.org/library/len-tilburger-and-chris-p-kale-nailing-descartes-to-the-wall-animal-rights-veganism-and-punk-cu (archived at https://perma.cc/A8T3-8SYN)

[13]   Anarchist Library. Available at: https://theanarchistlibrary.org/library/len-tilburger-and-chris-p-kale-nailing-descartes-to-the-wall-animal-rights-veganism-and-punk-cu (archived at https://perma.cc/A8T3-8SYN)

[14]   Economist (2018) Why people in rich countries are eating more vegan food, 11 October. Available at: https://www.economist.com/briefing/2018/10/13/why-people-in-rich-countries-are-eating-more-vegan-food (archived at https://perma.cc/EA57-KCN5) [Accessed 3 May 2022]

[15]   Peters, A (2019) Think fake burgers are just for vegetarians? (18 September) Available at: https://www.fastcompany.com/90396177/think-fake-burgers-are-just-for-vegetarians-95-of-impossible-foods-customers-are-meat-eaters (archived at https://perma.cc/DLG8-KKUN) [Accessed 3 May 2022]

[16]   Hancox, D (2018) The unstoppable rise of veganism: how a fringe movement went mainstream, The Guardian, 1 April. Available at: https://www.theguardian.com/lifeandstyle/2018/apr/01/vegans-are-coming-millennials-health-climate-change-animal-welfare (archived at https://perma.cc/U5YH-QPAY) [Accessed 12 September 2022]

[17]   Business Wire (2016) Available at: https://www.businesswire.com/news/home/20161115005674/en/Global-Packaged-Vegan-Foods-Market-to-Grow-at-a-CAGR-of-11-Through-2020-Reports-Technavio (archived at https://perma.cc/TYQ7-W2CF) [Accessed 21 June 2022]

[18]   Norwood, F (2022) 1 in 10 Americans say they don't eat meat, The Conversation, 1 March. Available at: https://theconversation.com/1-in-10-americans-say-they-dont-eat-meat-a-growing-share-of-the-population-176948 (archived at https://perma.cc/TAT4-LSDX) [Accessed 21 June 2022]

[19]   Statista (2022) Canadian willingness to reduce meat consumption 2020. Available at: https://www.statista.com/statistics/937738/consumer-attitudes-towards-reducing-meat-consumption/ (archived at https://perma.cc/ZZ2J-JW74) [Accessed 19 June 2022]

[20]   Vegan Society. Available at: https://www.vegansociety.com/news/market-insights/dairy-alternative-market/european-plant-milk-market/uk-plant-milk-market#:~:text=The%20UK%20has%20a%20strong,between%20the%20years%202020%2D2025 (archived at https://perma.cc/B7WY-ZF9B) [Accessed 21 June 2022]

[21] The Vegan Kind. Available at: https://thevegankind.com/news/germany-manufactured-less-meat-and-more-vegan-products-in-2020 (archived at https://perma.cc/MED4-PEBP) [Accessed 21 June 2022]

[22] Wood, Z (2021) Shares in alt-milk maker Oatly surge on US stock market debut, The Guardian, 20 May. Available at: https://www.theguardian.com/business/2021/may/20/shares-alt-milk-maker-oatly-us-stock-market-debut-investors-alternative (archived at https://perma.cc/Q96Q-PPYV) [Accessed 12 September 2022]

[23] Glotz, J (2021) Can the vegan eating boom continue at pace? The Grocer, 14 January. Available at: https://www.thegrocer.co.uk/plant-based/can-the-vegan-eating-boom-continue-at-pace/652112.article#:~:text=ING%20forecasts%20meat%20and%20dairy,%E2%82%AC4.4bn%20in%202019.&text=Kantar%20consumer%20insight%20director%20Tesni,Covid%20will%20curb%20the%20movement (archived at https://perma.cc/L9CG-FJRM) [Accessed 21 June 2022]

[24] Press Association (2020) Almost one in four food products launched in UK in 2019 labelled vegan, The Guardian (17 January) Available at: https://www.theguardian.com/food/2020/jan/17/almost-one-in-four-food-products-launched-in-uk-in-2019-labelled-vegan (archived at https://perma.cc/E8YP-B5VN) [Accessed 21 June 2022]

[25] Statista (2022) UK: dietary habits 2019 [Online] Available at: https://www.statista.com/statistics/1085198/dietary-habits-in-the-uk/ (archived at https://perma.cc/6KUD-J7ZK) [Accessed 21 June 2022]

[26] Statistics for vegan population in the US, China, Germany and Europe come from this source: Statista (2020) Food consumption trends in leading world markets [Online] Available at: https://www.statista.com/study/69609/food-consumption-trends-in-leading-world-markets/ (archived at https://perma.cc/2U38-S5VX) [Accessed 3 May 2022]

[27] Hancox, D (2018) The unstoppable rise of veganism, The Guardian, 1 April. Available at: https://www.theguardian.com/lifeandstyle/2018/apr/01/vegans-are-coming-millennials-health-climate-change-animal-welfare (archived at https://perma.cc/U5YH-QPAY) [Accessed 3 May 2022]

[28] Craig, W (2009) Health effects of vegan diets, American Journal of Clinical Nutrition, 11 March. Available at: https://academic.oup.com/ajcn/article/89/5/1627S/4596952 (archived at https://perma.cc/L7AP-FK2T) [Accessed 3 May 2022]

[29] An example: Sharp, B and Romaniuk, J (2010) How Brands Grow, Oxford University Press, Melbourne

[30] Life And Times (2013) Available at: https://lifeandtimes.com/22-days-challenge (archived at https://perma.cc/NG26-AFFF) [Accessed 3 May 2022]

[31] Good Morning Britain, 20 December 2019. Available at https://www.youtube.com/watch?v=RQHVi78ZUmI (archived at https://perma.cc/8BTA-CQCJ) [Accessed 8 March 2021]

[32] Hicks, J (2014) Move over hackers, the biohackers are here, Forbes, 15 March. Available at https://www.forbes.com/sites/jenniferhicks/2014/03/15/move-over-hackers-biohackers-are-here/?sh=6856eae74de6 (archived at https://perma.cc/SE24-9ZHB) [Accessed 8 March 2021]

Chapter 2: Why modern mainstream marketing is a low-growth zone

[1] The Drum (2021) P&G's Marc Pritchard says its 'startup mentality' to brand building makes the grade. [Online] Available at: https://www.thedrum.com/news/2021/01/29/pg-s-marc-pritchard-says-its-startup-mentality-brand-building-makes-the-grade (archived at https://perma.cc/PRG2-2E9T) [Accessed 12 September 2022]

[2] Marketing Week (2017) GE's CMO Linda Boff: Marketing leaders must be 'growth hunters'. [Online] Available at: https://www.marketingweek.com/general-electric-cmo-linda-boff-leaders-adapt/ (archived at https://perma.cc/TER9-6HE2) [Accessed 12 September 2022]

[3] Euromonitor International. Splitting Hairs - Share of the hair care market in the U.S.

[4] www.fortunebusinessinsights.com (2021). Hair Care Market Size, Growth, Analysis | Industry Trends, 2026. [Online] Available at: https://www.fortunebusinessinsights.com/hair-care-market-102555 (archived at https://perma.cc/S6UT-PJC7). [Accessed 12 September 2022]

[5] IRI (2019) Beyond Price, Consumers Find Value in Private Brands

[6] Ibisworld US specialized industry report OD4099 Life Sciences January 2022, Dmitry Diment

[7] Firmenich (2022) Available at: https://www.firmenich.com/company/about-us (archived at https://perma.cc/M4ZK-7L5V) [Accessed 21 June 2022]

[8] Cowen, T (2011) The Great Stagnation: How America Ate All The Low-Hanging Fruit of Modern History, Got Sick, and Will (Eventually) Feel Better, Dutton, New York

[9] Gordon, R (2016) The Rise and Fall of American Growth, Princeton University Press, Princeton

[10] Dunning, H (2019) Eating insects makes sense. So why don't we? Imperial College London (15 May) Available at: https://www.imperial.ac.uk/news/191214/eating-insects-makes-sense-so-dont/ (archived at https://perma.cc/LE6T-JMAH) [Accessed 25 August 2022]

[11] Kelland, K (2021) Overcoming the 'yuck factor', Reuters (13 January) Available at: https://www.reuters.com/article/us-health-food-mealworm-europe-idUSKBN29I145 (archived at https://perma.cc/8JGM-GNLS) [Accessed 25 August 2022]

[12]   Eat Grub (2022) Available at: https://www.eatgrub.co.uk/shop/ (archived at https://perma.cc/5KPJ-XHYR) [Accessed 25 August 2022]

[13]   FoodyBug (2022) Available at: https://www.instagram.com/foodybug/ (archived at https://perma.cc/3DW6-M9ZB) [Accessed 25 August 2022]

[14]   Ento Kitchen (2022) Available at: https://www.entokitchen.com/pages/about-us (archived at https://perma.cc/X5YY-7TGP) [Accessed 25 August 2022]

[15]   University of Rochester Medical Center (2022) Available at: https://www.urmc.rochester.edu/encyclopedia/content.aspx?contenttypeid=76&contentid=23569-1 (archived at https://perma.cc/BDV7-VPBY) [Accessed 25 August 2022]

[16]   Gerretsen, I (2021) Insects are a nutrition-dense source of protein embraced by much of the world. Why are some of us so squeamish about eating them? BBC Future (21 April) Available at: https://www.bbc.com/future/article/20210420-the-protein-rich-superfood-most-europeans-wont-eat (archived at https://perma.cc/HG8P-D62V) [Accessed 25 August 2022]

Chapter 3: Going for growth: Why the margins? And why now?

[1]   Author team present at ANA 2019 presentation. This is corroborated by a Courier report that recorded the oat milk market growing 1946% between 2018 and 2020; Oat milk market graphic, Courier, 2020

[2]   Snead, E (2011) Steve Jobs on his Issey Miyake black turtlenecks, Hollywood Reporter, 11 October. Available at: https://www.hollywoodreporter.com/news/general-news/steve-jobs-his-issey-miyake-black-turtlenecks-i-have-last-rest-my-life-246808/ (archived at https://perma.cc/JE3M-625T) [Accessed 12 October 2021]

[3]   Lewis, M (2012) Obama's way, Vanity Fair, 11 September. Available at: https://www.vanityfair.com/news/2012/10/michael-lewis-profile-barack-obama (archived at https://perma.cc/4A8Z-3LM6) [Accessed 12 October 2021]

[4]   Scott, J (2014) My no soap no shampoo bacteria rich hygiene experiment, NY Times, 25 May. Available at: https://www.nytimes.com/2014/05/25/magazine/my-no-soap-no-shampoo-bacteria-rich-hygiene-experiment.html (archived at https://perma.cc/74EB-NH67) [Accessed 12 October 2021]

[5]   Zell Ravenheart, M (2010) A bouquet of lovers, Patheos, 13 April. Available at: https://www.patheos.com/resources/additional-resources/2010/04/bouquet-of-lovers (archived at https://perma.cc/D296-G92D) [Accessed 19 February 2022]

[6]   Hof, W (2020) The Wim Hof Method, Rider, London

[7]   Buijze, G *et al* (2016) The effect of cold showering on health and work, 15 September. Available at: https://www.ncbi.nlm.nih.gov/pmc/articles/ PMC5025014/ (archived at https://perma.cc/BK3Z-SNSG) [Accessed 4 May 2022]

[8]   Levin, D (2020) Green Bank quiet zone, NY Times, 6 March. Available at: https://www.nytimes.com/2020/03/06/us/green-bank-west-virginia-quiet-zone.html (archived at https://perma.cc/XM44-7VWR) [Accessed 4 May 2022]

[9]   Schulenberg, F (2018) New technologies are stirring up an anti-tech backlash, 20 November. Available at: https://www.rolandberger.com/en/ Insights/Publications/Tech-pioneers-and-the-neo-Luddite-revolution.html (archived at https://perma.cc/2JBW-Q9UE) [Accessed 4 May 2022]

[10] Chopra, D (1993) Ageless Body, Timeless Mind: A practical alternative to growing old, Rider, London

[11] Powell, A (2018) When science meets mindfulness, Harvard Gazette, 9 April. Available at: https://news.harvard.edu/gazette/story/2018/04/harvard-researchers-study-how-mindfulness-may-change-the-brain-in-depressed-patients/ (archived at https://perma.cc/6YTL-D5S6) [Accessed 22 June 2022]

[12] Valuation based on estimate using Calm figures

[13] Lowrey, A (2021) The app that monetized doing nothing, The Atlantic, 4 June. Available at: https://www.theatlantic.com/technology/archive/2021/06/ do-meditation-apps-work/619046/ (archived at https://perma.cc/BE6R-AGDU) [Accessed 4 May 2022]

[14] Halliwell, E (2015) Mindful Nation UK Report, 20 October. Available at: https://www.mindful.org/mindful-nation-uk-report-on-mental-health-in-public-policy/ (archived at https://perma.cc/7M5K-J5GE) [Accessed 4 May 2022]

[15] Spangler, T and Spangler, T (2020) 'Tiger King' Nabbed Over 34 Million U.S. Viewers in First 10 Days, Nielsen Says (EXCLUSIVE). [Online] Variety. Available at: https://variety.com/2020/digital/news/tiger-king-nielsen-viewership-data-stranger-things-1234573602/ (archived at https://perma. cc/9RPB-63RN) [Accessed 12 September 2022]

[16] Statista (2019) YouTube: hours of video uploaded every minute 2019 | Statista. [Online] Statista. Available at: https://www.statista.com/ statistics/259477/hours-of-video-uploaded-to-youtube-every-minute/ (archived at https://perma.cc/2W4V-MB4K) [Accessed 12 September 2022]

[17] Sheikh, M (2022) 17 TikTok stats marketers need to know in 2021, Sprout Social. Available at: https://sproutsocial.com/insights/tiktok-stats/ (archived at https://perma.cc/JF3Y-YHMA) [Accessed 12 September 2022]

[18]   Einstein, A (2016) I am not hippy drippy, Daily Mail (13 July) Available at:
https://www.dailymail.co.uk/femail/article-3688088/Mother-desperate-birth-
wild-delivers-baby-STREAM-without-midwife-footage-watched-52-million-
times.html (archived at https://perma.cc/RG8A-ZCC2) [Accessed 4 May
2022]

[19]   Available at: https://www.youtube.com/watch?v=EsNhCWsDVQI&t=97s
(archived at https://perma.cc/5KL3-ZMYE) [Accessed 19 February 2022]

[20]   Schmidt, C (2021) Trends in home birth information seeking, 17 May.
Available at: https://www.ncbi.nlm.nih.gov/pmc/articles/PMC8129816/
(archived at https://perma.cc/E3LB-BMDD) [Accessed 4 May 2022]

[21]   Muniz, A and O'Guinn, T (2001) Brand community, Journal of Consumer
Research. Available at: https://www.researchgate.net/
publication/278228776_Brand_Community (archived at https://perma.cc/
Z9FH-3RK8) [Accessed 4 May 2022]

[22]   Pang, X (2021) Trendy to be a witch, VG, 2 November. Available at: https://
www.vg.no/nyheter/innenriks/i/OrWpAA/naa-er-det-trendy-aa-vaere-heks
(archived at https://perma.cc/MW8T-5BV5) [Accessed 19 June 2022]

[23]   Moniuszko, S (2021) What's the deal with Witchtok? USA Today, 14
October. Available at: https://eu.usatoday.com/story/life/2021/10/14/
tiktok-witchtok-has-billions-views-witches-explain-why/6102147001/
(archived at https://perma.cc/CTA9-AS34) [Accessed 19 June 2022]

[24]   Parker, K and Igielnik, R (2020) On the cusp of adulthood, Pew Research,
14 May. Available at: https://www.pewresearch.org/social-trends/2020/05/14/
on-the-cusp-of-adulthood-and-facing-an-uncertain-future-what-we-know-
about-gen-z-so-far-2/ (archived at https://perma.cc/Y43D-FLQ8) [Accessed 7
December 2021]

[25]   Francis, T and Hoefel, F (2018) True Gen: Generation Z and its implications
for companies, McKinsey, 12 November. Available at: https://www.mckinsey.
com/industries/consumer-packaged-goods/our-insights/true-gen-generation-z-
and-its-implications-for-companies (archived at https://perma.
cc/6UGS-WLLJ) [Accessed 13 September 2022]

[26]   Raynor, L (2021) Gen Z and the future of spend, Forbes, 21 January.
Available at: https://www.forbes.com/sites/forbesbusinesscouncil/2021/01/21/
gen-z-and-the-future-of-spend-what-we-know-about-this-generation-the-
pandemic-and-how-they-pay/?sh=676965c821eb (archived at https://perma.
cc/5LRG-E9JD) [Accessed 5 May 2022]

[27]   Royal College of Midwives (n.d.) Clinical Briefing Sheet: Freebirth [Online].
Available at https://www.rcm.org.uk/media/3904/freebirth_draft_23-april-
v5-002-mrd-1.pdf (archived at https://perma.cc/5W9A-5JBX) [Accessed 18
January 2022]

Interviews with Leonie Rainbird Savin and Anna Clarkson conducted
January 2022.

Chapter 4: A smouldering fire in the fringes: the elemental beacons

[1] Cukaci, C *et al* (2020) Against all odds: the persistent popularity of homeopathy, 9 March. Available at: https://www.ncbi.nlm.nih.gov/pmc/articles/PMC7253376/ (archived at https://perma.cc/3V6H-FGYJ) [Accessed 7 December 2021]

[2] PA Media (2019) Head of NHS voices 'serious concerns' over homeopathy, The Guardian, 28 October. Available at: https://www.theguardian.com/society/2019/oct/28/head-nhs-voices-serious-concerns-about-homeopathy-simon-stevens (archived at https://perma.cc/W9XF-KS46) [Accessed 7 December 2021]

[3] Kelland, K (2011) Professor calls Prince Charles, others, 'snake oil salesmen', Reuters, 25 July. Available at: https://www.reuters.com/article/uk-medicine-alternative-charles-idUKTRE76O4IG20110725 (archived at https://perma.cc/2KB4-ZPCP) [Accessed 5 May 2022]

[4] Emory, S (2021) Homeopathy doesn't work: so why do so many Germans believe in it? Bloomberg, 12 October. Available at: https://www.bloomberg.com/news/features/2021-10-12/homeopathy-doesn-t-work-so-why-do-so-many-germans-believe-in-it (archived at https://perma.cc/BN78-CHSZ) [Accessed 5 May 2022]

[5] Loudon, I (2006) A brief history of homeopathy, JRSM Available at: https://www.ncbi.nlm.nih.gov/pmc/articles/PMC1676328/ (archived at https://perma.cc/3HUX-LZTM) [Accessed 7 December 2021]

[6] Schmidt, J (2010) 200 Years Organon of Medicine Available at: https://www.sciencedirect.com/science/article/abs/pii/S147549161000086X (archived at https://perma.cc/) [Accessed 5 May 2022]

[7] Grob Plante, S (2019) It's just a big illusion, Vox, 23 October. Available at: https://www.vox.com/the-highlight/2019/10/16/20910346/homeopathic-homeopathy-holistic-alternative-medicine-oscillococcinum-history (archived at https://perma.cc/F7T3-4SDB) [Accessed 5 May 2022]

[8] Cukaci, C *et al* (2020) Against all odds: the persistent popularity of homeopathy, 9 March. Available at: https://www.ncbi.nlm.nih.gov/pmc/articles/PMC7253376/ (archived at https://perma.cc/3V6H-FGYJ) [Accessed 7 December 2021]

[9] Morabia A (2004) Pierre-Charles-Alexandre Louis and the evaluation of bloodletting Available at: https://www.jameslindlibrary.org/articles/pierre-charles-alexandre-louis-and-the-evaluation-of-bloodletting/ (archived at https://perma.cc/RDA7-4DRJ) [Accessed 5 May 2022]

[10] Loudon, I (2006) A brief history of homeopathy, JRSM Available at: https://www.ncbi.nlm.nih.gov/pmc/articles/PMC1676328/ (archived at https://perma.cc/3HUX-LZTM) [Accessed 7 December 2021]

[11] Malerba, L (2011) Homeopathy: a brief history, HuffPost, 1 July. Available at: https://www.huffpost.com/entry/homeopathy-history_b_875653 (archived at https://perma.cc/QZ3S-UK3U) [Accessed 5 May 2022]

[12] Cukaci, C, Freissmuth, M, Mann, C, Marti, J and Sperl, V (2020) Against all odds—the persistent popularity of homeopathy. Wiener klinische Wochenschrift, 132(9-10), pp 232–42. doi:10.1007/s00508-020-01624-x (archived at https://perma.cc/U5EJ-5YJF). [Accessed 13 September 2022]

[13] McLeod, S (2018) Solomon Asch Conformity Experiment, Simply Psychology, 28 December. https://www.simplypsychology.org/asch-conformity.html (archived at https://perma.cc/9M4T-ZXX7) [Accessed 5 May 2022]

[14] For violent vegan activism in the UK, look at these sources: Gayle, D (2021) Vegan activists block dairy distribution centre in Buckinghamshire, Guardian, 31 August. Available at: https://www.theguardian.com/environment/2021/aug/31/vegan-activists-block-dairy-distribution-centre-in-buckinghamshire (archived at https://perma.cc/D4CA-YBZ5) [Accessed 13 September 2022]. Also, Wynarczyk, N (2018) They smash up butchers, attack farmers and say milking a cow is the same as rape: meet the vegan mafia, The Sun, 20 July. Available at: https://www.thesun.co.uk/news/6808001/the-world-of-militant-vegans/ (archived at https://perma.cc/5D84-KKSR) [Accessed 13 September 2022]

[15] AFP (2019) French anti-meat activists sentenced for vandalising shops, The Guardian, 8 April. Available at: https://www.theguardian.com/world/2019/apr/08/french-anti-meat-activists-sentenced-for-vandalising-butchers-and-restaurants (archived at https://perma.cc/8DK5-ZUMS) [Accessed 5 May 2022]

[16] Blumetti, J (2019) Purists v partiers, Guardian, 25 November. Available at: https://www.theguardian.com/lifeandstyle/2019/nov/25/nudism-naturism-florida-pasco-county (archived at https://perma.cc/C8F5-JUSH) [Accessed 5 May 2022]

[17] Statista. Available at: https://www-statista-com.lbs.idm.oclc.org/statistics/767516/view-french-fashion-of-life-naturism/ (archived at https://perma.cc/C9ZH-WDQJ) [Accessed 19 June 2022]

[18] Landesman, C (2021) Would you go to a naked dining club? Spectator, 23 October. Available at: https://www.spectator.co.uk/article/would-you-go-to-a-naked-dining-club (archived at https://perma.cc/WA47-X5VJ) [Accessed 5 May 2022]

[19] Berger, H (2021) What is wicca? The Conversation, 30 August. Available at: https://theconversation.com/what-is-wicca-an-expert-on-modern-witchcraft-explains-165939 (archived at https://perma.cc/PU8V-45H7) [Accessed 7 December 2021]

[20] Brewer, M (n.d.). The Social Self: On Being the Same and Different at the Same Time. Personality and Social Psychology Bulletin, [Online] p 475. Available at: https://ezproxy-prd.bodleian.ox.ac.uk:2246/doi/pdf/10.1177/0146167291175001 (archived at https://perma.cc/86Y7-LM7J) [Accessed 13 September 2022]

[21] Obituary: Morning Glory Zell Ravenheart (2014), Sunday Times, 27 July. Available at: https://www.thetimes.co.uk/article/morning-glory-zell-ravenheart-g8nx3gwdvb6 (archived at https://perma.cc/C3KM-RV8U) [Accessed 24 May 2021]

[22] Haskell, R (2019) Justin and Hailey Bieber open up, Vogue, 7 February. Available at: https://www.vogue.com/article/justin-bieber-hailey-bieber-cover-interview (archived at https://perma.cc/WV4W-KGF3) [Accessed 17 May 2021]

Interview with Mary Crumpton conducted in Manchester, February 2022.
Interview with Emma Smith conducted in London, February 2022.

Chapter 5: What's hidden, what's there and what could be: the revelatory beacons

[1] Tversky, A and Kahneman, D (1981) The framing of decisions and the psychology of choice, Science, 30 January. Available at: https://www.science.org/doi/10.1126/science.7455683 (archived at https://perma.cc/8ADP-KACQ) [Accessed 23 June 2022]

[2] Coghlan, A (2012) Hail Jeremy Hunt, the new minister for magic, New Scientist, 5 September. Available at: https://www.newscientist.com/article/dn22241-hail-jeremy-hunt-the-new-minister-for-magic/ (archived at https://perma.cc/M6S6-PJCZ) [Accessed 13 September 2022]

[3] Cukaci, C, Freissmuth, M, Mann, C, Marti, J and Sperl, V (2020). Against all odds—the persistent popularity of homeopathy. Wiener klinische Wochenschrift, 132(9–10), pp 232–42. doi:10.1007/s00508-020-01624-x (archived at https://perma.cc/U5EJ-5YJF) [Accessed 13 September 2022]

[4] Goldacre, B (2008) Bad Science, Fourth Estate, London

[5] Robson, D (2022) The expectation effect: how your mindset can change your world, Henry Holt and Company, New York

[6] Sutherland, R (2019) Alchemy: The surprising power of ideas that don't make sense, WH Allen, London

[7] Covey, S (1989) The 7 Habits of Highly Effective People, Free Press, New York

[8]   Whyte, W (1952) Groupthink, Fortune. Available at: https://fortune.
      com/2012/07/22/groupthink-fortune-1952/ (archived at https://perma.cc/
      SF8P-BS5H) [Accessed 9 May 2022]

[9]   Janis, I (1982) Groupthink: Psychological studies of policy decisions and
      fiascoes, Houghton Mifflin, Boston

[10] Sunstein, C (2009) Going to Extremes: How like minds unite and divide,
      OUP, Oxford

[11] Beck, A T (2012) A Conversation with Aaron T Beck, YouTube. Available at:
      https://youtu.be/POYXzA-gS4U (archived at https://perma.cc/C3J9-D4NK)
      [Accessed 13 September 2022]

[12] For Aaker's work, look at any number of his blogs on the website of the
      Prophet. An example: Aaker, D (2014) 3 Ways to Re-frame Your Category |
      Aaker on Brands. [Online] Business Transformation Consultants | Prophet.
      Available at: https://www.prophet.com/2014/04/189-3-ways-to-re-frame-
      your-category-and-win/ (archived at https://perma.cc/8E7S-K784) [Accessed
      13 September 2022]

[13] O'Neill, S (2016) I slept for just 20 minutes at a time, New Scientist,25 May.
      Available at: https://www.newscientist.com/article/2088409-i-slept-for-just-
      20-minutes-at-a-time-for-6-months/ (archived at https://perma.cc/
      P2V4-YPK4) [Accessed 2 March 2021]

Chapter 6: Shakers of place and pace:
the opportunity beacons

[1]   Statista research dept (2022) Share of tattooed people in selected countries
      worldwide in 2018 [Online] Statista. Available at: https://www-statista-com.lbs.
      idm.oclc.org/statistics/941731/share-of-people-with-tattoos-in-selected-countries/
      (archived at https://perma.cc/3R76-6F6Z) [Accessed 13 September 2022]

[2]   Cox, D (2016) The name for Britain comes from our ancient love of tattoos
      [Online] www.bbc.com. Available at: https://www.bbc.com/future/
      article/20161110-the-name-for-britain-comes-from-our-ancient-love-of-tattoos
      (archived at https://perma.cc/T6F4-DD7S) [Accessed 13 September 2022]

[3]   DeMello, M (2000) Bodies of Inscription: a cultural history of the modern
      tattoo community, Duke University Press, Durham NC. p 49

[4]   www.vfw.org (2016) A Short History of Military Tattoos [Online] Available
      at: https://www.vfw.org/media-and-events/latest-releases/archives/2016/8/
      a-short-history-of-military-tattoos (archived at https://perma.cc/D2NQ-
      M9Z6) [Accessed 13 September 2022]

[5]   Brady, C (1993) From Punishment To Expression: A History Of Tattoos In
      Corrections | Office of Justice Programs. [Online] www.ojp.gov. Available at:
      https://www.ojp.gov/ncjrs/virtual-library/abstracts/punishment-expression-
      history-tattoos-corrections (archived at https://perma.cc/4ZTA-RK69)
      [Accessed 13 September 2022]

[6]   DeMello, M (2000) Bodies of Inscription: a cultural history of the modern tattoo community, Duke University Press, Durham NC.

[7]   Menswear Style (2017) The Real History Behind Sagging Pants [Online] Available at: https://www.menswearstyle.co.uk/2017/07/26/the-real-history-behind-sagging-pants/7788#:~:text=Although%20laws%20were%20passed%20locally (archived at https://perma.cc/5KBY-MS5J) [Accessed 13 September 2022]

[8]   DeMello, M (2000) Bodies of Inscription: a cultural history of the modern tattoo community, Duke University Press, Durham NC. p 67

[9]   BBC News Online (2014) Army eases rules on hand and neck tattoos, 2 October. Available at: https://www.bbc.co.uk/news/uk-29455849 (archived at https://perma.cc/K2NR-FPCZ) [Accessed 13 September 2022]

[10]   Olsen, MB (2018) Met Police relaxes tattoo ban to recruit more officers to the force, Metro, 26 September. Available at: https://metro.co.uk/2018/09/26/met-police-relaxes-tattoo-ban-to-recruit-more-officers-to-the-force-7981187/ (archived at https://perma.cc/Q75C-K79J) [Accessed 13 September 2022]

[11]   Bradley, G (2019) AirNZ to back down on controversial tattoo rule. [Online] News.com.au, 10 June. Available at: https://www.news.com.au/travel/travel-updates/air-nz-to-back-down-on-controversial-tattoo-rule/news-story/746a0940b4622ad8e166cc39af53c7b3 (archived at https://perma.cc/4PRS-BXNK) [Accessed 13 September 2022]

[12]   Statista research dept (2015) Public opinion of people with large tattoos in the United Kingdom (UK) as of 2015, by age group. [Online] Statista. Available at: https://www- statista-com.lbs.idm.oclc.org/statistics/530576/public-perception-of-tattoos-by-age/ (archived at https://perma.cc/D7ZE-8L45) [Accessed 13 September 2022]

[13]   Dangerous Minds (2017) Crime And Punishment In Japan During The Edo Period Included Tattooing The Faces & Arms Of Criminals [Online]. Available at: https://dangerousminds.net/comments/crime_and_punishment_in_japan_during_the_edo_period_included_tattooing_the_ (archived at https://perma.cc/4KAA-QDR6) [Accessed 13 September 2022]

[14]   Ox.ac.uk (2022) Shibboleth Authentication Request [Online] Available at: https://ezproxy-prd.bodleian.ox.ac.uk:2163/1843/2017/11/03/the-tattooed-hipsters-of-18th-century-japan (archived at https://perma.cc/NJ9R-C9V9) [Accessed 13 September 2022]

[15]   CNN, J M, Junko Ogura, Chie Kobayashi (n.d.). Did Japan just ban tattoos? [Online] CNN. Available at: https://edition.cnn.com/2017/10/18/asia/tattoos-japan/index.html (archived at https://perma.cc/8PEZ-Q4LM) [Accessed 13 September 2022]

[16]   BBC News Online (2019) Tattoos in Japan: Why they're so tied to the yakuza, 21 September. Available at: https://www.bbc.co.uk/news/newsbeat-49768799 (archived at https://perma.cc/Y79A-THH3) [Accessed 13 September 2022]

[17] BBC News Online (2019) Tattoos in Japan: Why they're so tied to the yakuza, 21 September. Available at: https://www.bbc.co.uk/news/newsbeat-49768799 (archived at https://perma.cc/Y79A-THH3) [Accessed 13 September 2022].

[18] Hida, H (2022) Shifting norms on tattoos in Japan, NY Times, 23 April. Available at: www.nytimes.com/interactive/2022/04/23/world/asia/japan-tattoo-norms

[19] Baumeister, R and Leary, M (1995) The Need to Belong Available at: https://www.researchgate.net/publication/15420847_The_Need_to_Belong_Desire_for_Interpersonal_Attachments_as_a_Fundamental_Human_Motivation (archived at https://perma.cc/J3XR-QT9B) [Accessed 9 May 2022]

[20] Thompson, K (2021) Has lockdown led to more subcultures? 28 April. Available at: https://revisesociology.com/2021/04/28/has-lockdown-lead-to-more-subcultures/ (archived at https://perma.cc/GJG9-P4F2) [Accessed 9 May 2022]

[21] Baumeister, R and Leary, M (1995) The Need to Belong. Available at: https://www.researchgate.net/publication/15420847_The_Need_to_Belong_Desire_for_Interpersonal_Attachments_as_a_Fundamental_Human_Motivation (archived at https://perma.cc/J3XR-QT9B) [Accessed 9 May 2022]

[22] Agrawal, N (2017) Thinking about getting into cryptocurrency? Be warned: it comes with a lot of social pressure to only eat meat for some reason, Twitter, 18 August. Available at: https://twitter.com/NeerajKA/status/898652838087213057 (archived at https://perma.cc/5DZV-ZS5B) [Accessed 9 May 2022]

[23] Fadiman, J (2011) The Psychedelic Explorer's Guide, Park Street Press, Vermont

[24] Kuchler, H (2017) How Silicon Valley re-discovered LSD, Financial Times, 10 August. Available at: https://www.ft.com/content/0a5a4404-7c8e-11e7-ab01-a13271d1ee9c (archived at https://perma.cc/E8HE-3KBN) [Accessed 2 February 2021]
Interview with "Alex" conducted in London, September 2021.

Chapter 7: An irresistible momentum: the growth beacons

[1] Edwards, P (2015) When running for exercise was for weirdos, Vox, 9 August. Available at: https://www.vox.com/2015/8/9/9115981/running-jogging-history (archived at https://perma.cc/2TVK-XV6Q) [Accessed 1 September 2022]

[2] Latham, A (2013) The history of a habit: jogging as a palliative to sedentariness in 1960s America. cultural geographies, 22(1), pp 103–26. doi:10.1177/1474474013491927 (archived at https://perma.cc/KRB4-MC4C) [Accessed 1 September 2022]

[3] Edwards, P (2015) When running for exercise was for weirdos, Vox, 9 August. Available at: https://www.vox.com/2015/8/9/9115981/running-jogging-history (archived at https://perma.cc/2TVK-XV6Q) [Accessed 23 June 2022]

[4] Boston Athletic Association. Available at: https://www.baa.org/races/boston-marathon/history (archived at https://perma.cc/VH4G-N5JN) [Accessed 23 June 2022]

[5] Lacke, S (2018) How running went mainstream, Women's Running, 13 August. Available at: https://www.womensrunning.com/culture/how-running-went-mainstream/ (archived at https://perma.cc/8MVW-7G6P) [Acessed 23 June 2022]

[6] Lieberman, D (2020) Exercised: why something we never evolved to do is healthy and rewarding, Pantheon Books, New York, p 16

[7] Gordon, R J (2016) The Rise And Fall Of American Growth: the U.S. standard of living since the Civil War, p 255, Princeton University Press, Princeton

[8] Lieberman, D (2020) Exercised: why something we never evolved to do is healthy and rewarding, Pantheon Books, New York, p 41

[9] Fisk, D M (2003) American Labor in the 20th Century. [Online] Available at: https://www.bls.gov/opub/mlr/cwc/american-labor-in-the-20th-century.pdf (archived at https://perma.cc/63Z6-QVHG) [Accessed 1 September 2022]

[10] Gordon, R J (2016) The Rise And Fall Of American Growth: the U.S. standard of living since the Civil War, p 255, Princeton University Press, Princeton

[11] Tzvetkova, S and Ortiz-Ospina, E (2017) Working women: what determines female labor force participation? (16 October) Available at: https://ourworldindata.org/women-in-the-labor-force-determinants (archived at https://perma.cc/9XAH-B4VF) [Accessed 30 June 2022]

[12] Bellis, M (2019) The television remote control: a brief history, ThoughtCo, 20 September. Available at: https://www.thoughtco.com/history-of-the-television-remote-control-1992384 (archived at https://perma.cc/P4TN-JMGR) [Accessed 20 June 2022]

[13] Latham, A (2013) The History Of A Habit: jogging as a palliative to sedentariness in 1960s America. Cultural geographies, 22(1), pp 103–26 doi:10.1177/1474474013491927 (archived at https://perma.cc/KRB4-MC4C) [Accessed 1 September 2022]

[14] Knight, P H (2016) Shoe Dog: A memoir by the creator of Nike, p 196, Simon & Schuster, London

[15] registration.baa.org. (n.d.). Boston Marathon 2019: Statistics. [Online] Available at: http://registration.baa.org/2019/cf/Public/iframe_Statistics.htm (archived at https://perma.cc/B7TS-J2SS) [Accessed 15 September 2022]

[16] All statistics on the 2019 Boston marathon can be found from this source: registration.baa.org. (n.d.). Boston Marathon 2019: Statistics. [Online] Available at: http://registration.baa.org/2019/cf/Public/iframe_Statistics.htm (archived at https://perma.cc/B7TS-J2SS) [Last accessed 15 September 2022]

[17] For source on the participant wearing clown shoes: mbonner@masslive.com, M.B. | (2019). Boston Marathon 2019: See the best Race Day outfits. [Online] masslive. Available at: https://www.masslive.com/boston/2019/04/ boston-marathon-2019-see-the-best-race-day-outfits.html (archived at https://perma.cc/V9HZ-GWVX) [Accessed 15 September 2022]. For source on crawling participant: www.boston.com. (n.d.). 10 must-see moments from the 2019 Boston Marathon. [Online] Available at: https://www.boston. com/sports/boston-marathon/2019/04/15/2019-boston-marathon-moments/ (archived at https://perma.cc/K6F6-25M8) [Accessed 15 September 2022]

[18] Stone, M (2020) Gold's Gym has filed for bankruptcy protection after closing locations amid the coronavirus outbreak, Business Insider, 4 May. Available at: https://www.businessinsider.com/golds-gym-bankruptcy-coronavirus-pandemic-2020-5?r=US&IR=T (archived at https://perma.cc/ U8BD-VL83) [Accessed 15 September 2022]

[19] Knight, PH (2016) Shoe Dog: A memoir by the creator of Nike, Simon & Schuster, London

[20] Global Probiotic Drinks Market 2020-2024 (2020). [Online] Technavio Insights. Available at: https://insights-technavio-com.lbs.idm.oclc.org/index. php?route=product/product&product_id=212961 (archived at https://perma. cc/Z6NE-E874) [Accessed 15 September 2022]

[21] Dive deeper into Yakult—the Probiotic Drink Born in Japan, Loved Worldwide. (n.d.). History | Dive deeper into Yakult—the Probiotic Drink Born in Japan, Loved Worldwide. [Online] Available at: https://www.yakult. co.jp/english/inbound/history/ (archived at https://perma.cc/38RJ-ME26) [Accessed 15 September 2022]

[22] Bland, B and Soble, J (2013) On the trail of the Yakult ladies, FT, 27 November. Available at: https://www.ft.com/content/e8e517c8-5387-11e3-9250-00144feabdc0 (archived at https://perma.cc/5KUU-4UP7) [Accessed 23 June 2022]

[23] Dive deeper into Yakult—the Probiotic Drink Born in Japan, Loved Worldwide. (n.d.). History | Dive deeper into Yakult—the Probiotic Drink Born in Japan, Loved Worldwide. [Online] Available at: https://www.yakult. co.jp/english/inbound/history/ (archived at https://perma.cc/38RJ-ME26) [Accessed 15 September 2022]

[24] Mackowiak, PA (2013) Recycling Metchnikoff: Probiotics, the Intestinal Microbiome and the Quest for Long Life. Frontiers in Public Health, [Online] 1. doi:10.3389/fpubh.2013.00052 (archived at https://perma. cc/5KXU-VM69) [Accessed 15 September 2022]

[25]   Davis, K and Montag, C (2019) Selected principles of Panksepp's Affective Neuroscience, 17 January. Available at: https://www.frontiersin.org/articles/10.3389/fnins.2018.01025/full (archived at https://perma.cc/FM87-7N93) [Accessed 9 May 2022]

[26]   Crampton, R (2020) Beta male: my year in stats, The Times, 4 January. Available at https://www.thetimes.co.uk/article/beta-male-my-year-in-stats-6g2rk7s8f (archived at https://perma.cc/37SU-U5VD) [Accessed 12 April 2022]

[27]   Wolf, G (2010) The Data-driven Life, NY Times, 28 April. Available at https://www.nytimes.com/2010/05/02/magazine/02self-measurement-t.html (archived at https://perma.cc/D2ZV-UL6U) [Accessed 2 November 2021]

[28]   Li, X (2017) Digital Health: Tracking Physiomes and Activity Using Wearable Biosensors Reveals Useful Health-Related Information, 12 January. Available at https://journals.plos.org/plosbiology/article?id=10.1371/journal.pbio.2001402 (archived at https://perma.cc/9ZTA-EY9G) [Accessed 12 September 2022]

Chapter 8: Entrepreneurs get it – they are marginals too

[1]   Kuratko, D, Fisher, G and Audretsch, D (2001) Available at: https://www.researchgate.net/publication/342254285_Unraveling_the_entrepreneurial_mindset (archived at https://perma.cc/JV5E-4A6M) [Accessed 20 June 2022]

[2]   Sarasvathy, S (2008) What makes entrepreneurs entrepreneurial? Available at: https://www.researchgate.net/publication/228145517_What_Makes_Entrepreneurs_Entrepreneurial (archived at https://perma.cc/G9BQ-EWDW) [Accessed 20 June 2022]

[3]   Mitchell, R K, Busenitz, L, Lant, T, McDougall, PP, Morse, EA and Smith, JB (2002) Toward a Theory of Entrepreneurial Cognition: Rethinking the People Side of Entrepreneurship Research. Entrepreneurship Theory and Practice, 27(2), pp 93–104. doi:10.1111/1540-8520.00001 (archived at https://perma.cc/6RLT-ZVN7)

[4]   Gladwell, M (2013) David and Goliath: underdogs, misfits and the art of battling giants, Little, Brown, Boston

[5]   Kuratko, D, Fisher, G and Audretsch, D (2001) Available at: https://www.researchgate.net/publication/342254285_Unraveling_the_entrepreneurial_mindset (archived at https://perma.cc/JV5E-4A6M) [Accessed 20 June 2022]

[6]   Knowledge at Wharton podcast (2019) Available at: https://knowledge.wharton.upenn.edu/article/role-of-feelings-in-entrepreneurship/ (archived at https://perma.cc/8MM4-4LEL) [Accessed 23 June 2022]

[7]   Huang, T Y, Souitaris, V and Barsade, S G (2019). Which matters more? Group fear versus hope in entrepreneurial escalation of commitment. Strategic Management Journal, 40(11), pp 1852–81. doi:10.1002/smj.3051 (archived at https://perma.cc/Q4DS-BS4Q)

[8]   Kuratko, D, Fisher, G and Audretsch, D (2001) Available at: https://www. researchgate.net/publication/342254285_Unraveling_the_entrepreneurial_ mindset (archived at https://perma.cc/JV5E-4A6M) [Accessed 20 June 2022]

[9]   Kuratko, D, Fisher, G and Audretsch, D (2001) Available at: https://www. researchgate.net/publication/342254285_Unraveling_the_entrepreneurial_ mindset (archived at https://perma.cc/JV5E-4A6M) [Accessed 20 June 2022]

[10] Eisenmann, T (2021) Why start-ups fail, Harvard Business Review (May-June edition) Available at: https://hbr.org/2021/05/why-start-ups-fail (archived at https://perma.cc/ATU8-HXZH) [Accessed 23 June 2022]

[11] The Founder Hour podcast (2021) Available at: https://www. thefounderhour.com/episodes/bjorn-oste-oatly (archived at https://perma.cc/ GXN9-SXBZ) [Accessed 23 June 2022]

[12] Oatly (2021) Available at: https://investors.oatly.com/static-files/0bfad979- 62b9-4d3d-84aa-6b112ee5c41b (archived at https://perma.cc/R92M-C4WL) [Accessed 23 June 2022]

[13] Estimated from: NielsenIQ (2016) Americans are nuts for almond milk [Online] Available at: https://nielseniq.com/global/en/insights/analysis/2016/ americans-are-nuts-for-almond-milk/ (archived at https://perma.cc/B4SW- 7A3G) [Accessed 13 September 2022]

[14] Meyers, A (2021) Demand for Alternative Dairy Is Here to Stay, as Consumers Seek Balance Between Sustainability, Health and Taste, Morning Consult, 30 March. Available at: https://morningconsult.com/2021/03/30/ alternative-milk-non-dairy-popularity/ (archived at https://perma.cc/ PA6Q-LJ88) [Accessed 13 September 2022]

[15] Oatly (2021) 2Q21Earnings presentation [Online] Available at: https:// investors.oatly.com/static-files/af76858e-ea58-45f5-9479-be6cfce312e1 (archived at https://perma.cc/973N-7J3G) [Accessed 14 September 2022]

[16] Roberts, C (2020) Oregon legalizes psilocybin mushroms, Forbes (4 November) Available at: https://www.forbes.com/sites/ chrisroberts/2020/11/04/oregon-legalizes-psilocybin-mushrooms-and- decriminalizes-all-drugs/ (archived at https://perma.cc/MW6M-ZGME) [Accessed 23 June 2022]

[17] Psych Global (2020) Gwell and the untapped opportunity in functional mushrooms (02 December) Available at: https://psych.global/gwella-and-the- untapped-opportunity-in-functional-mushrooms/ (archived at https://perma. cc/Y57H-Q9TG) [Accessed 23 June 2022]

[18]   Yakowicz, W (2020) Field Trip Health, another psychedelic company, goes
            public, Forbes, 7 October. Available at: https://www.forbes.com/sites/
            willyakowicz/2020/10/07/psychedelic-therapy-company-field-trip-health-
            goes-public-to-revolutionize-mental-health- treatments/?sh=60ad196779a5
            (archived at https://perma.cc/9V27-E9A6) [Accessed 23 June 2022]

[19]   Kerwin, N (2022) Insect agriculture company raises $2.5 million, Pet Food
            Processing, 2 November. Available at: https://www.petfoodprocessing.net/
            articles/15504-insect-agriculture-company-raises-25-million (archived at
            https://perma.cc/HQR2-KSVV) [Accessed 23 June 2022]

[20]   Cronin, M (2021) Startup that turns ashes of deceased loved ones into
            diamonds raises $10m, BizJournals, 27 July. Available at: https://www.
            bizjournals.com/twincities/bizwomen/news/latest-news/2021/07/eterneva-
            closes-oversubscribed-10m-series-a-round.html?page=all (archived at https://
            perma.cc/2XSE-5QPC) [Accessed 27 June 2022]

[21]   Nomads Campervan Creations. (n.d.). We're Nomads - Nomads Campervan
            Creations | Holly & Chris [Online] Available at: https://www.
            nomadscreations.com/we-are-nomads/ (archived at https://perma.cc/
            WW9K-84AH) [Accessed 28 August 2022]

[22]   Heijden, M van der (2018) Seven Continents, 1 Leap of Faith [Online] www.
            ted.com. Available at: https://www.ted.com/talks/mark_van_der_heijden_7_
            continents_1_leap_of_faith (archived at https://perma.cc/89HA-K6M6)
            [Accessed 28 August 2022]

[23]   Mansoor, S (2019) A sustainable snack, Time. Available at: https://time.com/
            collection/best-inventions-2019/5734537/akua-kelp-jerky/ (archived at
            https://perma.cc/GY3H-YQWL) [Accessed 23 June 2022]

[24]   Warren, K (2018) A 34 year old woman says spending 20% of her income
            has changed her life for the better, Insider, 15 March. Available at: https://
            www.insider.com/this-woman-says-extreme-frugality-changed-her-life-how-
            she-saves-money-2018-3 (archived at https://perma.cc/286E-67HY)
            [Accessed 3 July 2021]

[25]   Boyle, M (2010) The Moneyless Man, Oneworld Publications, London

[26]   Schwermer, H (2013) Moneyless world, TedX-Reset Available at: https://
            www.youtube.com/watch?v=i1rTu_cOT5k (archived at https://perma.cc/
            GX5L-GRZU) [Accessed 2 February 2022]
            Interview with Will Allen-Mersh conducted in London, February 2022.

Chapter 9: Growth from the margins: a marketer's playbook

[1]   Syed, M (2019) Rebel Ideas: the power of diverse thinking, John Murray,
           London

[2] Harvard Business Review (2017) How 'Brainwriting' Can Get Better Ideas Out Of Your Team - Sponsor Content From Kellogg Executive Education. [Online] Available at: https://hbr.org/sponsored/2017/05/how-brainwriting-can-get-better-ideas-out-of-your-team (archived at https://perma.cc/GTH4-QT8B) [Accessed 15 September 2022]

[3] Akua (2022) Available at: https://akua.co/ (archived at https://perma.cc/9CW7-H5PT) [Accessed 30 June 2022]

[4] Toussaint, K (2020) Every $1 invested in ocean sustainability generates $5 of benefits for the planet, 13 July. Available at: https://www.fastcompany.com/90527192/every-1-invested-in-ocean-sustainability-generates-5-of-benefits-for-the-planet (archived at https://perma.cc/M9QV-2RG5) [Accessed 30 June 2022]

Chapter 10: The M2M advantage: seven things every leader should know

[1] Katz, D R (1994) Just Do It: The Nike Spirit In The Corporate World, Random House, New York

[2] Bower, J L, and C M Christensen, Disruptive Technologies: Catching The Wave, Harvard Business Review 73, no. 1 (January–February 1995): 43–53. Available at: https://www.hbs.edu/faculty/Pages/item.aspx?num=6841 (archived at https://perma.cc/AS8A-W5NS) [Accessed 14 September 2022]

[3] Schumpeter, J A (1942) Capitalism, Socialism, And Democracy, Harper & Brothers, New York

[4] Stewart, R (2021) P&G's Marc Pritchard says its 'startup mentality' to brand building makes the grade, The Drum, 29 January. Available at: https://www.thedrum.com/news/2021/01/29/pg-s-marc-pritchard-says-its-startup-mentality-brand-building-makes-the-grade (archived at https://perma.cc/8GDX-HVXA) [Accessed 14 September 2022]

[5] Lorenzo, R (2020) How diverse leadership teams boost innovation, BCG Global. Available at: https://www.bcg.com/publications/2018/how-diverse-leadership-teams-boost-innovation (archived at https://perma.cc/R24P-LWW3) [Accessed 14 September 2022]

[6] Daykin, J (2022) Inclusive Marketing: Why Representation Matters To Your Customers And Your Brand, Kogan Page, London

[7] www.eea.europa.eu (2021) Growth without economic growth — European Environment Agency, 11 January. Available at: https://www.eea.europa.eu/publications/growth-without-economic-growth (archived at https://perma.cc/5NKE-XYBV) [Accessed 13 September 2022]

[8] Miller, J (2022) Liberté, Égalité, Nudité: France's new sexual politics, The Spectator, 13 August. Available at: https://www.spectator.co.uk/article/ libert%C3%A9-%C3%A9galit%C3%A9-nudit%C3%A9-frances-new-sexual-politics (archived at https://perma.cc/ELQ4-4JHZ) [Accessed 14 September 2022]

INDEX

Note: Page numbers in *italics* refer to figures

CPSIA information can be obtained
at www.ICGtesting.com
Printed in the USA
JSHW062240210223
38085JS00006B/28